The Pro-Life/Choice Debate

Recent titles in
Historical Guides to Controversial Issues in America
Ron Chepesiuk, Series Editor

Gun Control and Gun Rights
Constance Emerson Crooker

The Pro-Life/Choice Debate

Mark Y. Herring

Historical Guides to Controversial Issues in America
Ron Chepesiuk, Series Editor

GREENWOOD PRESS
Westport, Connecticut • London

Library of Congress Cataloging-in-Publication Data

Herring, Mark Y.
  The Pro-Life/Choice Debate / by Mark Y. Herring.
    p. cm.—(Historic guides to contemporary issues in America, ISSN 1541–0021)
  Includes bibliographical references and index.
  ISBN 0–313–31710–0 (alk. paper)
  1. Abortion—United States—Public opinion. 2. Pro-choice movement—United States.
  3. Pro-life movement—United States. I. Title. II. Series.
HQ767.5.U5 H467   2003
363.46'0973—dc21   2002032073

British Library Cataloguing in Publication Data is available.

Library of Congress Catalog Card Number: 2002032073
ISBN: 0–313–31710–0
ISSN: 1541–0021

First published in 2003

Greenwood Press, 88 Post Road West, Westport, CT 06881
An imprint of Greenwood Publishing Group, Inc.
www.greenwood.com
Printed in the United States of America

The paper used in this book complies with the
Permanent Paper Standard issued by the National
Information Standards Organization (Z39.48–1984).

10 9 8 7 6 5 4 3 2

For Carol
mulierem fortem quis inveniet procul et de ultimis finibus pretium eius

Contents

List of Illustrations

Preface

The writer of the book of Ecclesiastes in the Old Testament complains like a weary catalog librarian: "Of the making of books," he opines, "there can be no end." Just so. Certainly, the ring of truth is a resounding one in the case of abortion. Abortion is one of the single-most researched topics in high schools, and the most talked about issue in colleges and universities, especially at the freshman level.[1] Abortion is the same for all of us, young or old: an inexplicably difficult topic about which there seems to be no end of angles, twists, turns, and debates. Of course, when writing about a life-or-death issue, one would hope to find one's culture demonstrably worried, focused, even monomaniacal (one-track minded, if you will) about so important a topic. We wouldn't want to become as callous about abortion as the communist dictator Josef Stalin was about his own people: one death is a tragedy, he said; 1 million deaths are a statistic.

Some of the people who helped me on this excursion must be named in heartfelt appreciation. In doing so, I wish to make it clear, however, that they are in no way responsible for the content of this book. The errors and defects of this book are all mine, unfortunately; any seeming good should, however, be attributed to them.

I start with the editor of this series, Ron Chepesiuk, for having the confidence to ask me to lend a helping hand. Of the writing of books, Ron knows no end himself for he has written more than a dozen books, and more than three thousand articles for magazines of nearly every persuasion (serious, popular, liberal, conservative) to make him one of the most versatile writers I know.

Emily Birch at Greenwood Press should also be named. On Ron's recommendation, she gave me the contract. Ms. Birch is the kind of editor every author should be lucky enough to have. She never despairs, always makes improvements, even, and especially, when it means cutting substantial portions of text. Add to this a perdurably sunny disposition. This book is doubtless better because Ms. Birch made it so.

Finding what one needs to write a book can be as tedious and as exasperating as looking for the proverbial needle in a haystack. Samuel Johnson, the great eighteenth-century essayist, once said that man will turn over a whole library to write a book, and so I have. As a librarian, I have no excuses for missing important material (though there was much that I turned up that I could not use). In vocation, I have been exceedingly fortunate since I come to the process ready to seek and sometimes to find.

In profession, too, I have been doubly lucky as I have been able to call upon those who are better at finding materials than I am. Two such reference librarians have helped in this research, Susan Silverman and Lois Walker, both of whom work, or worked, for me. While the lion's share of this task fell to Ms. Silverman, both women have been instrumental.

I would be remiss if I did not also mention David Weeks, Ann Thomas, and later Jackie McFadden, of the Interlibrary Loan Department of Dacus Library at Winthrop University. It would be hard to find better sleuths, not only because I experienced their sleuthing ability firsthand, but also because it has been said time and again by Winthrop faculty who have marveled at their expertise. Dot Barber and the late Peggy Crouch also come to mind. My associate dean, Larry Mitlin, must also be named.

My own boss, Melford Wilson, proved especially helpful and supportive, as did our president, Anthony DiGiorgio. Winthrop is a teaching university, and while publication matters, teaching matters far more. Both Dr. Wilson and Dr. DiGiorgio have encouraged this work. Dr. DiGiorgio also provided additional research funds upon which to draw at critical times. When it comes to support at every level, however, Winthrop is the best place any faculty member could hope to be. We are supported at every level, beyond what one would expect or even hope.

Last, but hardly least and easily the best, is the woman to whom this book is dedicated: my wife of thirty years and counting, Carol Lane. We live in a different time and age than decades ago, when women, specifically wives, assumed certain roles they may or may not have sought. Fortunately, and only

God knows why, Carol took on a lifetime with me and has never wavered in the task. Yes, she has her own career, but her family has always come first. That she has remained with me for three decades is one of life's great mysteries. Only I, and our now-grown daughters, know just how many sacrifices she has made.

NOTE

1. The best evidence of this is EbscoHost's TOPICSearch, a database created by high school teachers and librarians. Among the fifteen or so broad topics is abortion. This database finds it way in the libraries of many, if not all, high schools. Since the chosen topics are putatively selected to reveal what's on the minds of high school students, this statement cannot be far from the truth.

Introduction

It's laughable to presume to present to the discriminating reading public a nonpartisan book about abortion. How can anyone, even an academic, remain unmoved by a topic so heartfelt on both sides? But perhaps it isn't so absurd after all. A nonpartisan approach may be the only way left to address this issue.

Abortion touches politics, of course, but is not (if only marginally) consumed by it. (Politics does, however consume virtually every public discourse about abortion, as we shall see.) Rather, abortion views, pro or con, generally consume the life of the individual holding them. Aristotle had it only half right when he wrote, "Men by nature are political."[1]

This may be true about nearly every other issue in American life. When it comes to the abortion debate, however, it is the men and women themselves who are often consumed by their views, and that, in turn, drives their politics. Is it possible, then, for any person to remain nonpartisan? Probably not, but it's a game worth the candle and here's why.

John Stuart Mill may have some important advice to offer when it comes to studying the abortion debate in a nonpartisan fashion. Wrote Mill, "The only way in which a human being can make some approach to knowing the whole of a subject is by hearing what can be said about it by persons of every variety of opinion and studying all modes in which it can be looked at by every character of mind. No wise man ever acquired his wisdom in any mode but this" (*On Liberty*). Every attempt to provide a large collection of minds on this topic from both sides of the abortion controversy has been provided in what follows.

A nonpartisan approach may prove the best, too, because it presumes to divorce itself from emotions that cloud reason. If a person is pro-life, it's likely that he or she cannot discuss the issue either rationally or well with a person who is not. Likewise for a person who is pro-choice. Both sides tend to inflate their positions, when necessary, and diminish the other side when convenient. It is because the views are so fully felt, because they so completely occupy the lives of the individuals who hold them that to deny those views is tantamount to denying the existence of the people who espouse them. A nonpartisan approach is the only way that allows a full airing of both views, warts and all.

One question that confronts us immediately is this: Why is there such bitterness on both sides of this debate? I've mentioned one reason already: the principals holding them hold them almost to the exclusion of everything else. Both sides tend to be single-issue people.[2] But language drives the bitterness as well. We're already knee deep into this part of the language controversy. It goes like this. The pro-life side will contend that the term *pro-choice* is an altogether unfair designation. What their opponents really are, they will argue, is pro-abortion. On the other hand, pro-choice proponents will likely argue that the term *pro-life* is an unfair, partisan description. Pro-choicers are just as much pro-life as their opponents, they'll say. Pro-choice advocates will argue that they just happen to be pro-life about the mother. Their opponents are "anti-choice" or "anti–reproductive rights."

No matter what terms are used, both sides are likely to object. "To say they're pro-life is to say that we're anti-life or pro-death," says Kate Michelman of the pro-choice National Abortion and Reproductive Rights Action League (NARAL–Pro-Choice America). But Judie Brown of the decidedly pro-life American Life League banters back, "Pro-choice? That baby does not get to have a choice."[3] This sort of one-upmanship gets us exactly nowhere, of course, so I have opted to use the terms preferred by pro-life advocates to designate themselves, and the term preferred by pro-choice advocates to designate themselves. In the latter case I have rejected the term *abortion rights* because it has recently become more political than descriptive. My choice of terminology is in accord with Mary B. Mahowald, a pro-choice critic who defends her use of the same terms by arguing that it aligns with popular use and popular understanding.[4] In the end, pro-choice advocates do stress the choice of the mother to have or not to have children over other considerations. Pro-life advocates stress the life of the unborn over all else in the argument. I can only plead forbearance.

Debate over the designation of principals' views is only the beginning of the linguistic debate. There is even argument over what the term *abortion* means. Even in books favorable to the topic, the word is likely to arouse nitpicking disagreements. Consider the following in a widely used text on the topic:

1. DEFINITIONS A. "*Abortion*" The new focus on abortion as a medical technique has brought about modernized legal definitions, usually of the term "abortion" but sometimes of "miscarriage" or "feticide." A few states content themselves with defining abortion as termination of pregnancy while others specify methods in a comprehensive way.

Abortion implies intent or purpose, but statutes frequently spell it out anyway, either generally or in terms of intent to produce fetal death. More frequently, the intent element is stated inversely, that is, a purpose other than to induce live birth or to remove a dead fetus. Only rarely does a definition of abortion include references to viability or period of gestation; such matters usually are dealt with in substantive provisions.[5]

Only the pro-choice Naomi Wolf has had the temerity to attack the question on these terms. Other pro-choice advocates argue over whether abortion actually means taking a life when the "organism" in question has yet to achieve, in their minds, legally defined personhood.

Earnest views, earnestly held, however, describe a number of much-debated social issues. Language wars, too, characterize nearly every important disagreement. Neither are exclusive to abortion. Given this, why has this particular issue been so hotly and zealously contested for so many years? The final reason lies in our history, and it is because of this history that the nonpartisan approach may be the best way to tackle this admittedly difficult subject.

Abortion as an issue of public debate is largely a twentieth-century phenomenon. But the debate began much earlier, not over abortion, but over how social issues (of which abortion is certainly one) would later be viewed. Two camps emerged as noteworthy: the Federalists and the Anti-Federalists. Both viewed government very differently by viewing social issues with strikingly different presuppositions. Both saw the Constitution as a document that either gave birth to a federal government or limited the same (giving the states more power) to just those powers named in the Bill of Rights. The two sides warred over this interpretation and, in many ways, the abortion debate reflects that ongoing struggle. Here's how.

The Federalists wanted a central government. The Anti-Federalists wanted something more akin to state government and a strict interpretation of the Constitution, that is, the federal government had only those rights specified in the Constitution and no others. The Bill of Rights reflects the compromise struck to pacify the Anti-Federalists, who feared a too-powerful central government.

Some recent writers have argued that our Founding Fathers were motivated more by religious, even Christian viewpoints, and it is this that has
shaped the debate. This view is too simplistic, and too prone to error.[6] While
a generous number of our Founding Fathers held deeply felt religious beliefs,
these beliefs, influencing as they did *realpolitik* (politics from a pragmatic perspective as the only realistic governing option for a great state) in this country, cannot be said to have guided the country completely. For some, these
religious beliefs informed everything; for others, these religious beliefs remained peripheral to political pragmatism—often as much by design as by
default.

When it came to the founding documents, however, the men who wrote
them were not governed by orthodox religious beliefs, but by ideology, favoring either a centralized government and an expansive interpretation of the
Constitution, or state government and a much more strict interpretation of
the Constitution. They wrote their beliefs (save only for the most generaliz-
able of them, and therefore the least debatable) *out of,* not in, those documents. This can be confusing, especially when one reads, say, the preface to
the *Ordinance of 1802,* in which the writer makes bald-faced references to
God and Christian polity. The seeds of the abortion controversy, therefore,
though they did not sprout until modern times, were sown in the soil of political ideology from the beginning of our country. Had the competing ideologies not been present, it is likely this debate would find no audience, for
there would be no debate. The issue would have been settled on one side or
the other long before now.

Strongly held *political or spiritual* belief is the dividing line between Federalists and Anti-Federalists. *The Federalist Papers,* written as they were by James
Madison, John Jay, and Alexander Hamilton, formed the groundwork that
led to our adoption of a pluralist (and eventually secular) view of life in America. Above all, these men were pragmatists. Thomas Jefferson, for example,
was suspicious of anything that smelled like religious division. Religious belief may have been everywhere in early America, as Tocqueville observed in
his celebrated work, *Democracy in America.* Finding it in our governing documents, however, is another matter. When compared with other nations, our
country certainly allowed religious sentiment to insinuate itself into our political fabric, but not as much as some other countries.

Jefferson, as much as any other individual involved in our nation's founding, had more to do with the framework of the Constitution and the Declaration than anyone else. And Jefferson, while a deeply thoughtful man, was
not one governed by religious orthodoxy. His views regarding religion were
quite unorthodox. Jefferson's views, intellectual instead of spiritual, and influenced by the especially nonreligious (some would say anti-religious) views

Thomas Jefferson. (Courtesy of the Library of Congress.)

of the French Enlightenment, infuse and inform nearly all of our early documents. The seeds of both sentiments, religious and pragmatic, were therefore
present from the beginning. There were men (the term is descriptive, not sex-
ist) who wanted religious sentiment to inform politics, and men who did not,
and who greatly feared its presence. The latter camp, not the former, won the
day.

Were this tension not apparent from our earliest beginnings, the endgame
of abortion views in America would be very nearly incomprehensible. While
Washington might issue a farewell address that sounded like a sermon, or
Adams warn that the Constitution was in fact written for a people "bridled"
by religious sentiment, there was Jefferson warning that men of strong religious persuasion endangered the American experiment. He felt that if they
were not somehow co-opted, they would destroy the Republic with their
wrangling. This tension guaranteed that there would be men (and later

women) who would see a social issue exclusively from a pragmatical and political standpoint, and men (and later women) who would see the *same* issue
as entirely spiritual and religious.

This point is important because it's critical in understanding how a country that was basically religious at heart moved so rapidly from that viewpoint
on this issue to one that appears completely at odds with it.[7] Understanding
this early division helps us to understand why that division, implanted in our
politics, shows up two hundred–plus years later. If, from the beginning, we
had such debates about whether social issues were moral and spiritual or pragmatic and political, then it only stands to reason that today we would still
have men and women lining up on both sides of that divide. This may further help to explain why men and women considering the same issue can see
constitutional reasons for viewing an issue as morally neutral, and those who
see constitutional reasons why it should be viewed as "obviously" moral alone.
Both views are part of the warp and woof of our political consciousness;
hence, a nonpartisan look at the issue allows both sides to make their case.

In the end, that is why the terms *pro-life* and *pro-choice* designate so well
where we are in this argument. Except for a small minority (and it is indeed a
radical and vocal one), no one argues that we're not performing enough abortions in this country. Rather, those in the pro-choice camp argue that choice
must remain at the heart of the issue, that privacy should override all other
concerns and somehow limit the outcome. Likewise, those favoring the pro-
life position see a moral issue only, and argue that the morality of an issue
must guide its solution. Then, to further cloud the abortion debate, those
who began by viewing it as neutral sometimes jump to the moral view of the
debate (and here I do not refer to politicians who do it only for votes). Jefferson, who feared a strong centralized government, voted *with* the Federalists.
In our own modern times, a devout defender of choice has moved entirely to
the pro-life side because the sheer number of abortions suddenly boggled his
mind.[8]

Given the rancor and argumentativeness on both sides of the abortion debate; given that both sides, pro and con, hold their views passionately at the
very soul of their beings; given that abortion is a life-or-death matter whether
we speak of the real death of the unborn child (pro-life argument), or the real
or figurative (emotional, economic, psychological) death of the mother (pro-
choice argument)—given all that, framing this debate in terms that will bring
both sides to the table is more than a matter of passing concern: it is critical
to reception by the antagonists. How then, to present this book that in all
likelihood will anger both sides, yet end with something akin to a broad read-
ership across the spectrum of the debate?

A narrative that seeks to tell where this debate began, how it arrived at its present state, and where it might go in the future will provide not only for an explanation of facts, but also for the venting of opposing arguments. Following that line of thinking, the first three chapters examine the abortion debate from the earliest of times to 1972, just prior to the landmark *Roe v Wade* decision handed down by the Supreme Court in January 1973.

Chapter 4 examines *Roe v Wade* in detail. While this landmark decision is the feature or theme of this chapter, it isn't the only Court decision discussed. Other decisions handed down at or near the same time (for example, *Doe v Bolton* was handed down on the same day as *Roe*) are also discussed in detail. Since chapter 4 may be said to represent the crowning triumph of the pro-choice side against all odds, chapter 5 assesses what the pro-life side did in retaliation, and may be seen as its crowning achievement.

Chapter 6 tackles what is referred to as the "morning after bills." If *Roe* is seen as the first shot fired by pro-choice advocates, and *Humane Vitae et al.* the volley returned by their pro-life counterparts, decisions presented here represent a jockeying for position. *Webster* represents the keystone case. Other decisions leading up to it represent how we got there and what happened afterward as a result.

Chapter 7 spotlights *Casey*. While most books focus on *Webster* as the "denouement" of the abortion debate, *Casey* appears to me equally important because it frames the debate following *Webster* on both sides. It also registers how much politics has seasoned, and spoiled, this debate.

Chapter 8 examines the highly controversial, highly contentious issue of what is referred to as "partial-birth" or "late-term" abortions. As with all chapters, both those who favor and those who wish to restrict these abortions get to vent their spleen.

The last chapter of the book attempts to indicate where the debate now stands. While it may be thought that there is no untying of this difficult knot, that is hardly the case outside the United States. Our debate has been a bitter, even deadly, one. In other countries, however, the democratic process has paved the way for a compromise. Granted, unlike the United States, they do not have abortion on demand; yet nevertheless they have found a way to retain abortion while limiting its frequency.

Whatever one's position on abortion, that position is likely heartfelt. It's also likely to have been arrived at after much anguish and soul-searching. Very few on either side of this great debate, a debate that has played a significant role in the last seven presidential elections, are completely happy where we are. The debate itself mimics not only the schizophrenic nature of the national consciousness about it—at once pro-life, then pro-choice—but also mimics what has been sowed in our national consciousness from the beginning—wars based on religious and spiritual beliefs with pragmatic, political concerns. Both sides see evidence of their own conclusions in the very fabric of our American-ness, and both sides remain unhappy with the status quo.

I began this introduction by saying that it was somewhat ludicrous to write a nonpartisan book on a topic about which people on both sides hold such partisan views. And yet perhaps the only way to think about abortion is to look at where we began in order to see where we have come, to watch how we progressed as a nation in order to understand why we arrived at this particular juncture. One reason—perhaps the only reason—it's so hard for anyone to remain nonpartisan on this issue is because this issue really comes down to a life-and-death matter. In the end, perhaps all we can do to understand the debate, and to understand one another, is to come to understand better how our past has been prelude to our unfortunate and cantankerous present. This book is an attempt to do just that while also attempting to set a course for a very different future.

NOTES

1.   Aristotle, *Politicus,* Book I: "Hence it is evident that the state is a creation of nature, and that man is by nature a political animal. And he who by nature and not by mere accident is without a state, is either a bad man or above humanity; he is like the tribeless, lawless, hearthless one, whom Homer denounces—the natural outcast is forthwith a lover of war; he may be compared to an isolated piece at draughts."

2.   Of the literally hundreds of places where this is discussed, here are a few: http://www.trinityonline.org/k/issues/issue5_9/baoill/; http://www.religion-online.org/cgi-bin/relsearchd.dll/showarticle?item_id=1331; C. Joffe, "Abortion as Single-Issue Politics," *Society* 34, no. 5 (July/August 1997): 25–29; Ellie Lee, "Don't Mention the A-Word," http://www.spiked-online.com/Articles/000000005457.htm, accessed January 24, 2001.

3.   Marcus D. Rosenbaum, "The Name Game: More Than Mere Nuance," *CQ Editorial Research Reports* (January 26, 1990): 51.

4.   Mary B. Mahowald, "As If There Were Fetuses without Women: A Remedial Essay," in Joan C. Callahan, ed., *Reproduction, Ethics and the Law: Feminist Perspectives* (Bloomington, Ind.: Indiana University Press, 1995), 199 note 1.

5.   B.J. George Jr., "State Legislatures versus the Supreme Court: Abortion Legislation into the 1990s," in J. Douglas Butler and David F. Walbert, eds., *Abortion, Medicine and the Law,* 4th ed., (New York: Facts on File, 1992), 23–24.

6.   For an altogether different view of this, readers are directed to David Barton, *The Myth of Separation: What Is the Correct Relationship between Church and State?: A Revealing Look at What the Founders and Early Courts Really Said,* 8th ed. (Aledo, Tex.: WallBuilder Press, 1992).

7.   See John B. Judis, *The Paradox of American Democracy: Elites, Special Interests, and the Betrayal of Public Trust* (New York: Pantheon Books, 2000).

8.   Bernard Nathanson, who after running one of the largest and most lucrative abortion clinics in the world, tergiversated the cause (in the minds of pro-choicers) and has become one of the most outspoken opponents of abortion today. His film, *Silent Scream,* both shocked and outraged the pro-choice movement.

1

The Past as Prologue to the Present: Abortion from the Classical Period to 1750

Resorting to historical evidence, at least for the first four thousand years of abortion history, we find that from the earliest times this issue has been less about abortion and more about life—its value and its sanctity. This is true whether we examine either the secular or the sacred ancient record. It could be argued that the issue, historically anyway, has never *really* been about abortion per se, but about how one side argues about, and values, potential life, and how the other side argues about, and values, the quality of life of those already living. Nevertheless, for pro-choice advocates, invoking the historical record is hardly a way to move their argument forward even though this is precisely what *Roe v Wade* did. While the historical record is hardly absolute (it can be tricky for either side, depending on the century), the preponderance of evidence from the earliest historical record comes down decidedly in favor of life.

What makes this of critical importance at the outset of our debate is that the Supreme Court managed to miss or ignore the historical record in *Roe v Wade* by calling that history "ambiguous." By doing so, it made certain that *Roe v Wade*'s scholarly legitimacy would be questioned from that moment to this.

The great legal scholar John T. Noonan Jr. called the testament of history on life to be "an almost absolute value."[1] Indeed, in surveying the historical landscape of abortion, it is much easier to note the exceptions than to list conformities to the rule. The number of writers, with or without religious leanings, who favor life exceeds those who favor, or allow for, abortion (or abortifacients—those herbs or chemicals that cause a woman to abort—as is the case more often than not) by more than three to one. At least on this topic, history may be said to be a record of various races, cultures, and religions all speaking in unison: abortion is to be avoided. Even when we encounter those few cases where abortion is allowed, the number of conditions necessary to meet qualified acceptance expresses, at the very least, the culture's uneasiness about the practice and the uncertainty of its appropriateness.

This does not necessarily mean that the pro-life side "wins" this part of the debate. In some ways this is unsurprising since large families were required to manage the agricultural nature of life. It does mean, however, that the case *for* abortion cannot be made from a nonpartisan reading of the historical record. Ancient writers were anything but comfortable with abortion. Could science have attenuated this view had it developed more quickly? The known science of abortifacients is made up of a combination of both pessaries (vaginal suppositories meant to cause a pregnant woman to abort) and emmenagogues (herbs that cause a woman's period to begin). These were at once so numerous and so well-known that any woman wishing an abortion by either method could have had one at any time.[2] In fact, by the time of Roman civilization (first century A.D.), women were so well aware of abortion-causing herbs that could be used alone or combined with other commonplace ones (even household products) to produce the hoped-for abortion effect, that abortion could have been had on demand, if only it would have been 100 percent effective.[3] If by some strange coincidence a woman did not know about these herbs, she could be pointed in the direction of a woman who did. That woman most likely lived down her street, or in a nearby neighborhood.

With the means of abortion available, and pregnancy often kept secret (during this early history, women could "hide" their pregnancies [because of baggy clothing] until they wanted anyone, especially men, to know), it is astonishing that abortion was not *more* widely practiced and more widely accepted. We will look at both the biblical and nonbiblical records to substantiate a claim that some will think is not only surprising but also quite shocking.

THE OLD TESTAMENT TESTIFIES

It should come as no surprise that the biblical Old Testament fully supports life. Although some have tried in recent years to write a revisionist treatment of later biblical testimony on the topic, the Old Testament record is unceasingly in favor of life.[4] Indeed, almost nowhere else is pathema (strong religious feeling) so powerful than on the subject of life, its holiness before God, and its presence as a "proof" of God's blessing to humankind. Let's begin at the beginning.

The first commandment of God (and also his first blessing) is a simple one: "Be fruitful and multiply" (Genesis 1:22). This is critical to understanding the nature of Jewish thought about life and really frames everything else mentioned in the Old Testament. Life was something to be celebrated and honored. Never as something to be taken for granted. In the book of Exodus, we encounter the first instances or references to what can be generally called abortion.[5] Exodus 21:22–23 offers the first penalties and, curiously enough, sets the stage for the first abortion debate to be resurrected in our own century: "And if men strive together, and hurt a woman with child, so that her fruit depart, and yet no harm follow—he shall surely be fined, according as the woman's husband shall lay upon him; and he shall pay as the judges determine. But if any harm follow—then thou shall give life for life." The passage, read as one would characteristically read any passage in literature, seems straightforward enough: if you jostle a woman with child and she and/or her unborn are harmed, a penalty shall follow depending on whether the "harm" is fatal. Scholars are, however, as is their wont, divided on the meaning of "harm" and so the pro-life/pro-choice debate ensues. The Septuagint (the Latin translation of the Bible) applied the "harm" spoken of here to the unborn child. Philo was in agreement and specifically prescribed, as shall be later pointed out, a death penalty for causing an abortion, especially when the fetus was fully formed but not yet delivered.

Talmudic scholars, however, argue that the term refers rather to the woman and not to her offspring, taking this interpretation from an earlier passage (Exodus 21:21), where a man who "smites" another man is put to death. Interestingly, this interpretation mimics other literature of the period with one colossal exception: when a woman willfully seeks her own abortion, in which case the penalty is always her death.[6] On the surface, the text appears to pit the woman against her unborn. The argument is not merely an academic, "inside baseball" sort of musing. If the interpretation refers to the woman, then the fetus may be seen as accidental and abortion may be allowed in certain cases, though hardly in the *Roe v Wade* sense. If the interpretation falls on the side of the fetus, then there can be no mistaking that Jewish thought saw abortion as murder. Regardless of the interpretation chosen, the passage clearly gives the fetus the status of a human being.

In both cases, the debate focuses entirely on known biology and the nature and meaning of "quickening" (when the first movements of the unborn child are felt by the mother). It is not entirely possible to say which side has it exactly right. It is clear throughout this part of the literature that abortion *accidentally* caused does not end in a death penalty, but in a fine, the determining factor resting on whether the unborn has reached the time past "quickening," or that time when the unborn gives evidence of its own life, say by kicking or moving. Pay careful attention, however, to the adverb, *accidentally*. Jewish literature is unequivocal when making the case that when pregnant women are around warring men, both must be careful. That is, if a woman is harmed in some way, her husband can levy the fine according to the judges.

This sounds like a "case closed" argument for the pro-choice side, and favors the "ambiguous" contention of *Roe v Wade*. A fine is not as severe a penalty as death, so obviously the loss must not be as meaningful; therefore, the culture did not abhor abortion, just certain kinds of it, or so the pro-choice argument goes. But alas, take note: it is equally clear that in every case this argument is made with respect to *accidental,* not premeditated, harm. Thus, it is clear that when abortion is purposeful or self-inflicted, it is considered evil, a "case closed" argument for the pro-life side. The early historian Josephus makes this point very clear: "[T]he Law has commanded [us] to raise all the children and prohibited women from aborting or destroying seed; a woman who does so shall be judged a murderess of children for she has caused a soul to be lost and the family of man to be diminished" (*Against Apion* 2:202).

The book of Leviticus in the Old Testament is often dismissed, even by the pious, as having little to offer but ordinary and extraordinary rules about foods. But Leviticus is really more about two major principles used to set apart the community of Israel. Written between 1450 and 1410 B.C., the book of Leviticus seeks to show, "that all of life, both human and animal, and its processes, are sacred to Yahweh [the Old Testament Hebrew word for *God*], and that the Israelites must be free to serve Yahweh.... "[7] In chapter 12 of Leviticus, purification rites are given regarding a woman after childbirth. Some have made much of the differences required: "If a woman becomes pregnant and gives birth to a boy, she will be unclean for seven days...If she gives birth to a girl, she will be unclean for two weeks..."[8] But the differences are in keeping with later purifications for a woman when the onset of her menses occurs. Chapter 18 contains elaborate prohibitions against sexual offenses, especially adultery and incest (in neither case is abortion recommended), while chapter 20 expounds on those regarding adultery.

Throughout the book of Leviticus, the transmission of life, whether through male or female children, is presented as holy, a blessing from Yahweh. It is impossible for anyone who reads the book as literature to come away from it with any other notion than that life is to be valued because it is holy to Yahweh. Throughout all of these prohibitions, regardless of what one may think of them, one is struck by the tenderness to the individual, and the holiness with which life is viewed. Life is neither to be expected as guaranteed (its vicissitudes are governed by diseases, wars, disasters) nor ignored as insignificant (Yahweh created it). Rather, it is to be honored by all. Later, in the book of Deuteronomy, extreme prohibitions are laid down for those who rape a woman. Both respect for the woman and for her unborn child are accorded the highest regard. (This is later elevated once more in Mary, the mother of Jesus, in the New Testament.)

Throughout the Old Testament, women who bear children are praised and considered blessed (Genesis 16:2; 29:31–34; 30:1; 2 Kings 4:14; and Psalms 127: 3–5). In a passage from the Psalms, the man whose wife is "a fruitful vine" is blessed above all else. The same idea is echoed in a later proverb in which the happy man is he whose "quiver" (family) is full of "arrows" (children). Barrenness and widowhood are on the same plane in the Old Testament as conditions that should evoke both our pity and our consolation.

A remarkable extrabiblical myth bears mentioning here, since it came along about the same time. Coming from the pages of the *Chronicle of Jerahmeel,* it underscores the preciousness of life as the Jews understood it.[9] A special angel, Lailah, we are told, presides at the very moment of conception. Under his auspices the *embryo* (the word used in the myth) is brought before God and his (or her) future is determined, his station in life is set even to the extent of who he's going to marry. Upon the invocation of God himself, a spirit enters the sperm and the union with the egg is returned to the mother's womb. The child is enfolded there with its head between its knees. Two unnamed angels are charged with its care. A light is set at the head of the fertilized egg in which it can see from one end of the world to the other. Here the embryo is taught all the joys of heaven, all the tortures of hell. When the child is at last ready to come forth, it is struck (the crease in the upper lip bearing the mark), extinguishing the knowledge gleaned during prebirth. The newborn child forgets all he has learned.

While we cannot make much of what is, after all, a myth, it does offer a number of useful insights. First, the understanding of biological development is very much present even in the earliest of times. Conception is considered to occur when egg and sperm unite. Finally, the Socratic notion of heuristic learning (learning in which all that is known has been previously taught before birth but forgotten during birth) is obviously present. It's easy to see, with stories of birth like this circulating, why ancient cultures had little place for abortion, accidental or otherwise.

Two other passages from the Old Testament need to detain us. The first is found in Psalms 139. Here David cries out, "You created my inmost self, knit me together in my mother's womb. For so many marvels I thank you; a wonder am I, and all your works are wonders" (verses 13–14). Here David ascribes to God the very act of creation in his mother's womb. The image is not an accidental one: God knits humans together from the beginning. God is omnipotent, according to David, and his hand is ever at work, from the minutest of creation—the formation of the embryo—to its most grand—the formation of the mountains. Later on in the same song, David makes the point even more clearly about God: "You could see my embryo. In your book all my days were inscribed, every one that was fixed is there." One does not have to subscribe to the spiritual beliefs of David to understand what he's saying. God made him from the beginning (see the myth mentioned above) and God has His hand in life from its earliest formation and ordains it as holy.

Ecclesiastes 11:5 contains the second passage. The book discusses the wisdom of God and his omnipotence. The contrast is between the finitude of man's knowing, and the vast omniscience of God. The passage runs as follows: "You do not understand how the wind blows, or how the embryo grows in a woman's womb." This sort of comparing and contrasting between the finite and the infinite is not unusual in the Old Testament (it occurs frequently in Psalms and in Proverbs). What is unusual is the choice of the comparison. The implication here is that Yahweh understands the nature of life and its wonder; humanity does not understand this and so should remain silent. The word translated as *embryo* in this translation has been variously translated as *fetus,* or *life-breath* in other translations.

These are not, of course, the only places in the Old Testament that speak of the preciousness of life, of its value and its holiness. Abortion, especially if purposeful and self-inflicted, is *always* condemned. Deuteronomy 30:19 spells out the ethical statement clearly when Yahweh says, through Moses, "Today I call heaven and earth to witness against you: I am offering you life or death, blessing or curse. Choose life, then, so that you and your descendants may live.... " Elsewhere, children are called a blessing from God (Psalms 127:3–5; 113:9; Genesis 17:6). Further, God is at work in the womb of a pregnant woman (Psalms 139:113–16; Isaiah 49:1, 5, 15; Jeremiah 1:5). The Isaiah passages are particularly impressive: "Can a woman forget the baby at her breast, not have pity for the child in her womb?"[10] The only occasion in which we can find any record that there may be another view is in the case of accidental abortion. Building a case on exceptions, however, is not a good practice. From these passages and others, it's easy to see how the early church later came to embrace what can be called the pro-life view.

Pro-choice advocates do point to much of the Old Testament's specific silence about the practice of abortion per se, and have made a case that rests on quickening (when the mother feels the unborn move), mentioned above. An argument can be made based on the ambiguity regarding the unformed fetus as opposed to a formed one. Even if we grant this, however, no case can be made to accept abortion as it is practiced in the United States today by basing it on the practices of biblical Israel. At best, pro-choice advocates can claim only the ambiguity about the translation in the Genesis 21:22–25 passage mentioned above. About the other passages there is no disagreement.

But there are other passages that pro-choice advocates point to. In the ones below, pro-choice advocates argue that the Bible not only treats abortion, it treats it favorably.[11] A passage in 2 Kings 15:16 reads, "At that time Menahem sacked Tappuah...and ripped up all the women who were with child." The pro-choice argument here is that if Menahem did this, how could abortion be wrong? Hosea 9:14 reads, "Give them, O Lord—What will you give? Give them a miscarrying womb and dry breasts." The pro-choice proponent argues that here the prophet (Hosea) is calling for God to afflict the women of Ephraim with miscarriages and since a prophet calls for this it must be something "acceptable." Later on in the same book (13:9) we find "Samaria['s]...little ones shall be dashed to pieces, and their pregnant women ripped open." Here some pro-choice advocates argue that it appears that the Bible endorses both abortion and infanticide. The passage found in Numbers 5:11–31 is often cited by pro-choice advocates as well. In this passage a woman suspected of adultery (there are no witnesses) may be taken before the priest who makes her take an oath that asks God to make her barren, followed by drinking a potion that will essentially kill her. Is this not a passage that favors abortion, or at least abortion in some cases?

Pro-life advocates are quick to rescue these passages by arguing that, for example, Menahem in his battle at Tappuah behaved brutally and it is recorded but not taught.[12] They further argue that the passages in Hosea and Amos are prophetic passages and are hardly prescriptive at all. The Numbers passage, they contend, really reflects upon the evil of adultery, not abortion. The curses found in verses 20–25 are meant to frighten women who might otherwise be "lured" into adulterous relationships as a crime against both their husbands and God.[13] The curses found in this passage merely reaffirm a long-standing Old Testament tradition that calls upon God to witness infidelity and curse it accordingly. To make this passage speak in favor of, or remain neutral to, abortion would be to argue that the Bible speaks in favor of prostitution because it also speaks favorably of sexual intercourse between husband and wife.

Although some Middle Assyrian Laws (around 1600 B.C.) appear to allow for a small difference, the laws of ancient Israel speak only of unwitting abortion, not abortion on demand. In the case of the former, where abortion was willful, the stringent Middle Assyrian Laws called for the mother's trial and prosecution (see info-center.ccit.arizona.edu/~ws/ws200/fall97/grp2/part4.htm for more on this). When the trial was ended and she was found guilty, she was to be impaled on stakes. Strikingly, even if she died in the process of a self-inflicted abortion, her body was *still* to be impaled on stakes after her death(!) and she was to be denied a proper burial. In the Code of Hammurabi, if a man unwittingly caused another man's pregnant daughter to abort, and she later died, his own daughter was to be put to death. On the pro-choice side, there is the exception made for malformed children. They can be aborted. Our own Americans with Disabilities Act would frown on such an allowance. Lycurgus and Solon (neither were considered especially pious) both enacted laws that prohibited abortion and punished its practice.

In addition to these restrictions on abortion, little relief is gained when the eye is turned to the Far East. It has been said that "In antiquity the people of the East opposed abortion with intensity."[14] Buddhism punished offenders with severity. In India, the Aryas law books condemned abortion as nothing short of homicide. The Parsees's religion of Avesta forbade abortions with the utmost stridency. And we have already seen what awaited Assyrian women who broke the code by having abortions.

Nowhere in the Old Testament is abortion praised as worthy, right, or acceptable as a practice. That we know it was practiced is hardly an exception worth pondering since so many of the commandments found in the Bible address the breach of those commandments. The pro-choice view is forced to accept these for what they are, along with the rest of the testimony of the period. That view, as we shall see, will change, especially as we move closer to our own time. As matters stand in this part of the historical record, however, the pro-choice view finds little to rest its arguments upon. This is not to imply that the pro-choice view is wrongly held. It is rather to examine the record left us and bring forward that record. That record in the Old Testament, and in literature written from other cultures during the same time, is clearly one that favors life.

In agricultural societies, where males especially are needed to tend the farm, this is hardly surprising. Indeed, to interpret this record in light of our own knowledge, we can say that it would be most extraordinary to find cultures that have not moved beyond Maslow's hierarchy of survival need entertaining values that can only occur after survival can be taken for granted. And, in fact, that *is* what we encounter. As cultures grow more sophisticated, and survival is no longer a daily concern, we do see different values emerge, ones that are more in concert with the pro-choice view.

THE NEW TESTAMENT RECORD

Abortion is not so easily treated when it comes to the New Testament. Given the record of the Old Testament, which does not seem ambiguous at all, the record of the New Testament is less clear. Some pro-life advocates find the deafening silence in the twenty-seven books that constitute this record disarming at the least, problematic at most. The disconcertment is not without reason. There are no *verses* that lead us to certainty about the New Testament position on abortion. The only views that can be gleaned from the New Testament are by decoding or interpretation.

The passage most often referred to in connection with the New Testament, and the one familiar to most readers, is found in Luke 1:42–44. The passage is just before Mary's "Magnificat" song. Mary has gone to visit her cousin, Elizabeth, who will soon be the mother of John. When the two meet, Elizabeth cries out, "Of all women you are the most blessed, and blessed is the fruit of your womb. Why should I be honored with a visit from the mother of my Lord? Look, the moment your greeting reached my ears, the child in my womb leapt for joy." Pro-life advocates claim that this proves life in the womb, a point that may have been argued early on but has since been dispelled by both medical science and every pregnant woman. Further, if truth be told, this argument, if anything, would be a very weak defense of late-term abortions at most, something that neither side is willing to concede.

In the first place, there is the fact that all the writers, save one, of the New Testament are Jewish. Of course, it is possible that these writers could be departing from the tradition (the record of the New Testament is, in fact, a record of revealing the "hidden" Messiah of the Old Testament). Then there is the problem of New Testament teachings on sexual immorality. For example, the Pauline letters are replete with prohibitions against fornication, *or any kind of uncleanliness*.[15] Perhaps Jewish thought, while four-square against abortion on demand in the Old, is now attenuated in the New? This would be possible except for what we know about the period. Early Jewish thought recorded in extrabiblical literature outside the New Testament upholds the Old Testament teaching against abortion.

For example, the *Sentences of Pseudo-Phocylides* (written sometime between 50 B.C. and A.D. 50) argue in favor of the Old Testament view in unambiguous language. "A woman should not destroy the unborn babe in her belly, nor after its birth throw it before the dogs and vultures."[16] It's hard to argue from this statement that there is another view or interpretation here. *The Sibylline Oracles* contains a brief statement that further augments this one by casting as "wicked" or "evil" not only those who seek out abortions, but also those who "produce abortions and unlawfully cast their offspring away." Here the charge is against not only the woman who seeks the abortion, but also the abortionist who aids her. In the same text, readers are warned about "sorcerers" who dispense abortifacients (things that cause a woman to abort).

In the first century B.C. (some scholars place it in the second century), 1 *Enoch* records a rather startling admission. Here we are told that an "evil" angel taught mankind how to "smash the embryo in the womb." Again, reading this as an unbiased observer, it's hard to make this seem like something other than an admission that this practice is neither acceptable nor praiseworthy. Additionally, Philo of Alexandria (mentioned earlier), who lived between 25 B.C. and A.D. 41, and who is also accepted as a standard-bearer of

Jewish thought and practice, rejected in plain language the idea that the embryo or the fetus was merely a part of the mother's body. Philo saw the two—the mother and the child—as separate entities and claimed both to be protected not only by Jewish law, but also by the prevailing ethic that found abortion an abominable practice. Further, Philo advocated the death penalty for women who had abortions.

Finally, to make the extrabiblical testimony complete, Josephus, a first-century Jewish historian respected by virtually every writer of the period, throws his weight to the pro-life side of the argument. There is no ambiguity about Josephus: "The law orders all the offspring be brought up, and forbids women either to cause abortion or to make away with the fetus."

Now, however, comes the more difficult part of the New Testament argument. Granted, all these positions are clear and one-sided, incontestably favoring the pro-life side. Yet none of these arguments are *from* the New Testament itself. In order to make the pro-life claim from the New Testament, it must be made by inference from other texts. For example, it can be claimed that Paul, in his letter to the Romans, does not include infanticide in his list of sins in the first chapter of that book. Infanticide was, in fact, a common practice. Parents throughout Greece and Rome had the bizarre right to kill their infants for just about any reason.[17] Since Paul mentions quite a long list of bad behaviors in the first chapter to the book of Romans, why does he fail to mention infanticide and abortion? There are no "case closed" arguments to be found in the New Testament for either side—no outright condemnation or approval.

Although there is little in the New Testament about abortions of any kind, one could point to the many New Testament passages about life and its celebration as possible evidence that abortion is condemned. However, if infanticide is not condemned by Paul, we must reach such conclusions without concrete evidence. We do see how precious life is in the New Testament, and with what regard it is to be esteemed.[18] Further claims could be made on the New Testament's numerous references to children, their special place in God's economy, and their care.[19] Moreover, this celebration is not only for children who have been born, but for mothers who are with child. In the end, we are back to the place where we started: there simply are no outright condemnations of the practice. By the time 1 John 4:20 (where hatred of individuals cannot co-exist with an expressed love of God) was written, the Christian condemnation of both suicide and infanticide was well-known. It would be odd to find abortion and infanticide embraced by this same faith without explanation. Finally, arguments from silence are always questionable arguments. Thus, both the pro-life side and the pro-choice contingent, if they resort to the New Testament, will not find ready resolutions to their arguments. While the New Testament record is silent on abortion per se, it would not be fair not to point out, "that Christianity in a very general sense, by its insistence on compassion and on the sanctity of the human body, had a tendency to soften or abash the more extreme brutalities and flippancies of the ancient world in all departments of life, and therefore also in sexual matters, may be taken as obvious."[20]

Finally, there is one more obstacle the pro-choice side has in making its case that the New Testament doesn't care one way or the other about abortion. To get this to work, pro-choice advocates rely on their understanding of the Scriptures better today (two thousand years removed from the time of the New Testament) than those who lived only a few years after (or even while) it was being written. All the literature we have about the time of the New Testament favors the pro-life side.

IMPORTANT EARLY CHURCH COUNCILS

A number of early church councils occurring in or around the time of the first five centuries after Christ serve to confirm the pro-life claim on this part of history. Abortion is featured as the subject of some of these councils, though it is usually connected with the product of sexual impropriety.[21] The Spanish Council of Elvira around A.D. 300 condemned abortion with the penalty of exclusion from communion until death. Fourteen years later, the Council of Ancyra required that women who had unlawful intercourse followed by abortion must serve a decade in penance. Ancyra proved most influential in both the East and West and was cited as the pro-life precedence many years later.

Contraception of any kind was condemned in the Council of Guarnicia and had the force of Canon Law in Gratian's *Aliquando*. It contains a passage that rejected lustful intercourse via contraception.[22] Gratian, however, incorporated Augustine into the basic canon, *Aliquando*. For Gratian, abortion constituted homicide only if the fetus was fully formed.[23] By the thirteenth century, Augustine's influence was universal. Contraception had gained the force of murder, primarily from the placing of the *Si aliquis* (*If someone*) of Regino of Prum and by its description by Burchard as a canon of the Council of Worms nearly a century later.[24] Heresies against the church regarding both virginity and marriage figure largely into the second, third, fourth, and fifth Lateran Councils that occurred between the twelfth and the sixteenth centuries. The Council at Mainz in the early thirteenth century reserved for the bishop any absolution from, among other things, those who "procure . . . abortion." The view of some sects that Satan resided in a woman's womb might have encouraged abortion had it not been roundly condemned as heresy by the Council of Tarnovo in 1211.

Other councils and decrees occurred as well, but these stood out as having the effect of force in the church. The *Si aliquis* passage mentioned above, for example, continued in place in the Catholic Church until just prior to the First World War. The other councils continued to exercise influence on the history of abortion in the Catholic Church, but also influenced Protestant thought.

THE TESTIMONY OF ANCIENT LITERATURE

We come now to the remaining testimony of the literature of the early period. This includes both the writings of the early church fathers, as well as the writings of nonbiblical authors who spoke out on the topic in some way. While the record is far from being entirely one-sided, it is clear about one thing. Abortion of some kind was practiced while abortion on demand was condemned. Herbs and other means (pessaries, for example) were widely used and were common knowledge. Within the ancient record there exist a number of writers who approve of abortion and also of infanticide. It was not until the fourth century A.D. (about the time Augustine wrote) that Roman Emperors began to enact measures to protect the lives, not of the unborn, but of the newly free-born.[25] Such exceptions, however, are clearly in the minority.

Before sampling the record on abortion found in ancient literature, take a look at Table 1.1. While this is not an exhaustive listing, it provides enough depth and variety to indicate that not only did the early church writers find abortion repugnant but so did a number of secular writers. Further, they found the practice hard to understand even though many of them knew about it, and doubtless knew of those who had undergone the procedure. What the table cannot show, however, is what will later become more important. Quickening becomes increasingly significant as time goes on, and not simply to secular writers, but also to Christian ones, most notably Augustine and Aquinas, and those who followed them. This quickening moment later came to be developed into a philosophical moment of "ensoulment," or that time in which the unborn child received his or her soul from God.[26]

Hippocrates is one of the most celebrated nonbiblical figures in ancient literature. From Hippocrates (or from his namesake; scholars are divided whether this is the work of a "quilt" of authors, or a single author) we get the celebrated "Hippocratic Oath." Thomas Rutten clearly dramatizes its importance:

The *Oath* is said to present the most telling evidence for bioethical rigidity of so-called modernism. Similar to the way Christian doctrine developed according to the tradition of the Ten Commandments, medical ethics, following the tradition of the

Table 1.1
Classical Writers and Their Positions on Abortion

Name	Date	Work	Disposition on Abortion
Ambrose	c. AD 340–397	*Hexameron*	No
Aquinas, Thomas	1225–1274	*Summa Theologica*	No (feared intercourse during pregnancy might cause abortion)
Aristotle	384–322 BC	*History of Animals*, Books VI & VII; *Politics* Book VII	Yes
Athenagoras	c. A.D. 133–190	*Embassy for the Christians*	No
Augustine (Aurelius Augustinus)	AD 354–430	*De nuptiis et concupiscentia; De origine animae*	No
Avicenna	A.D. 980–1037	"De regimine abortus," in *Canon Medicine*	Yes (but only if mother's life in jeopardy)
Basil of Cappadocia, also Basil the Great	A.D. 329–379	*Letters*, 188	No (if deliberate, guilty of homicide)
Cicero	106–43 B.C.	*De Oratore; Tuscalanae Disputationes*	No
Clement of Alexandria	c. A.D. 150 – 211 or 216	*Pedagogus*	No
Council of Ancrya	A.D. 314	*Canon 21*	No
Council of Elvira	c. A.D. 300	*Canon 5*	No
Cyprian, Saint (Thascius Caecilius Cyprianus)	c. A.D. 200–258	*Epistle 52*	No
Galen (Galenos) of Pergamum	A.D. 129–c.216	*On Natural Faculties*, Book III	Yes
Aulus Gellius	c. A.D. 130–180	*Noctes Atticae*	Yes
Gratian	b 11th Century, d. before 1159	*Decretum*	Yes (but not after fetus is formed)
Hippocrates	469–399 BC	*Nature of the Child; On Airs, Waters and Places*, Part IV; *Aphorisms* Sections III, V, VII; *On the Sacred diseases; Fistulae; Oath; Of Epidemics*, Books I & II	No

Oath, seemingly found unity, clarity, continuity, truth, logic, and coherence, that is, precisely those characteristics which, while condemning them, post-modernism attributes to modernism.[27]

Rutten goes on to point out that by pulling the Oath out of its historical context, medical science garnered for itself a means of creating a *pro forma* allegiance to life. The Oath itself is short and includes this line: "I will give no

Table 1.1 (Continued)

Hippolytus	c. A.D. 170–c. 235	*Elenchos*	No
Jerome (Eusebius Hieronymus)	c. A.D. 347–420	*On Ecclesiastes; Epistle 22; To Eustochium 13*	No
St. John Chrysostom	d. A.D. 407	*Homily 24 on the Epistle to the Romans*	No
Juvenal (Decimus Junius Juvenalis)	Between 50 & 70–127 B.C.	*Satira*	Yes
Lactantius, Lucius Caelius (Caecilius) Firmianus	c. A.D. 245–c. 325	*Institutiones divinae,* Book 6	No
Minucius Felix, Marcus	flourished A.D. 190 – 240	*Octavius*	No
Old Testament		*Deuteronomy 6:5; Leviticus 19:18*	No
Ovid (Publius Ovidius Naso)	43 B.C. –A.D. 17	*De amoribus*	Yes and No
Peter Lombard	c. A.D. 1095–1160	*Sententiarum*	No
Philo (Philo Judaeus)	30 B.C.–c.45 A.D.	*Special Laws*	No
Plato	427–347 B.C.	*Republic*	Yes
Plautus, Titus Maccius	c. 250 B.C – 184 B.C.	*Truculentus*	Yes
Plutarch (Lucius Maestrius Plutarchus)	c. AD 46 – c.120	*Romulus*	No
Seneca the Younger (Lucius Annaeus)	c. 4 BC – c. 65 A.D.	*De Ira*	Yes (but elsewhere he praises his own mother for not aborting; and, later, warns against destroying any offspring)
Soranus	A.D. 98–138	*Gynecology*	Yes
Suetonius	A.D. c. 69–122	Various	No
Tacitus, Publius Cornelius	A.D. 56–57–c.117	*Annals*, Book XIV; *Historiae 5*	No
Tertullian (Florens Quintus Septimius Tertullianus)	A.D c. 160–c.255	*Apologeticum ad nationes* and *De Anima*	No
Unknown		*Apocalypse of St. Peter; Didache; Epistle of Barnabus 19:5*	No

deadly medicine to any one if asked, nor suggest any such counsel; and in like manner I will not give a woman a pessary to produce abortion."

The debated words are in the Greek, *pesson phthorion,* and have been rendered here "will not give a woman a pessary to produce an abortion." Literally translated, the phrase is "poisonous pessary" (a pessary, remember, is a vaginal suppository meant to induce abortion). Hippocrates knew that pessaries were a well-known and a favored formed of inducing an abortion.[28] On

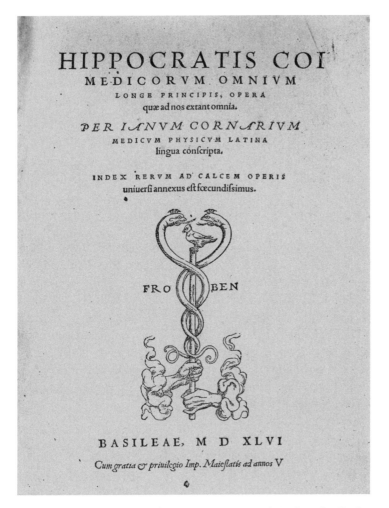

Title page of *Opera quae ad nos extant omnia,* with Froben family device of cadeceus clasped by two hands (complete extant works). (Courtesy of the Library of Congress.)

the other side of the argument is the fact that physicians of the period did not find so objectionable other forms of abortion, or other activities that induced abortion, such as manually puncturing the womb, drinking abortion-causing herbs, or violent physical exercise. We not only know these were in fact used, but we also have ancient records to prove that physicians, midwives, and necromancers (magic dabblers) were aware of them and regularly prescribed them. Add to this that we are unsure who Hippocrates is, and you have the makings of a scholarly free-for-all that allows various laypersons to take whichever side they prefer.

The ambiguity, however, is less unclear if we resort to Hippocrates's other writings. In his *Aphorisms,* Book V, Hippocrates warns against purging a pregnant woman unless "there be any urgent necessity." He also warns against bleeding a pregnant woman because she may abort if she is taken with "violent diarrhoea." These may have been, however, warnings for women who wanted their children, not for those who wanted abortions. Also, it may be that the scholar Paul Carrick is right when he argues, that the "poisonous pessary" was merely symbolic of all forms of abortion and thus restricted physicians from practicing an art that could just as easily (and more likely) have ended in the unintended death of the woman as in death for the unborn.

Of other well-known ancient philosophers, Socrates, his secretary, Plato, and Plato's student, Aristotle, on the other hand, allow for abortion but not without qualification. Socrates is recorded as arguing for its use to remedy overpopulation in Plato's celebrated *Republic.*[29] Plato is also shown there as endorsing the idea, along with other eugenic measures. In Plutarch (*De Placitis Philosophorous* 5.15), however, Plato is presented as rejecting abortion. In addition to Plato and Aristotle, some Stoics and the Pythagoreans, two philosophical sects, allowed for abortion, even endorsing it for certain reasons. Philosophers as a group, though there are exceptions, may be said to have come down on the side favoring abortion.

In his *History of Animals,* as well as in Book VII of his *Politics,* Aristotle is an advocate of abortion. Not only does he see it as a means of limiting the population, but he also proposes it to couples who might otherwise have too many children for the state's well-being. While he does not appear to pass judgment on the act of abortion, he is nervous about when it should be done, calling for the procedure to occur before there is "sensation and life," what would later be referred to as quickening. One could argue then that Aristotle allowed for abortion during the first three months of a pregnancy but not afterwards. What he outlines in the *History of Animals* allows for abortion up to fifty days, or thereabouts. It is possible that Aristotle influenced later rabbinical teaching on the subject. The famed Talmudist Rashi (1040–1105) taught that "Whatever has not come forth into the light of the world is not a full human life." Further, other rabbis adopted the same thought that the embryonic fluid was "dispensable" up to forty days.[30]

Other writers of the period are less unrestricted. In a second-century treatise known as the *Didache,* the warnings are more straightforward: "You shall not murder a child by abortion nor shall you kill a newborn." Both abortion and infanticide are warned against. In the *Epistle of Barnabus,* we find, "You shall not murder a child by abortion, nor shall you kill a newborn" (*Barnabus* 19:5), again echoing the words of the *Didache* (2.2). In the *Apocalypse of Peter,* Peter, describes Hell containing "women who produced children out of wedlock and who procured abortions" (*Apocalypse* 26). On the other side, Aelius Theon, a first-century Stoic philosopher, reported that one of Lysias's orations focused on whether the fetus was human and whether abortions were subject to penalty.[31]

Writings treating abortions up to the late Middle Ages come mainly from councils, encyclicals, and other Christian writings. It will come as no shock that nearly all of these are ceaselessly opposed to abortion. By the time we reach Thomas Aquinas (1225–1274), the matter remains unchanged. Aquinas calls it a mortal sin to have intercourse with a pregnant woman because the risk for abortion was too high. In the case of deliberate abortion, Aquinas is of no help, even if the reason for inducing it is to baptize the unborn and prevent its eternal damnation. Aquinas argues the contrary: better to let the child be born and die than to commit this "sin." He cites Paul from the book of Romans, saying that we cannot do evil so that good may come.

By the end of the latter Middle Ages and the beginning of the Renaissance, we find a slow, evolving change. The many different ways abortions were performed during the Middle Ages find ready use throughout the period. All may be effective if administered correctly; but all are just as likely to cause the mother's death if administered incorrectly. "Science" is also beginning to formalize itself, though not, of course, as we find it even one hundred years later.[32] St. Antoninus of Florence found abortion to be "allowed" in the case of the dying mother by relying on an obscure thirteenth-century theologian, John of Naples. We don't know if Antoninus adopted this opinion himself, but he did publish it.[33]

Tomás Sanchez (1550–1610), the remarkable Spanish marriage casuist, condemned the Onan-like behavior of "spilling the seed" to allow sex for the sake of pleasure (Onan is a character in the Old Testament who was condemned for this), but did allow for abortion in the case of rape. Sanchez took this distinction and added a further exception—the case of a young girl trapped by illegitimate intercourse and facing certain death by her father or others when they discovered it. She could terminate the pregnancy in order to save her own life. Further, if she were impregnated by one man but betrothed to another and knew he might kill her upon discovery, she could abort to save her life. Sanchez is clear, here, too: she could abort because the loss was so great as to be not a mortal, but a venial, sin. Even here, however, the lines of distinction are weakened. She could not abort merely to save her own reputation.[34]

By the beginning of the Renaissance, the Immaculate Conception of Mary began to take on new life, so to speak. At the turn of the century,

1701, Pope Clement XI makes the Immaculate Conception a celebration of universal obligation (required belief). The prevailing view is clear: ensoulment is no longer at issue.[35] There's no discussion about the number of days until ensoulment for it is obvious to him that at the Immaculate Conception of Mary, Jesus is Lord at the very moment of conception. He is not, according to the theologians, declared to be "the Christ" forty days later, or even a few days later. Mary, in the Lucan passage according to Clement, understands Jesus to be God's son the *moment* she is visited by the angel Gabriel.[36] If so, ensoulment occurs immediately for Jesus; the Christ could not be called Lord without a rational soul, according to Clement.

It should be remembered that this opinion regarding abortion, coming at the close of the seventeenth century, occurred when abortion, or its means anyway, was readily at hand. Herbs flourished everywhere, and women and midwives were quick to recommend them. Soranus warns against their use because of the possible dangers. He argues that it is better not to conceive than to kill the fetus. We cannot know for certain today the amounts of herbs that were used, nor can we determine whether today's herbs, if correctly identified, were the same strength now as then.[37]

CONCLUSION

From ancient times up to the close of the eighteenth century we can spot two immediately recognizable trends. On the one hand, abortion and infanticide were both practiced. On the other hand, history presents an almost unbroken record of condemning or, at the very least, stringently discouraging abortion, and, yes, even contraception. That abortion is found to have been practiced during a most spiritual age, like the Middle Ages or the early Renaissance, is not surprising. The existence of the practices should not necessarily be seen as condoning abortion.

This is where the issue of abortion rests at the end of the 1700s. Taking the historical period as a piece, history sees birth as an "absolute value." With the exception of a few voices, the preponderance of evidence appears to favor the pro-life side. It is no wonder that many people, especially on the pro-life side, were baffled by the inexplicable assertion of the Supreme Court in *Roe v Wade* that the historical record is ambiguous as it is found in the ancient texts.

If there is any ambiguity to be noted, it must come down on the side of the practice of abortion as allowed, if at all. From the Jewish Decalogue (the Ten Commandments) to the ethical teachings of Jesus in the "Sermon on the Mount," to the Middle Ages, to the Renaissance, the preponderance of evidence indicates that abortion was certainly practiced. It also, however, indicates that the practice of abortion, both willful and accidental, was a morally inferior practice; at worst, a morally reprobate one. This four-thousand-year history covers much of human social behavior, and in that time it is not surprising to find various exceptions to a given rule. The rule that does emerge is one unquestionably against the practice at all, or against it save for only the narrowest of reasons. In the end, even if we allow for abortions through the first trimester (as some in the latter part of this history appear to allow for), we are still no closer to resolving the debate, for neither side is willing to allow for the one, and prohibit the others.

The turn of the new millennium into the nineteenth century, at least at the beginning, does not provide much in the way of pro-choice advocacy, as we shall see. But we will also see, amid laws and severe punishments, a strong, loud voice emerges that leads us to *Roe v Wade*. But the way there is as circuitous as it is difficult. The way there is through another hundred years of abortion disapproval and prohibition.

NOTES

1. John T. Noonan, "An Almost Absolute Value in History," in John T. Noonan, ed., *The Morality of Abortion: Legal and Historical Perspectives* (Cambridge, Mass.: Harvard University Press, 1970), 1–59. Much of this chapter draws upon Noonan's impeccable research.

2. The word *emmenagogue* has to do with the menstrual cycle and, therefore, in this case, means the onset of the menses. An emmenagogue was something that would precipitate or cause the menses to begin, interrupting the pregnancy cycle and thus acting as an abortifacient.

3. John M. Riddle, *Eve's Herbs: A History of Contraception and Abortion in the West* (Cambridge, Mass.: Harvard University Press, 1997).

4. I am thinking here of Daniel A. Dombrowski and Robert Deltete, *A Brief, Liberal, Catholic Defense of Abortion* (Urbana, Ill.: University of Illinois Press, 2000).

5. There is another passage, Genesis 38:2–4, 9, regarding Onan and his "spilling his seed upon the ground." This seems beyond the scope of a book on abortion.

6. See, for example, the article "Abortion," in *The Jewish Encyclopedia* (New York: Funk & Wagnalls Co., 1901–1906).

7. *The New Jerusalem Bible*, reader's ed. (New York: Doubleday, 1990), 92.

8. Ibid., Leviticus 12: 2, 5.

9. For the full rendition of this, see the entry under "Birth (Jewish)" in James Hastings, *Encyclopedia of Religion and Ethics* (New York: Charles Scribner's Sons, 1918), vol. 2, 654.

10. This particular verse was used by Mother Teresa as the springboard for her uncompromising anti-abortion stance.

11. See John M. Swomley, "The Pope Versus the Bible," in *Compulsory Pregnancy: The War Against American Women* (Amherst, N.Y.: Humanist Press), 84–87.

12. For the full effect, see Mordecai Cogan and Hayim Tadmor, *II Kings: A New Translation with Introduction and Commentary,* Anchor Bible Series (New York: Doubleday, 1988), 171ff.

13. See Jacob Milgrom, *The JPS Torah Commentary: Numbers* (Philadelphia: The Jewish Publication Society, 1990), especially excursuses 8–10. See also G. W. Clarke, ed. and trans., *The Letters of St. Cyprian of Carthage, Ancient Christian Writers* series, vol. 43, Letter 4: "The crime she has committed (adultery) is not against a husband; she has committed adultery against Christ and, therefore, only when there has elapsed what is judged an appropriate period and she has publicly confessed, may she return to the church" (60).

14. Tomas J. Silber, "Abortion: A Jewish View," *Journal of Religion and Health* 19, no. 3 (Fall 1980): 231.

15. See, for example, Revelation 17:2; 18:3, 9; Galatians 5:19; Ephesians 5:3; Colossians 3:5; Matthew 15:19ff; and Mark 7:21ff, to name but a few of many. It is intellectually indefensible to argue that if the act that results in the product of a thing is prohibited on moral grounds, an act to erase the act producing it would be granted.

16. See Michael Gorman, "Why Is the New Testament Silent About Abortion?" *Christianity Today* (January 11, 1993): 27–30. Also see Scott Klusendorf's "Answering the Theological Case for Abortion Rights," http://www.issuesetc.com/resource/archives/klsdorf2.html. Both argue these texts and the Enoch one below in the same manner.

17. Paul Carrick, *Medical Ethics in Antiquity: Philosophical Perspectives on Abortion and Euthanasia* (Dordrecht, Netherlands: D. Reidel, 1985), 101.

18. Some are John 1:4; 11:25; 10:10; 14:6; 1 John 5:11; Revelation 22:1, 7.

19. Some of these would include Matthew 19:14; Mark 10:14; Luke 18:16; Hebrews 12:5; Ephesians 5:8; 1 Peter 1:14.

20. C. S. Lewis, *The Allegory of Love: A Study in Medieval Tradition* (London: Oxford University Press, 1958), 8.

21. Although mentioned by others, the chief source used here for the councils is John T. Noonan, *Contraception: A History of Its Treatment by the Catholic Theologians and Canonists* (New York: Mentor-Omega Books, 1965).

22. Noonan, *Morality of Abortion,* 16, 21. Much of this section follows Noonan closely. The passage came from Augustine but was incorporated by Gratian into Canon Law. It remained in place until the new Canon Law in 1917, according to Noonan.

23. Ibid., 20. Noonan points out that this came about through a spurious quotation from Augustine.

24. Ibid., 21ff.

25. Carrick, 101.

26. Table 1.1 has been pieced together for this book from the research done for it. While similar information may be found elsewhere, I have not yet found one with this kind of detail.

27. Thomas Rutten, "Receptions of the Hippocratic *Oath* in the Renaissance: The Prohibition of Abortion as a Case Study in Reception," *Journal of the History of Medicine and Applied Sciences,* 51 (1996): 457.

28. An excellent discussion of this and other points may be found in Carrick, especially 77–88.

29. Noonan makes this same point in *Morality of Abortion,* 5.

30. Riddle, 232–234; 237.

31. Noonan, *Morality,* 10.

32. Bernard Nathanson, "Abortion Cocktail," *First Things* (January 1996): 23–26.

33. Noonan, *Morality of Abortion,* 26.

34. Ibid., 26–28.

35. Ibid.

36. Read the passage in Luke 1:26–38.

37. Riddle argues that contraception was widely used by the lower classes as a means of limiting family size. But a compelling and opposite conclusion is offered by Bruce W. Frier, "Natural Fertility and Family Limitation in Roman Marriage," 1994.

2

Before There Was *Roe:* 1750–1899

The century and a half that is the subject of this chapter is represented in Table 2.1. The divisions in the table are partially arbitrary. A great deal goes on during the more than one hundred years of this great debate, filled as it is with colorful figures and early abortion laws. While the first hundred years is occupied mainly by those on the pro-life side of the debate, pro-choice advocates take the stage and hold it, owing to the demonstrativeness of their representatives. Indeed, the first figure we meet, the Marquis de Sade, is a devout, if not outrageous, pro-choice advocate. Toward the close of this period—roughly the last fifty years prior to the *Roe v Wade* decision—the number of pro-choice advocates begins to equal the number of their counterparts for the first time in this history.

At the close of the eighteenth century and the commencement of the next, abortions remained rare but available. Unfortunately, "safe abortions" were missing during this period. When it was practiced at all, abortion was practiced by those whose medical knowledge rarely exceeded the nostrums, or fake potions, they sold. Medieval priests who gave unsuspecting young maidens amulets to ward off unwanted pregnancy may strike us as amusing on one level, sad on another. At the beginning of the 1800s, however, abortion remedies lost all humor because they were so often fatal and equally as ineffective as those amulets. When women were not stuffing a pessary of gunpowder into their vaginas, they were using any number of other equally dangerous, equally deadly, concoctions to ward off birth.

In the early years, when survival could not be taken for granted, abortion proved extremely rare when it was practiced at all. As society advanced,

Table 2.1
Abortion Events, History, and Important American Documents

Decade	Events relating to Abortion	Other American Historical Events	Important American Documents (nonabortion related)
1790-1810	Sade's works; Lord Ellenborough's Act	First U. S. Census (1790); Work on the White House begins; New York stock exchange organized (1792); Whiskey Rebellion breaks out (1794); Adams elected second president (1796); Northwest Territory divided, (1800); John Marshall appointed chief justice of the U.S. Supreme Court.; Jefferson elected twice; Madison elected (1808) first hotel in Saratoga, N.Y.; John Randolph admits to illegitimate child; Sacagawea helps lead Lewis & Clark	Proclamation on the Whiskey Rebellion; Washington's Farewell Address (1796); Alien and Sedition Acts (1798); Land Act of 1800 (allows credit); Cession of Louisiana (1803); *Marbury v. Madison* (1803); Embargo Act (1807); Act to Prohibit the Importation of Slaves (1807)
1811-1830	*Commonwealth v. Bangs*, Massachusetts Supreme Court decides in Bang's favor; Connecticut Law; Missouri Law; Illinois Law; Lansdowne Act; New York law outlawing abortion after quickening; Connecticut outlaws instrumental abortion	Trade with Britain interrupted; Huge earthquake in MO; steamboats appear; University of Maryland chartered; Lucy Brewer disguises her sex (as Nicholas Baker) serves on abroad the *Constitution* for three years; American Bible Society founded; MS admitted to Union (1817); Monroe Doctrine enunciated by Monroe; horse racing becomes popular; American colonization of Texas; Creek Indian treaty signed; first railway steam locomotive prototype; fiery Andrew Jackson elected	*Dartmouth College v Woodward* (1819); Missouri Compromise; Land Law, 1820 (overturns 1800); Monroe Doctrine (1823); *Gibbons v. Ogden* (steamboat case); Massachusetts High School Law (1827); South Carolina protests against tariffs
1831-1850	Ohio Law; Great Britain modifies its abortion law; almost half the states have abortion laws; Madame Restell, Costello become [in]famous; Massachusetts passes law to deal with abortion separately–now crime to advertise; AMA founded and work to gain control of abortions;	*Young Man's Guide.* moralistic work by William A. Alcott (1832); Jackson reelected; transcontinental railroad suggested; Webster's bowdlerized Bible published; Congressional Temperance League founded; Post Office Department accepts newspapers, magazines; First covered wagon trail to	Jackson's message on the removal of Southern Indians, 1835; Jackson's veto of Bank Bill, 1832; Texas Declaration of Independence; Compromise of 1850; Clayton-Bulwer Treaty; Horace Mann on Education and welfare (1848); Oregon Treaty (1846); Dorothea Dix on insane asylums (1843);

medical needs moved from mere survival to enhancement. In the United States, while the East developed, the West, at least west of the Mississippi, remained unsettled. Until the Union and Central Pacific railroads snaked their ways across the middle of the United States, and towns sprang up around them, abortion remained on the back burner of social issues.[1] As

Table 2.1 (Continued)

		CA; liberalization of Christian teachings begins; Charles Dickens tours US; Sons of Temperance founded; Alcott's books pandemic; Polk elected president (1845); 1st female medical school opened; *Harper's Monthly Magazine* begins	Texas Annexation
1851-1870	Storer and Comstock begin work; declining birth rates in Protestants attributed to abortions; Offenses Against the Person Act is passed; Horatio Storer begins his campaign; Anthony Comstock rises to power; AMA establishes anti-abortion article award; Dr. Edwin M. Hale publishes *The Great Crime of the Nineteenth Century*, in which he charges 75% of all "conceptions" are criminally aborted; Storer & Fiske publish *Criminal Abortion*; Pope Pius IX issues excommunication stance for those procuring abortions	School attendance law passed; yellow fever outbreak in LA (5,000 die, 1853); Gadsden Purchase (gave us Arizona and Mexico); barroom dangers showcased everywhere; Crittenden Compromise (attempt to prevent Southern secession); Yale confers first Ph.D.; Civil War begins, first casualty recorded; Dorothea Dix serves as head of nursing for Union Army; John D. Rockefeller invests $4,000 in oil refinery business at age 23; Sherman leave Atlanta in flames (1864); 13th Amendment passes (1865); Lincoln assassinated (1865)	Trial of Mrs. Douglas for teaching colored [sic] children to read (1853); *Dred Scott v Sandford* (1857); Lincoln-Douglas Debates; Secession of MS, SC; Homestead Act; Pacific Railway Act; Morrill Act; Emancipation Proclamation; Gettysburg Address; Lee's Farewell to his Army; Johnson's Amnesty; Veto of First Reconstruction Act; Impeachment of President Johnson; Purchase of Alaska ("Steward's Folly"); Ku Klux Klan: Organization & Principles;
1871-1890	AMA steps up anti-abortion campaign; Comstock Law passed; Restell commits suicide; Hegar dilators invented (metal rods used to dilate the cervix for abortions); More than three dozen states now have anti-abortion laws; Canada restrict "obscene" materials. This also includes materials or items relating to contraceptives and abortifacients; Japan makes it a crime to have an abortion	James McNeil Whistler exhibits *Arrangement in Grey & Black*; Susan B. Anthony arrested for voting (1872); Prohibition Party forms; "Boss" Tweed convicted, escapes to Cuba, captured in Spain; Biblical creationism dismissed; El-trains made their way throughout New York; Coney Island, once a mere heap of sand, becomes famous; First Tournament of Roses held on January 1 1890	Civil Rights Act (1875); Powell's Report on the Arid Region of the West (1878); Chinese immigration regulated; Wabash Case (forerunner to the Interstate Commerce Act); Sherman Anti-Trust Act
1891-1920	Pelletier cries out for women to have reproductive control; Sanger seconds this; Comstock continues his work until he falls ill and dies; Soviet Union views abortion as necessary evil	Indian land opened in OK; Ellis Island opens for immigrants; Metropolitan Opera House destroyed by fire; Women's Suffrage adopted in CO; Eugene Debs nominated, Social Democratic Party; Langley attempts to fly a lighter than air machine to much ridicule; Panama Canal	Chinese Exclusion Act; Annexation of Hawaii; *U.S. v. Debs* et al; *Plessy v. Ferguson* (1896); Gold Standard Act; Wilson's appeal for Neutrality;"Peace Without Victory" Address; Wilson declares war; Wilson's Fourteen Points; Child Labor Act; National Prohibition Cases
		Construction; Social Creed of the Churches written, thus liberalizing church polity; Woodrow Wilson elected president, 1913	(1920);Volstead (Prohibition) Act; *Schenck v. U.S.*

Source: Some of the material in column 2 is repeated in Maria Costa, *Abortion: A Reference Handbook* (Santa Barbara, Calif.: ABC-CLIO, 1991); The rest has come from research done for this book. The documents and related events given in columns 3 and 4 come from Henry Steele Commager, *Documents of American History,* 9th ed., vols. 1–2 (Englewood Cliffs, N.J.: Prentice-Hall, 1973) and Robert Blake, ed., *World History from 1800 to the Present Day,* vol. 4 (Oxford: Oxford University Press, 1988).

these railways developed, towns matured, urbanization increased, and abortions became more numerous.

In a developing and mainly agrarian nation that demanded large numbers of men to till the soil or protect the land, it is unsurprising that abortion remained localized to large cities. While it is true that large families strained most households, these same families could rely on the soil for support and had ready-made "workers" to till it. In the East, however, where urbanization had begun to crowd out farms, abortions became more numerous, one reason being that large families proved a financial burden in an era when jobs were scarce. Since contraception remained in its infancy, sexual union often resulted in children.[2] The growing need for women—married or not—to secure abortions, and their willingness to risk everything to get them, pressured the politics of a still-developing nation to change its position regarding abortion.

Dozens of personalities and laws stand out during this century. Events or individuals on the one hand stress the need for an abortion policy, while those on the other curse its presence as indicative of moral decline. Both sides war with one another while the issues lay siege to the American moral consciousness.

America has always been influenced by Europe and, in the case of abortion, nothing could be more obvious. Europe, in particular Great Britain, proved most influential, either for what it did or did not do. In many ways, America made greater social progress by importing or rejecting certain mores from Europe.

The Marquis de Sade, a French nobleman, wrote during one of the most tempestuous of political times. His work, whatever else may be said about it, was always provocative, always extraordinary, and usually pornographic.[3] Nevertheless, he stood as an important and extremely vocal proponent of abortion. Works like *Justine* and *The 100 Days* could be discounted as the ravings of a mad and sexually perverted man. His *La Philosophie dans le boudoir* (*Bedroom Philosophy*), however, provided some insight into the formulation of abortion as a social concern.[4] Written at the close of the eighteenth century, Sade argued for abortion not only as a means of population control (echoing Plato), but also managed to bring it forward as a social concern. Sade's work stood as an effrontery to the Augustinian view of sexual intercourse, whose sole purpose was procreation. He interjected into the mix the idea that relations between a man and a woman—in his view, any man, any woman—should be for the purpose of pleasure alone. Children simply got in the way.

It is against this backdrop that nineteenth-century America begins. We know that Jefferson and Franklin, for example, were largely influenced by the work of the deists, Voltaire and Diderot especially.[5] The work of Rousseau, another deist, figured into America's understanding of education even down to the present day. For example, Rousseau's novel *Emile* focused on the principles of what he called "natural education" and have been embodied in our own educational system. Focus on the environment, the need to learn from new experiences, and the value of each person's individuality—Rousseau's ideas all—are easily recognizable in today's educational theory.[6] As the century developed, whether consciously or not, the presence of all these arguments became increasingly important, and Rosseau's "footprints" turned up everywhere.

Not everyone was ready to change, of course. Daniel Defoe, an English novelist, a writer of pamphlets, and the author of *Robinson Crusoe,* made a very strong case against abortion.

... [T]hat all the while the *Foetus* is forming...even to the Moment that the Soul is infused, so long as it is absolutely not in her Power only, but in her right, to kill or keep alive, save or destroy the Thing she goes with, she won't call it Child; and that therefore till then she resolves to use all manner of Art, to the help of Drugs and Physicians, whether Astringents, Diuretics, Emeticks, or of whatever kind, nay even to Purgations, Potions, Poisons or any thing that Apothecaries or Druggists can supply.[7]

Soon thereafter many Americans stepped up to the plate to argue the abortion question. But it took our neighbors across the Atlantic to codify their opposition before we in the United States codified our own.

ELLENBOROUGH AND LANSDOWNE ACTS

Barely ankle deep into this period, Lord Ellenborough's Act in Great Britain emerged. The Act served to underscore the fact that abortion had been thoroughly criminalized by many nations. On June 24, 1803, the Act became English law. Its preamble is worth repeating. The spellings and italics are in the original.

An Act for the further Prevention of malicious shooting, and attempting to discharge loaded Fire-Arms, stabbing, cutting, wounding, poisoning, and the malicious using of Means to procure the Miscarriage of Women; and also the malicious setting to Fire Buildings; and also for repealing a certain Act, made in *England* in the twenty-first year of the late King *James* the First, intituled [sic] *An Act to prevent the destroying and murthering of Bastard Children;* and also an Act made in *Ireland* in the sixth Year of the Reign of the late Queen *Anne,* also intituled [sic] *An Act to prevent the destroying and muthering of Bastard Children;* and for making other Provisions in lieu thereof.[8]

Lord Ellenborough was a chief justice of England. Almost single-handedly, he captured the sentiment of a people and pushed through passage of his law in 1803. An earnest conservative upset at what he saw as the continuing and relentless "liberalization" of English law on the subject, he brought forward this omnibus bill with nearly a dozen felonious crimes.[9] As seen from the preamble, the law against abortion *both before and after quickening,* made any abortion illegal in Great Britain. As Mohr points out, this influenced the American debate, but Americans did not make abortion a criminal offense until later. By the time abortion was criminalized in the United States, it had, by 1860, become almost as frequent in practice as it is today.[10]

Ellenborough's law, while making abortion criminal before quickening no matter the method, made it criminal after quickening only if poisons were used. Lord Lansdowne's Act, twenty-five years later, eliminated the inconsistencies by making the use of instruments equivalent to the use of poisons.[11]

Ellenborough's Act was an interesting piece of legislation for it underscored the view of abortion by many at the time: abortion was the equivalent of arson, murder by handgun, as well as knifings. The Act further specified abortion as, "heinous Offences, committed with Intent to destroy the Lives of his Majesty's Subjects by Poison, or with Intent to procure the Miscarriage of Women..."

The Act set the stage against any pro-choice viewpoint, and made certain its practitioners, if caught, would face severe punishments. And while abortion did became common in the United States, it was only a matter of time before numbers exceeded tolerance, the usual history of criminal law in the United States. The laws of the various states did, until around 1860, provide a measure of escape for abortionists. The first piece of American abortion legislation, however, was found in the Georgia Penal Code for 1811. The Code viewed abortion as nothing short of a peccant (sinful) act: performing an abortion made one an accessory to murder.[12]

Prosecution proved difficult. The Massachusetts Supreme Court dismissed charges against one Isaiah Bangs, because Bangs had not prepared the abortifacient or administered it but had made it available. In a sense, Bangs won his case on a technicality because the woman's unborn had not "quickened." The Augustinian and Thomist distinctions of quickening proved the rule of law instead of its exception. Bangs went free because he was not guilty according to the letter of the law. Although the forty-day rule established by Augustine (and even Aristotle before him) was overturned by the church fathers, the idea of quickening figured largely in America law, again as much a function of biology as anything else.

John Burns's 1808 book, *Observations on Abortion,* however, did not.[13] The modern reader is doubtless shocked to read:

Such medicines, likewise, as exert a violent action on the stomach or bowels will, upon the principle formerly mentioned, frequently excite abortion; and very often are taken designedly for that purpose in such quantity as to produce fatal effects; and here I must remark, that many people at least pretend to view attempts to excite abortion as different from murder, upon the principle that the embryo is not possessed of life, in the common acceptation of the word. It undoubtedly can neither think nor act; but, upon the same reasoning, we should conclude it to be innocent to kill the child at birth.

Whoever prevents life from continuing, until it arrive at perfection, is certainly as culpable as if he had taken it away after that had been accomplished. I do not, however, wish, from this observation, to be understood as in any way disapproving of those necessary attempts which are occasionally made to procure premature labor, or even abortion, when the safety of the mother demands this interference, or when we can thus give the child a chance of living, who otherwise would have none.[14]

Burns clearly means to instruct the medical profession (a profession later commandeered by Margaret Sanger for the pro-choice cause) not to be party to these wars unless under very strict conditions. We can extrapolate from this that at least as early as the first decade of the 1800s, abortion in this country, while certainly occurring, was not generally acceptable, at least not to the medical profession. The Burns text remained the standard one for the next half-century.

At the same time as the *Bangs* decision, a much more important legal matter was raging, known as *Marbury v Madison* (1803). In it, Justice John Marshall held that the dispute over federal appointments (Adams appointed William Marbury Justice of the Peace, but the appointment was withheld by Jefferson), denied in the Constitution by Article III, found remedy in this statute: Marshall argued that the Court's authority exceeded that of the Constitution's. It was the first such decision to invalidate an act of Congress while vastly expanding the power of an unelected judiciary. This establishment of the Court's right to judicial review would, of course, figure greatly in the *Roe v Wade* decision, one that essentially overturned the laws of all state legislatures and underscored the power of the judicial branch of government over the other two, at least as far as abortion was concerned.

While Ellenborough's Act ruled English abortion law, in the hands of Lord Lansdowne, Henry Petty-Fitzmaurice (1780–1863), the law became clearer. Lord Lansdowne's Act, enacted in 1828, standardized the language of Ellenborough:

If any person, with intent to procure the miscarriage of any woman then being quick with child, unlawfully and maliciously shall administer to her, or cause to be taken by her, any poison or other noxious thing, or shall use any instrument or other means

whatever the intent, every such offender, and every person counseling, aiding or abetting such offender, shall be guilty of felony, and being convicted thereof, shall suffer
death as a felon; and if any person, with intent to procure the miscarriage of any
woman not being or being not proved to be, then quick with child, unlawfully and
maliciously shall administer to her, or cause to be taken by her, any medicine or other
thing, or shall use any instrument or other means whatever the like intent, every such
offender, and every person counseling, aiding or abetting such offender shall be guilty
of a felony.

Two things stand out here. Under this Act, both aiders and abettors were
charged, including those who *counseled* abortion. Surely this had some impact
on pro-life advocates in later debates against Planned Parenthood and its allies, at least in the sense that both those who perform abortions and those
who counsel them were in their partisan eyes anyway, equally guilty. Everything changed while remaining the same.

Second, and this appears more striking, was the issue of the importance of
a woman "quick" with child. What this Act appeared to do was clear up this
matter as one that alluded more to biology than to either philosophy or the-
ology. Recall that in the previous chapter, a woman had full control of her
pregnancy in the sense that no one really knew she was pregnant unless she
told them, or until she began to show. The latter proved easily hidden from
untrained and even trained eyes. By the first quarter of the nineteenth century, little had changed. Neither Burns nor any of the other medical writers
of the time—including Joseph Brevitt, who wrote *The Female Medical Repos-
itory* (published in 1810) and Thomas Ewell, the Navy Hospital's surgeon
who wrote *Letters to Ladies* in 1817—could determine a woman's pregnant
state without examination, unless she admitted it. Walter Channing, who lec-
tured at the Harvard Medical School in the 1820s, taught his students that
diagnosis with complete accuracy might be impossible. So did John Beck, a
devoutly adamant opponent of abortion at any stage of gestation.[15] At least
one other explanation of the quickening laws in this country may have far less
to do with not seeing the embryo as human (it is clear that the medical and
theological professions did view the embryo as human), than it did with having no other scientific means for determining accurately the pregnant condition of a woman. A woman, therefore, seeking medical help would be far less
likely to admit quickening at all, since this would clearly indicate the status of
her unborn child.

The Acts of Ellenborough and Lansdowne both figured prominently in the
history leading up to *Roe v Wade*, as did *Commonwealth v Bangs*. It is crucial
in this discussion to understand the historical importance of these events, and
the Acts behind them as they influenced American law.

Whatever its legal status, colonial America saw abortion in an unsavory light.[16] Yet abortions did occur. It is impossible to know the exact number of abortions being performed prior to 1860, but we do know that abortions occurred, though not with the frequency they were during and immediately following the Civil War. We also know that about one-third of all colonial brides were pregnant.[17]

Following the *Bangs* case, Connecticut passed a law in 1821 that prohibited the inducement of abortion though the administration of "dangerous poisons." While the penalty was not death, it did specify life imprisonment, and from this law two things could be gleaned. Quickening again played a role, as the law applied to those women who were "quick" with child. The Connecticut law (and its revision in 1831) also served to point out that insofar as abortion was practiced, it had to be regulated, since it more often than not ended in the death of the woman. On the face of it, the law would appear to place abortion in the hands of the medical professionals. But on second glance we see that there was no provision for abortifacients or pessaries, whether administered by midwives or anyone else, presumably even the woman herself, after the quickening of the child.

The Connecticut law was quickly followed by similar laws in Missouri (1825), Illinois (1827), and New York (1828). These laws were all patterned on the Connecticut law, but the New York law also took into consideration the Lansdowne Act of 1828. All of these laws sought to criminalize poisons used in abortions. The Lansdowne Act, which treated abortion *by any means and by anyone,* much influenced the New York law.

The New York law (passed in 1828, made public a year later, and enacted the year after that) added that there must be a death either of the woman herself or the unborn child for a charge to be brought.[18] Without one or the other, the law argued, the abortion did not take place. This probably helps to explain why so few abortionists were prosecuted. Essentially a third party had to witness the abortion and presumably neither the physician performing it nor the woman seeking it would likely do so. Section 21 of Title VI, Chapter I, Part IV, the third section of the New York law also adds a maximum penalty for the abortionist: one year in jail and/or $500 in fines.[19] The death of the "unborn quick child" meant second-degree manslaughter for the abortionist, not the woman. Perhaps under the influence of *Bangs*, the New York law added an interesting provision: "...unless the same shall have been necessary to preserve the life of such woman, or shall have been advised by two physicians to be necessary for that purpose..." In other words, the law did not punish abortions performed when the mother's life was at risk.

This was an important qualifier. Many pro-choice advocates and their proponents have seen this as part of the modern law in *Roe v Wade*. But clearly the

New York law did not include any of the additional provisions in *Roe v Wade* (which provided for abortion on demand, a phrase that means abortion can be had whenever it is sought). Of course, circumventions of this law abounded. We can deduce, from the number of abortions we know were being performed, that some physicians could be persuaded (say for the right dollar amount?) to agree that the mother's life was at stake. Legally, however, the mother had to be dying from the pregnancy for abortion not to be a crime.

Perhaps in response to the Lansdowne Act, Connecticut revised its statute in 1830, just two years following the adoption of the English law. While the Lansdowne Act punished all abortions for any reason and by any method before or after quickening, the Connecticut revision outlawed them after quickening alone. In all the laws of this period, then, common practice neatly guided the criminal code. This is hardly surprising or unusual. Indeed, it is not until we arrive at modern Supreme Court justices who find "penumbra" (shadows) in the law, that common practice ceased to influence the criminal code while the criminal code established what became common practice.

Table 2.2 serves as a laconic representation of laws up to and following this time.[20] It is interesting to note not only the number but also the wide variety of legislation. Clearly, abortion occupied a central concern. But were people concerned about it because of its frequency, or because medical practitioners desired to maintain their close control of any medical practice? It is not easy to say for certain.

It is not, however, clear that these are the only reasons. As has been previously noted, pregnancy handbooks and guides were abundant. Newspapers contained "curing" ads for virtually every kind of disease. And quacks with their fake wares made rounds promising all kinds of freedom from disease and guaranteeing long life. This fact of early nineteenth-century life did not change with the passage of laws. Today, medical practitioners have used the strong arm of their political action committee through their professional association to bring pressure to bear on what could be seen as modern-day nostrums: herbalists and those who distribute vitamins. Yet both physicians and vitamins are ubiquitous in spite of, or perhaps because of, legal tampering.

Laws passed after the Connecticut revision need not concern us much. These laws drew heavily on the Connecticut and New York laws and sought to formalize common law procedure at work, or so it seemed. The common law of Sir Edward Coke in his *Institutes of the Laws of England* (1641) argued that the abortion of a quickened fetus is "a great misprision [i.e., evil], [but] no murder."[21] Blackstone concluded in his *Commentaries on the Laws of England* that while abortion was a "heinous" act, it remained a misdemeanor. New York law recognized this but ratcheted the pressure up, not down. The

Table 2.2
Early Abortion Laws

Name of Law or State	Year	Law
Ellenborough's Act (England)	1803	10 criminal laws including abortion
Georgia	1811	Criminalized abortion
Massachusetts	1812	Isaiah Bangs found not guilty of abortion
Connecticut	1821	Prohibits abortion after quickening
Missouri	1825	Anti-poison act
Illinois	1827	modeled after Connecticut's
Lansdowne's Act	1828	Standardized Ellenborough's Act and sought to prevent all abortions before or after quickening
New York	1828	Prohibits abortion by any means after quickening
Connecticut	1830 (revision)	Prohibits abortion after quickening; fines abortionist
Ohio	1834	Follows Connecticut; adds that attempted abortion is a misdemeanor. The death of either the quick unborn child or the mother is a felony.
Indiana	1835	Follows Connecticut
Arkansas	1837	Follows Connecticut
Offenses Against the Person Act, Great Britain	1837	Revises its law and removes the reference to quickening; eliminates the death penalty for abortion
Iowa Territory	1839	Follows Connecticut
Alabama	1840	Follows Connecticut
Maine	1840	Follows Lansdowne; the law makes attempted abortion a criminal offense whether the child is quick or not. It further adds a provision for therapeutic abortion.

common law casuistry (rightness or wrongness of a practice) seemed to be to make the moral observance more, not less, in the New York offering.

The New York law received much of the discussion not only because so much more was known about it, but doubtless, too, because it sought to provide an anodyne between practicing physicians on the one hand, and illegal abortions on the other. The New York law provided legal means for limiting a killing practice, perhaps to protect women. Medicine still lacked sophistication. Any number of quacks (persons claiming to have medical knowledge) could not be pursued legally until such laws allowed for prosecution. There

Sir Edward Coke. (Courtesy of the Library of Congress.)

appears to be less of an insistence during these years on providing for abortion than on preventing or prohibiting those who would perform what they could not by practice excel in doing. Oddly, years later and just prior to *Roe,* the number of abortionists who were practicing what they had not been trained in, abortion, exceeded those who had been taught to perform them.

When one reads through the major medical manuals of this time period (Burns's *Observations on Abortion,* noted above, for example) one is struck by the ill-informed nature of physicians. If medical doctors could be so ill-informed about science (Burns believed that soft bed lines could bring on a miscarriage), then what was the medical knowledge of those who had received little or minimal training? A woman who placed herself in the hands of one of these quacks for any reason, much less a complicated procedure like abortion, courted death. Childbirth in the early 1800s also proved dangerous. Mohr is, however, surely wrong when he argues that childbirth outstripped abortion in danger.[22] Childbirth, however dangerous, remained far more commonplace than abortion. Penicillin had not yet been developed and abortions performed without it often meant death from infection. Pioneer women had themselves delivered the children of their neighbors with success.

By the middle of the 1800s, almost half of the twenty-six states posted statuary prohibitions on abortion. Quickening figured as often in these laws as it did not and, again, for reasons of biology as much as anything else. Most abortion laws were part of larger bills. Although some writers have concluded that the laws remained unenforced, or were enforced inconsistently, they nevertheless remained. Further, some pro-choice advocates have argued that the presence of the laws without any substantial pro-life protestations was significant.

Meanwhile, English law was changed once again under the Offenses Against the Person Act of 1837. The Act has particular importance and its material part, Section 6, is quoted here in full:

Whosoever, with intent to procure the miscarriage of any woman, shall unlawfully administer to her or cause to be taken by her any poison or other noxious thing, or shall unlawfully use any instrument or other means whatsoever with like intent, shall be guilty of felony.

Although the law's intent was to prevent either the dispensing of poisons or to formalize the practice of medicine, it nevertheless strengthened the casuistry (the determination of right and wrong) of common law by keeping abortion a felony rather than a misdemeanor.

By 1840, other matters had begun to shift the abortion debate away from what pro-life advocates would consider in their favor, and more to what pro-choice advocates would consider theirs. After 4,500 years of nearly exclusive control over the abortion question, pro-life advocates (though, of course, they were not called such until modern times) occupied the mainstream view. Whether it was the influence of the church (which is most likely, whether it be Roman Catholic or Protestant), or just a social consciousness, cannot be said for sure. Pro-choice advocates do make much of the fact that abortion has been practiced since the beginning of time. The fact of a practice does not vouchsafe its acceptance, however.[23] The tide began to turn more obviously to the pro-choice side around the 1840s.

One thing is certain. Abortion moved from a practice that occurred behind closed doors and only for a select portion of the population (generally the more wealthy), to a practice that virtually skyrocketed among the general populace, rich or poor. Both pro-life and pro-choice advocates agree on this point. If abortion occurred with a kind of illegitimacy before this time, it moved to a wide open, widespread practice, not at once, but gradually and rather quickly. Abortionists competed for what seemed to be an "open market" in the trade. If abortion had been the bailiwick or domain of the rich and unknown among the poor, it began occurring more frequently among the middle class.

If earlier laws, like the Connecticut and New York laws, represented a movement among the medical profession to underscore the seriousness of this medical procedure, by the 1840s, the medical profession had open competition for these services. Newspapers quickly jumped on this as a source of advertising revenue, much as they do today with "personals" that seem to showcase the love lives of the forlorn.[24] Since these abortion advertisements were not illegal, physicians quickly discovered that the "market" was not theirs alone.

RESTELL, RESTELLISM, AND MORE

Among abortionists of this time, one name towers above all the rest: Ann Trow Lohman (1811–1878, a.k.a., Madame Restell). Restell, an English immigrant from Gloucestershire, dealt exclusively in abortions for her livelihood. Restell performed so many abortions that at least one citizen argued that "recourse to Lynch law" may be the only way to stop her, and her prosecutor seconded that by pleading that "lust, licentiousness, seduction and abortion would be the inevitable occurrences of every day" unless she ceased and desisted. Restell, like Capone later, was prosecuted on minor technicalities.[25]

Restell married a tailor and had one daughter. They immigrated to New York City in 1831, in search of opportunity in the land that promised same. Unfortunately, in August of that year, her husband, Henry Summers, contracted a "bilious fever" and died, leaving Ann to raise their only daughter alone. The now-single mother took a job as a seamstress. A few years later, in 1836, she met Charles Lohman, a printer, and they married. Although Ann had little education, she and her husband considered themselves freethinking intellectuals. Soon this freewheeling couple took to selling medicines by mail, hoping to get rich quick. They did. Not long thereafter, Ann, certainly medically illiterate, began performing abortions. It is unclear where and how she learned this trade. Charles may have been a true intellectual, however. In any case he was certainly very clever and began advertising for her under what became her notorious pseudonym, Madame Restell. He took on the name Dr. Mauriceau.

Restell promised to cure all abortions, which she euphenized as "derangement of the stomach" or "deathly, sallow and inanimate complexion." The "remedies," which rarely worked, ranged from mere placebos (tansy oil) to deadly potions (turpentine). When these failed, women rushed to New York for a "painless operation" that involved using a wire to pierce the amniotic sac. Women were charged according to their ability to pay, from $20 to $100.[26] Restell made the ads upbeat and service-oriented. She also used very modern arguments to persuade the public of the value of her services. Women could abort because they loved their husbands (fidelity); pregnancy had risks (health care issue); abortion proved easy (medical technology); abortion made life better (quality of life issue); and abortion really only removed fluids (not a baby, just tissue).[27]

Restell advertised her services in the *New York Sun* and the *Boston Daily Times.*[28] Her business prospered beyond any expectation. It flourished to the extent that by 1845 she opened "clinics" in Boston and Philadelphia. She even had traveling salesmen distributing her "pills." When these did not do the trick (and they usually did not), she authorized them to refer women to her main clinic in New York. Restell was not the only such figure but merely the celebrated court case of the times. Newspapers throughout the East promised "relief" from "female complaints." Mohr, for example, mentions a Dr. Caswell, Dr. Louis Kurtz, Dr. Dow, "Sleeping Lucy" (a clairvoyant), and others who also practiced the trade.[29]

Given the early history, oddly most of the early objections to these practitioners did not come from the clergy. Newspapers (although, as pointed out, they rushed to this revenue source) criticized the clergy for remaining silent. The *National Police Gazette* opined, "Would that we might hear some strident tones from the pulpits about this phase of evil."[30] The clergy, however, did not take this matter lying down. When a woman died at the hands of an abortionist, her minister blamed the *Gazette* for having offered "rose water balderdash" and "cream-cheese platitudes" rather than strict warnings against abortion as a means of escape from pregnancy. But his words sang alone with one rather surprising exception: the Presbyterian Church in the United States.[31] Most Presbyterian clergy rushed to the defense of abortion by making the same argument they do today: "It is less criminal to kill children before they are born, than to curse them with an unwelcome existence."[32] Restell became at the very least a self-promoting master of Madison Avenue, before that name became synonymous with advertising. One 1845 advertisement from the *New York Sun* ran:

MADAME RESTELL, FEMALE PHYSICIAN, office and residence 148 Greenwich street, between Courtland and Liberty st, where she can be consulted with the strictest confidence on complaints incidental to the female frame.

Madame Restell's experience and knowledge in the treatment of cases of female irregularity, is such as to require but a few days to effect a perfect cure. Ladies desiring proper medical attendance will be accommodated during such time with private and respectable board.

Madame Restell would apprize ladies that her medicines will be sent by mail, or by various expresses, to any part of the city or country. All letters must be postpaid, except those containing all enclosure.... [33]

Advertisements such as these did cost money, even then, and it is estimated that her advertising budget by the 1870s topped more than $50,000 annually. The advertisements cloyed the language but little. Restell's ads competed against those offering "French Lunar Pills," "French Periodical Pills," and "Portuguese Female Pills."[34] The language of these ads grew increasingly bold and straightforward. Restell had to fight for more than just her abortion activities. She saw allegations of all sorts leveled against her, including stealing and selling infants. When a young woman charged her with stealing her child, the rabble awaiting her could only be dispersed when the mayor of New York City, William Havermayer, promised to have her arrested. At one point, Restell's clinic where single women could have children was thought to have a special sewer that disposed of the evidence into the Hudson River. Restell always managed to escape prosecution, since conviction relied on eyewitnesses who were, of course, too involved to come forward.[35] Until one fateful day.

A former patient, Maria Bodine, charged Restell in 1847 under the 1845 Abortion Law that made it a felony to kill an unborn quickened child. The trial proved sensational and made all the New York papers, garnering for Restell a dubious title: "the most evil woman in America." Restell escaped the felony charges but was found guilty of a misdemeanor and served one year at Blackwell Island. The stay Restell found easy because she was able to use her huge fortune to avoid the hard labor of prison. Instead, she slept on feather beds and dressed in fine silk. She returned to New York upon her release and resumed her practice. After imprisonment, Restell turned to the affluent exclusively, and while her competition charged $10 per abortion, Restell made $2,000 each, mainly off wealthy New York's single, affluent women who did not want the stigma of a child out of wedlock. After Restell's second husband died, things went downhill quickly. While many of her abortions were successful, she made the tactical mistake of crossing swords with Anthony Comstock.

The New York papers ran scathing stories on abortionists, including Restell, and Comstock, using his celebrated Comstock Law of 1873, finally caught up with her in the 1870s. Comstock's law, among other things, made it a crime to advertise anything obscene, or anything that could terminate a pregnancy. On April Fool's Day 1878, when Restell saw that she would go back to prison without the ability to avoid prison's harshness, she took an ebony-handled knife, and, sitting in her tub, committed suicide at the age of 67. Ironically enough, the charge proved a minor one but enough to cause her to take her life. Comstock, when he heard of her suicide, called it "a bloody ending to a bloody life." She left an estate valued at upwards of $1 million. Her flamboyance, her diamonds, and her silk finery made her an easy target for those who disliked her.[36]

Although Madame Restell exploited women for money, she was not alone. Sarah Sawyer, who came to be known as the "Restell of Boston," dressed so lavishly that her clothes alone cost more than most people made in a year. Of course, men joined these ranks as well, making as much as $2,000 a month as abortionists in the 1870s.[37] At the close of the Civil War, abortion won a hearing legislatively because so many women complained about being exploited. The rich could afford it and did not care; indeed, they sought out the Restells of New York and Boston and assured them of a livelihood. Because there was so much money to be made, abortionists of this time could offer their services for as little as $8, putting abortion within the reach of all but the most indigent. It did not help the cause of abortionists when it became publicly known that they posted bail at amounts three times what university professors were making.[38]

As the costs increased at every level, so did moral sensitivity. Some tolerated wealthy debutantes who had gotten themselves "in trouble" and sought "Lunar pills" for relief, but married women who sought the skills of the abortionists were not tolerated so lightly. As early as 1844, medical journals noted the practice with nothing that resembled moral neutrality. The editor of one journal excoriated the practice as "deplorable." He also referred to Madame Restell as "the vampire of New York."[39] As most physicians saw it, there was no excuse for married women "killing their own children," as they often put it.

The argument is often made that what physicians wanted was not that abortion be stopped but that the medical profession control it. Perhaps so. Some physicians saw it differently:

Awful as these recitals [of abortions] are, of the name of heathen a nation, the deeds of darkness repeated in our own cities, in a professedly Christian country, beyond the cognizance of any police, are, if possible, still more deplorable. Such are the willy movements of these professed abortionists, that, although their acts, according to common report, are exceedingly frequent, no one can be found who will boldly face the foe and arraign them at the bar of insulted justice.... Law is disregarded, and those who have become expert...in stifling human life *in utero* neither fear the frowns of man nor the avenging arm of God.[40]

Physicians up and down the East Coast lamented the practice: in Atlanta, Vermont, Boston, New York, Maine, and Massachusetts. The *Boston Medical and Surgical Journal* also criticized abortionists.[41]

Obviously, the trend to accept abortion tended in the opposite direction. If abortions among single, affluent women were tolerated, the practice was never without complaint. By all accounts it was still considered wicked by most. And lest we too quickly resort to political correctness to defend the practice by charging that it was men who pressed their moral obligations upon their more free-thinking counterparts, it should be added that the earliest of the women's movements during the last quarter of the 1800s also opposed abortion, not because it was forced on them by men, but because they saw it as morally wrong.[42]

Early feminist leaders rushed to disabuse the public that their movement favored abortion. Feminists such as Victoria Woodhull, Susan B. Anthony, Emma Goldman, Alice Paul (author of the Equal Rights Amendment in the early twentieth century), and Elizabeth Cady Stanton, spoke for its elimination, suggesting adoption instead, or impugned abortion's immorality. Woodhull, who defended the reasons women might resort to abortion, was no ordinary woman or feminist. With her sister, Tennessee Clafin, she became the first female stockbroker. Later, she was the first woman to open a bank on Wall Street, and, later still, she declared her candidacy for the U.S. presidency on the Equal Rights Party ticket with none other than Frederick Douglass as her running mate![43] Most women, including feminists like Woodhull, looked at abortion as doing more harm than good in the debate for women's rights and distanced themselves from it as soon as they could. Up until the end of the nineteenth century, it was hard, if not impossible, to find even one feminist advocating abortion as a woman's right, or as a means to the end of sexual inequality. Feminists railed against men and their "sensuality" and called on them to exert more self-control. In fact, they turned the tables on the men and called on them to curb their appetites and quit forcing motherhood on their wives. In the end, however, early feminists opposed abortion. To many modern ears this will sound oddly offbeat, but feminists throughout this period saw the prevention of unwanted pregnancies as having but one solution: abstinence.

Although abortion became commonplace during this time, it became so not because moral sentiment against abortion waned. William A. Alcott (1798–1859), a doctor and an educator, rose to fame during these years and wrote one of the most important set of books ever.[44] Alcott was raised on a farm so his schooling occurred only during the winter. Before entering Yale College, he taught school in the area. Once licensed in 1826, he added numerous medical innovations, served on the local school committee, and established a library. He later went to Boston where he and W. C. Woodbridge established *Juvenile Rambler,* the first weekly periodical for children published in this country.

Alcott was an indefatigable, tireless writer, publishing more than one hundred books and scores of articles. His *Confessions of a Schoolmaster* established him as an educator, but none of his books were as important as four aimed at young men and women, whether single or married: *The Young Man's Guide; The Young Woman's Guide; The Young Mother;* and *The Young Husband, or Duties of Man in the Marriage Relation.* The books took a fiercely moral and didactic tone. For example, in *The Young Man's Guide,* Alcott warned young men against gambling ("it produces nothing"), lotteries ("the *worst* species of Gaming"), the evils of the theater, and smoking. He spoke positively of the benefits of early rising, obeying one's parents, and forming "temperate" habits early in life. Throughout the book were sprinkled Christian teachings.

Women were likewise warned or exhorted. *The Young Women's Guide* pointed out how they should use their time, how they could acquire the love of domestic concerns, followed by chapters on "self-command" and "self-government" or why women weren't expected to be "reasoners." Similarly, *The Young Husband,* for example, taught the male how to love his wife, and why he should not be overbearing in any capacity. A chapter on man's sexual behavior urged him to conquer the "devils," and not to defile his marriage bed by lust or an absence of purity. Alcott also instructed through anecdote how men, with all the advantages, should not be too hard on their wives who did not have the same opportunities.

The Alcott books were probably the most well-read books from the date of their publication (1834) through the end of the century. *The Young Man's Guide* went through more than fifteen editions in as many years. One would not want to overstress the ramifications of these books, but it is historically important to note that at a time when abortions were everywhere apparent, men and women both were counseled by the "best-sellers" of the time to behave themselves in a moral manner.

In 1861 Great Britain again revised its Offenses Against the Person Act. The revisions changed a number of things, not the least of which was the penalty for abortions. Sections 58 (administering drugs or using instruments to procure abortion) and 59 (procuring drugs and the like to cause abortion) are clear about intent:

Section 58

Every woman, being with child, who, with intent to procure her own miscarriage, shall unlawfully administer to herself any poison or other noxious thing, or shall unlawfully use any instrument or other means whatsoever with the like intent, and whatsoever, with intent to procure the miscarriage of any woman whether she be or not be with child, shall unlawfully administer to her or cause to be taken by her poison or other noxious thing, or shall unlawfully use any instrument or other means whatsoever with the like intent, shall be guilty of felony, and being convicted thereof shall be liable...to be kept in penal servitude for life.

Section 59

Whosoever shall unlawfully supply or procure any poison or other noxious thing, or any instrument or thing whatsoever, knowing that the same is intended to be unlawfully used or employed with intent to procure the miscarriage of any woman, whether she be or not be with child, shall be guilty of a misdemeanor, and being convicted thereof shall be liable...to be kept in penal servitude.... [45]

The law served notice of the seriousness of the offenses and also served as models for the United States. By 1869, Pope Pius IX demanded the excommunication of anyone who either had an abortion or who had performed one. Bishops had already made clear to American Catholic women that abortions were not only unacceptable practice, but also a sin against God.[46]

HORATIO STORER

An early voice of the pro-life camp rose during this time: the physician Horatio Storer.[47] Horatio Robinson Storer (1830–1922) was a practicing physician who followed in his father's footsteps by entering medicine.[48] A most unlikely pro-life champion, the surgeon Storer for most of his life studied the varieties of shellfish and dedicated his first identified species to his father.[49] Storer's father, a professor of obstetrics and medical jurisprudence at Harvard, became president of the American Medical Association. The younger Storer opened his practice in Boston in 1855 and in almost no time had established himself as a leading physician in the East. In order to better understand his practice, Storer also acquired degrees in medical jurisprudence and became the first physician in America to teach courses in gynecology and obstetrics as opposed to midwifery. His semi-annual lectures in Boston on the surgical diseases of women unconnected with pregnancy filled lecture halls with physicians from all over the world. He also maintained the most complete collection then in existence of medals, jetons, and tokens that illustrated the science of medicine.[50]

Storer may be counted as the physician who brought light to bear upon what became one physician's crusade against abortion. A prolific writer, Storer wrote seven books and more than two hundred articles on medical issues. He used his pen in the campaign against abortion by writing to physicians all over the United States, inquiring about their state's abortion laws. When Storer learned from them that the laws when present remained weak and unenforced, it motivated him to begin his campaign. Many physicians expressed regret that the practice took place in their states and wished something could be done about it. Did Storer and his fellow physicians fight this fight owing to the moral climate, the need to control medical practice, or the Hippocratic Oath? Most likely the Hippocratic Oath, given the decades in which Storer launched his efforts. Physicians did not like the idea of taking life, whether quickened or not, and blanched at the idea of a practice so rife with the opportunity for money that it made the practice of medicine seem more like commercialism. After gaining support from physicians throughout the country, Storer, in 1857, introduced to the Suffolk County Medical Society (Massachusetts) the call for a committee to consider whether further legislation was necessary to criminalize abortion.

Once Storer's committee was launched, a number of prominent physicians in Boston opposed the measure. The opposition was itself divided. Some opposed Storer on the grounds of his harshness toward physicians' acceptance of abortion, while others saw it as political suicide. In the end, most came around to Storer's views. He wrote articles for all the major medical magazines and garnered what became national support for his anti-abortion project.[51]

Storer's respect among physicians and his excellent practice and pedigree served him well. Storer's prize-winning essay, "The Criminality and Physical Evils of Forced Abortion" (1865) followed by its extended monographic form published by the AMA, *Why Not? A Book for Every Woman,* proved the key to the criminalization of abortion in this country. *Is It I? A Book for Every Man,* written for legislators, quickly followed.[52] Both books garnered exceedingly positive reviews in the press and gained wide audiences, proving once again that a government of the people, by the people, and for the people must be taken to them to *win* acceptance. Storer followed up these books with another he coauthored with attorney Franklin Fiske Heard, *Criminal Abortion: Its Nature, Its Evidence, and Its Law.* Storer brought to bear on the subject all his training in medical jurisprudence, hoping to win over lawmakers to his point of view. The book did.

Storer and Heard made their case plainly. They appealed to reason instead of the heart, and called upon the presumed dignity of their chosen professions, law and medicine, to take up their responsibilities in this matter:

Lawyers and physicians should stand to each other, in medico-legal matters, as associates working together for the common good of society, rather than as adversaries liable to be thought endeavoring to make the worse appear the better reason. The crime of unjustifiable abortion is now recognized by both professions as of frequent occurrence, and as going too often unwhipt of justice.... Argumentation, however, though cogent, and ethics, though divine, are insufficient, this side of eternity, to restrain the vices and passions of mankind.[53]

The point of the preamble was to rivet the reader's mind to reason in addition to facts. Storer and Heard did not argue that abortion could not be rationalized; indeed, they assumed that it could be. Their argument became most compelling when they asserted that there were some things we could do that we should not.

In the battle over abortion, both sides fought as if at war, and Storer stood at the center of the battleground. The editorial in the July 1869 issue of the *New Hampshire Journal of Medicine* shows why:

> We feel we may be pardoned for first speaking at length as we have, of the connection of the Massachusetts brethren with this subject, as the war seems first to have fairly begun with them; and will only say in addition, that we have personal knowledge that the evil [abortion] is no less prevalent in our own community. . . .
>
> Dr. H. R. Storer has taken a stand in this matter alike creditable to his head and his heart, and we feel that he will receive the hearty thanks of every *true* physician.[54]

Once launched, the AMA took up the gauntlet and promoted the campaign around the country. Soon local medical societies that Storer had alerted with his early letters to individual physicians took up the debate. States began changing or revising their statutes on abortion. The process was fascinating in an age that could not rely on e-mails and faxes. Storer, one man with a passion, forced the hand of a nation that had not looked hard at a practice with which it had never grown comfortable. The AMA referred, at times, to the *Storer Resolution* on criminal abortion, rather than using its legal name, much like the Comstock Law. But the AMA agreed with Storer—of that there can be no doubt. By 1859, the *Transaction of the American Medical Association* began, "The heinous guilt of criminal abortion, however viewed by the community, is everywhere acknowledged by medical men. Its frequency—among all classes of society, rich and poor, single and married—most physicians have been led to suspect; very many, from their own experience of its deplorable results, have known."[55]

This uneasiness, more than anything else, helped spur the pro-life elements in this country on to victory. If the populace had thought abortion to be adiaphorous—that is, morally neutral—then Storer would never have been able to achieve as much as he did. Because the practice of abortion proved loathsome to just about everyone involved, it remained in the shadows in a society that tried to tolerate it. When the slightest pressure to reject it pushed to the fore, the arguments for it, never having been very articulately made, fell away.

COMSTOCKISM

While Storer took his campaign to the professional community, Anthony Comstock (1844–1915), made his case to the general public.[56] Comstock came from very humble beginnings; his father was a farmer and a sawmill owner. His mother died when Comstock was only ten.

Comstock's success cannot be denied. He claimed once, in an interview with *Harper's Weekly* in 1915, that he had convicted enough people of sexual misconduct to fill a sixty-car passenger train, in addition to the destruction of "tons" of obscene materials.[57] Although he had served in the Union Army, Comstock hated the raucous behavior and vulgarity of barracks life. He did not appreciate the pluralistic values of the Republic that would, on the one hand, foster such high moral standards by individuals and yet tolerate such cavalier behavior (at least to Comstock's mind) sanctioned by the government.[58] Using the financial backing of prominent figures such as philanthropist Morris Jesup and congressman William E. Dodge, Comstock set up a vice squad, so to speak, of the Young Men's Christian Association. This developed later into the New York Society for the Suppression of Vice, modeled after the society established in Great Britain a hundred years earlier. Jesup provided the money while Comstock prosecuted those trafficking in pornography. In 1873, Comstock produced what is perhaps the jewel in the crown of his life's work, what has popularly been called "The Comstock Act."

The Comstock Act is still on the books, although slightly modified. The pertinent part of the original law read:

That no obscene... [thing]... or any *article or thing deigned or intended for the prevention of conception or procuring of abortion...shall be carried in the mail, and any person who shall knowingly deposit [it]...* shall be deemed guilty of a misdemeanor, and, on conviction thereof, shall...be fined not less than one hundred dollars nor more than five thousand dollars, or imprisoned at hard labor not less than one year nor more than ten years, or both, in the discretion of the judge.[59]

The italicized portions of the law indicate how Comstock tricked Madame Restell into confession.

The one-two punch of Storer and Comstock during the close of the nineteenth century bracketed what had been an abortion heyday, heyday referring to the number of performed abortions. As Comstock sought to cut off the source of advertising revenue and promulgation, Storer brought professional opinion to bear on the subject. Around the end of this century, Edward E. Conrad shone yet another light from the professional viewpoint. Writing about the practice of abortion, a topic he thought was overdone, he added:

The immediate and remote results of mismanagement forms a gruesome picture too vivid to be unnoticed, and far too serious to fail to impress a man possessed of a healthy amount of sentiment. And yet when the history of numberless cases [of abortions] proves the existence of a class of men who limit their treatment to an examination of the vessel that is supposed to contain the products of conception, the administering of ergot, and the collection of their fee, I think that every right-minded man will admit that there is still a crying demand for a further supply of literature that will aid the physician to form a clear conception of his duty toward these cases.[60]

Conrad proceeded to describe the proper procedure for this "awful" practice. Comstock certainly imbued the public with a sense of restraint necessary in sexual relations. And though a "Punch" cartoon prophesied that New York would be overrun with small children upon the death of Madame Restell, that prophecy never came true. In fact, abortions declined, deaths from abortions declined as well, and abortion as a practice became a criminal act, though convictions were few.

The curtailment of abortion through Storer and Comstock made the practice even less lucrative than it had been formerly. When mailings, advertising, and the sale of instruments for the purpose of abortion all became punishable offenses both here and in Great Britain, abortion had no other place to go but up.[61] With so much facing an abortionist, or an abortion provider, fewer and fewer takers stepped up to test the laws. Convictions still were few, even amid so strong an anti-abortion sentiment. Largely this was because so few reported it, even among physicians who disagreed with the practice. Many physicians who did not wish to make a name for themselves as abortion practitioners would perform abortions discreetly, and for a select few.[62]

CONCLUSION

These early years of abortion practice are bewildering. Why were so many abortions being performed, especially after the Civil War, while there was so much public sentiment against it? One answer resides in the lack of contraception. On the one hand, married couples sought the enjoyment of sexual intimacy. On the other hand, few families, especially in urban areas, could afford more than two children. Often, however, these couples would have five or six. Since contraception was often left in the hands of wives, women sought the limitation of families wherever they could find it. Contraceptives proved not only ineffective but also repugnant. As late as 1885, a woman who asked about the best way to prevent pregnancy was told, "The best way is for you to sleep in one bed and your Man in another.... "[63] The problem was twofold. Wives were expected to submit to their husbands' sexual demands and yet they had very few means by which to limit their families. Literature about reproduction had been limited, if not by the church, then by Comstock and others. In the end, the only way to limit the size of one's family was the abortionist.[64]

Since the abortionist turned out to be a man or woman untrained in the practice, deaths occurred quite frequently. These deaths forced the hands of those holding political power to make a statement. Because church teachings still guided mainstream opinion, and church teachings did not favor abortions, those in power often sided with popular sentiment, that is, with the pro-life point of view. This still does not explain, however, why, after the perfection of contraceptives, abortions continued to rise. For that answer we need to turn to the modern history of this practice that will lead us to *Roe v Wade.*

NOTES

1. For a fascinating discussion of the union of these two railroads, and the subsequent development of the West with its turn to saloons and houses of ill repute, see David Haward Bain, *Empire Express: Building the First Transcontinental Railroad* (New York: Viking, 1999).

2. Although the earliest mention of what Casanova called the "English riding coat," (what we would call a condom) occurred in the mid-1500s by Gabriel Fallopio, it was not until after the vulcanization of rubber in 1844 that condoms were in widespread use. Until then, a variety of largely unsuccessful contraceptive methods were used.

3. At the beginning of 2001, Hollywood attempted to portray the Marquis as the artist-victim of a repressive Catholic Church in its movie *Quills.* The priest who protected him in prison became in Hollywood's rendition a man himself beset with all sort of sexual secrets. History, however, left a much different record, for the Marquis celebrated a sexual ethic that included infanticide, the disemboweling of women, and more.

4. A. D. Farr, "The Marquis de Sade and Induced Abortion," *Journal of Medical Ethics* 6 (1980): 7–10.

5. A deist is one who believes in the existence of a supreme being while denying revealed religion. A deist bases his faith on reason and rejects the rest. God may have created the world but withdrew from it thereafter. All supernatural elements (for example, miracles) are rejected.

6. For more, see www.infed.org/thinkers/et-rous.htm. Accessed Fall 2000.

7. Quoted in Rosalind Pollack Petchesky, *Abortion and Woman's Choice: The State, Sexuality, and Reproductive Freedom* (Boston: Northeastern University Press, 1984), 1.

8. 43 Geo. 3, C 58. *Lord Ellenborough's Act,* C ap. LVIII, available at http://members.aol.com/abtrbng/lea.htm. Accessed Fall 2000.

9. James C. Mohr, *Abortion in America: The Origins and Evolution of National Policy, 1800–1900* (Oxford: Oxford University Press, 1978), 23.

10. Marvin Olasky, "Victorian Secrets: Pro-Life Victories in 19th-Century America," *Policy Review* 60 (Spring 1992): 31. There were 160,000 abortions in 1860 in a population of 27 million. This is the equivalent of the 1.6 million today in a population of over 270 million.

11. Mohr, 24–25.

12. Laurence H. Tribe, *Abortion: The Clash of Absolutes* (New York: W. W. Norton and Company, 1992), 28.

13. The full citation is John Burns, *Observations on Abortion Containing An Account of the Manner in Which It Takes Place, the Causes Which Produce It, and the Method of Preventing or Treating It* (Troy, N.Y.: Wright, Goodenow, and Stockwell, 1808).

14. Burns, 75–76.

15. Mohr, 14–15.

16. Olasky, *The Press and Abortion,* 30.

17. Janet Farrell, Brodie, *Contraception and Abortion in Nineteenth Century America* (Ithaca, N.Y.: Cornell University Press, 1994), 39.

18. Mohr, 26–27.

19. The statute reads: "...shall upon conviction, be punished by imprisonment in a county jail no more than one year, or by a fine not exceeding five hundred dollars, or by both such fine and imprisonment." For more on this see Mohr, 27.

20. Mohr, *Abortion in America;* Tribe, *Abortion: The Clash of Absolutes;* and the footnotes to *Roe v Wade* all make mention of these laws.

21. Samantha Halliday, "Medical Ethics and the Law, Handouts 1998," http://www.law.warwick.ac.uk/ncle/materials/mela.1.html. Accessed Fall 2000.

22. See Mohr's discussion on 26–45.

23. The Latin phrase *absus non tollit usum* is instructive here. Abuse of a thing does not prohibit its use any more than practice establishes a thing's acceptance.

24. This may seem harsh, at first, but any reading of these personals, especially in the intellectuals' publication of choice, the *New York Review of Books,* will quickly dispel the notion of harshness. Dozens of advertisements (for $5 a line), which plead that a "SWF, full of spirit and delight, who loves Thoreau and walks in the wood, seek SWM who enjoys the same," can hardly be described as anything but "unlucky." What else would drive a person to place such an advertisement but successive failures in amorous unions?

25. Mohr, 48.

26. Regarding this and the preceding paragraph, see Stacey Hamilton, "Lohman, Ann Trow," in John A. Garraty and Mark C. Carnes, eds., *American National Biography,* vol. 13 (New York: Oxford University Press, 1999), 849–850.

27. Marvin Olasky, *The Press and Abortion, 1838–1988* (Hillsdale, N.J.: Lawrence Erlbaum Associates, 1988), 4–6.

28. Dina A. LeClair, *The American Catholic Church and Its Evolving Position on Abortion During the Mid-Nineteenth Century.* Master's Thesis, Wright State University, Dayton, Ohio, 1999.

29. Mohr, 48–50.

30. See Olasky, *The Press and Abortion,* 32, for this and the following quote.

31. The fierce abortion opposition by the PCUS is surprising, for it is known by most today to be at the vanguard of social reform and pro-choice advocacy. It's "justice-love hermeneutic" is used to allow not only homosexual unions, but also very possibly extramarital affairs.

32. Olasky, *The Press and Abortion,* 32.

33. Keller, Allan, *Scandalous Lady: The Life and Times of Madame Restell, New York's Most Notorious Abortionist* (New York: Atheneum, 1981).

34. Mohr, 54–57.

35. Hamilton, 849.

36. Keller, 65ff.

37. Mohr, 98.

38. Mohr, 94.

39. "Criminal Abortions," *Boston Medical and Surgical Journal* 30, no. 15 (May 15, 1844): 302–303. Also quoted in Mohr, 87.

40. Ibid., 303.

41. "Procuring Abortions," *Boston Medical and Surgical Journal* 51, no. 10 (October 4, 1854): 224–205. (Emphasis added. The pages are obviously misnumbered.) Also quoted in Mohr, 88–92.

42. Pollitt, Katha, "Abortion in American History," *Atlantic Monthly* (May 1997), http://www.theatlantic.com/issues/97may/abortion.htm, accessed Fall 2000; see also, Mohr, *Abortion in America*; and Leslie J. Reagan, *When Abortion Was a Crime: Women, Medicine, and the Law in the United States, 1867–1973* (Berkeley, Calif.: California Press, 1997).

43. "Victoria Woodhull," http://americanhsty.miningco.com/homework/americanhistory/library. Accessed Fall 2000.

44. The biographical information about Alcott comes from Herbert Thoms, "Alcott, William Andrus." *Dictionary of American Biography.* Allen Johnson, ed. Vol. 1. New York, Charles Scribner's Sons, 1928, pp. 142–143.

45. *Offenses Against the Person Act of 1861,* http://members.aol.com/abtrbng.oatpa61.htm. Accessed Fall 2000.

46. LeClair, 31.

47. Betsy Clark, "Abortion in the Life and Times of 'The Most Evil Woman in New York, Madame Restell,'" http://world.std.com/~ljk/restell.htm. Accessed Fall 2000. The address is based on Betsy Clark's seminar "Women, Church, and State" and is decidedly pro-choice in tone.

48. Most of the biographical material comes from "Storer, Horatio Robinson," *The National Cyclopedia of American Biography,* vol. 10 (New York: T. J. White), 273–274; University Microfilms, Ann Arbor, 1967; and Frederick N. Dyer, *Champion of Women and the Unborn: Horatio Robinson Storer* (Canton, Mass.: Science History Publications, 1999).

49. Dyer, 4.

50. As, indeed, Storer himself was so honored by a token. See Dyer, 487.

51. Mohr, 150–155.

52. Mohr, 158.

53. Horatio Storer, and Franklin Fiske Heard, *Criminal Abortion: Its Nature, Its Evidence, and Its Law* (Boston: Little, Brown and Company, 1868), 1.

54. Dyer, 119. The italics are in the original.

55. Dyer, 149.

56. Most of the biographical material that follows is drawn from Robert D. Cross, "Comstock, Anthony," in John A. Garraty and Mark C. Carnes, eds., *American National Biography,* vol. 5 (New York: Oxford University Press, 1999), 306–307; and Mark Van Doren, "Comstock, Anthony," in Allen Johnson and Dumas Malone, eds., *Dictionary of American Biography* (New York: Charles Scribner's Sons, 1930), 330–331. See also Mohr 78–79, and Craig L. LaMay, "America's Censor: Anthony Comstock and Free Speech," *Communications and the Law* 19, no. 3 (September 1997): 1–59.

57. Ellen Chesler, *Woman of Valor: Margaret Sanger and the Birth Control Movement in America* (New York: Doubleday, 1993), 66.

58. Cross, ANB.

59. March 3, 1873 Ch. 258, section 148, 17 Stat. 599. (Italics added.)

60. Edward E. Conrad, *The Fin-de-Siecle Treatment of Abortion* (No publisher, circa 1900), 1.

61. Patricia Knight, "Women and Abortion in Victorian and Edwardian England," *History Workshop Journal* 4 (1977): 57–69.

62. Mohr, *sic* passim.

63. Brodie, 212. The woman in question was Rose Williams.

64. Brodie, 153, 182–183, 212.

3

Before There Was *Roe:* 1900–1970

By the turn of the twentieth century, pro-choice forces had gained substantial ground. No longer was abortion an entirely covert, under the table, operation or discussion. The Restells and the Sawyers of the world had made abortion a public conversation. Further, no longer were abortions limited to the wealthy alone. More and more middle-class women were seeking and acquiring them.[1] Although pro-life forces had won the public debate, if not the public war, the few making pro-choice arguments continued to make them loudly and long. Hurting the pro-choice cause, however, were the increasingly large number of botched abortions (even though performed by physicians) and the accompanyingly high patient mortality rates. Those physicians who refused to perform abortions still outnumbered those who did them; further, they did not mince words, one calling the procedure a "hideous excrescence of civilization."[2] Annie Besant called this "destruction of the fetus" the "destruction of life." Legislation, coupled with the testimony of the press, the laity, attorneys, and most physicians did not make abortion as the means of solving a "problem" easy for a woman—single or married. Women looked for a solution anyway and, not surprisingly, found one.

Why? For two reasons: urbanization and industrialization. Both continued to contribute to abortion as a commonplace practice. Although the church would have a measure of success in reducing the number of abortions, these two unseen forces, coupled with the expediency of improved communications, made a rise in the number of abortions inevitable. Throughout the country, prostitutes set up trade and the number of abortions increased. A woman could easily make more money working in a "massage parlor" than in most other places; she could further add to her income through full-fledged prostitution. If the pro-choice forces were to be successful, there would have to be at least a twofold approach: one that addressed the moral needs, and one that addressed the economic ones. Added to prostitution was the proliferation of establishments where drink was easy and cheap. The two in combination made the prospect of an increased need for abortion probable.

In France, meanwhile, physicians complained that abortion laws were too rigid, and one, Dr. A. Wylm, argued in 1907 that, at least in the case of rape, some allowance should be made for abortion.[3] Although France still forbade the *recherche de la paternite* (discovery of paternity; a pregnancy was the woman's sole responsibility, Article 340) and made abortion a crime (Article 317), the movement was away from these rigid codes.[4] Add to this some very public and outspoken critics of abortion laws and slowly but perceptibly, public sentiment about abortion began to change, abroad first, then at home.

OUTSPOKEN PRO-CHOICE ADVOCATE: MADELEINE PELLETIER

As much as anyone leading the debate was Dr. Madeleine Pelletier, a French physician and activist for abortion. In 1913 she made the feminist case for a woman being able to decide whether or not she wanted to carry her baby to term.[5] Pelletier ranked among the most militant suffragists of all time, invading polling "booths," editing feminist newspapers, writing feminist articles and pamphlets, and frequenting gatherings of Freemasons and communists (neither of which embraced her fully).[6] Pelletier argued for a nonsexist feminism. She advocated a more thoughtful, more philosophical feminism, embracing radical individualism and arguing that the identification of women by their sexual selves contradicted the very idea of individuality.[7] Using her training as a psychiatrist, she embarked on a project of re-presenting [sic] women "as they are."[8] She would use her knowledge of psychology to analyze the behavior of women and offer an antidote to it. Pelletier also argued in favor of women carrying handguns to make them feel more secure. "Apart from the uses it has in the cases of danger, the revolver has a psychodynamic power; simply the fact of feeling it one's self makes one braver."[9]

Pelletier advocated population control through contraception and abortion and, as Joan Wallach Scott points out, "on a belief in the importance of the individual's responsibility for the economic and social conditions of his or her life." Further, like Margaret Sanger later, the eugenic and Neo-Malthusian movement also influenced her thinking.[10] Although she performed abortions clandestinely, she never admitted it. In her book *La Rationalisation Sexuelle,* she made a familiar feminist claim repeated today as if it were new: "Is the wedding night legal rape?"[11] At the end of her life, when a stroke made performing abortions impossible, she was arrested for having supervised them. The judge sentenced her to a hospital instead of prison. She died in 1939.[12]

Abortionists, whether professional or not, could not deny the number of women who turned up ill from their practice. If abortions increased in frequency, not many abortionists practiced common-sense hygiene, and without penicillin, infections were inevitable. If women did not die from infections, they lived with punctured uteruses, pierced bladders, damaged livers, peritonitis, gangrene, or other organ failures brought on by various abortifacients. Although most herbalists' remedies were as safe as they were useless, some proved outright deadly, including turpentine, gin, gunpowder, quinine, lead, and boric acid.[13] Pelletier argued that this could be corrected with liberal abortion laws, which in turn would make them safe. She argued vehemently for abortions to be legal for the first trimester, and the decision left to the mother alone. Meanwhile, the Children's Aid Society and the New York Foundling Home begged women to consider adoption rather than abortion.[14] This particular plea began to find resonance with the populace by 1910. But so did another trend.

MORE PRO-CHOICE OUTSPOKENNESS: MARGARET SANGER

Press coverage of the pro-choice position changed dramatically with the emergence of Margaret Sanger (1879–1966). Sanger's encounter with Comstock catapulted her into the public eye. As much as any other American woman (with the possible exception of Restell), Sanger recast the public *Weltanschauung* regarding abortion. Sanger presented as unlikely a candidate for the pro-choice brigade, as Storer had been for the pro-life side.[15] Born Margaret Higgins in Corning, New York, she and her family barely subsisted as Irish-American immigrants. Her father, Michael Hennessy Higgins, was a free-thinking Irish stonemason; her mother, Anne Purcell, was a devout Roman Catholic. It's safe to say that the Catholicism of her mother had little influence on the free-thinking Sanger. After watching her family eke out a living from day to day, Sanger took a vow never to live in poverty, and kept it. From the time she worked for her nursing education at Claverack College to her marriages of convenience (both to wealthy men who supported her causes), Sanger never wanted for money again.[16]

This women's rights activist did not practice nursing long. In 1911, she married the architect William Sanger and settled down with children of her own in Westchester, New York. For ten years she and Sanger lived in what she called "tamed domesticity" until her second "great awakening." At Mabel

Margaret Sanger. (Courtesy of the Library of Congress.)

Dodge's salon and in classes in the evening at the very left-of-center Ferrer School, she listened intently to socialists and free-love advocates. Their accounts of erotic fulfillment overwhelmed her. As she recounts in her own autobiography, her living room bulged with anarchists, socialists, liberals, and others whose sole intent was to re-create America in their own image. By all accounts, she and they succeeded.

By 1887, the *New York Times* ran an editorial titled "The Comstock Nuisance." Comstock's funds by 1910 had begun to dry up, his health had become more precarious, and the *Times,* which had supported him, began to run stories less favorable to him.[17] The following year, Theodore Schroeder, founder of the Free Speech Society, cast Comstock as an ideologue. Comstock was his own worst enemy, and when he attacked French art, destroying several priceless works, his public grew weary. By 1912, Margaret Sanger (see below) had begun her series in the *New York Call* on "What Every Girl Should Know." Sanger stressed a number of points, chiefly involving female anatomy and reproduction, and concluded that sex was as natural as it was clean and healthful. Comstock ignored this, but when Sanger turned to a graphic description of venereal disease, Comstock declared it "unmailable." The matter was "kicked upstairs" and, as Craig L. LaMay points out, forgotten, or rather recycled. Not only was it eventually mailed, but Sanger's tract was reprinted for U.S. troops during World War I.

By 1915, Comstock felt he could no longer ignore Sanger and arrested her for publishing a pamphlet about birth control titled "Family Limitations."[18] Sanger fled the country to avoid prosecution, so Comstock arrested her husband when he gave Comstock a copy of the pamphlet. Although the case was clearly a matter of entrapment, Sanger was convicted but Comstock had spent his last energies. He fell ill after the highly public, very celebrated trial (it pitted frequent exchanges between Comstock and his forces against the Sanger and pro–birth control crowds that flocked to the trial) and never recovered. The public could not believe that pamphlets about contraception were entirely or altogether evil. Further, Sanger benefited—and Comstock suffered—from a shift in public sentiment at the end of the nineteenth and the beginning of the twentieth centuries: at that time even the *National Police Gazette,* once a mainstay of anti-abortion sentiment, changed its views without warning and opened its advertising pages to both abortion and pornography.[19] There is no record showing us why the same newspapers that had called such actions "sinful" and "vile" suddenly found them acceptable. Revenue dollars doubtless provide a persuasive argument.

The *Gazette*'s more modern approach brought in literally tens of thousands of advertising dollars. Now, not only did women who did not want more children benefit from abortions, but so did the economy. Sanger captured this sentiment and wrote in her autobiography that she saw lines of fifty to a hundred women standing "with their shawls over their heads waiting outside the office of the five-dollar abortionist."[20] While most journalists were aware of this, they did not write about it, but their papers took the advertising, small at first, but later by the handfuls. Sanger doubtless exaggerated her claims with respect to numbers, as even sympathetic historians have indicated. When women began to die at the hands of abortionists in higher numbers, the press ignored the stories, giving them all but the scantiest of coverage. Less well-known papers than the *New York Times* did run headlines, and soon stories started circulating that women were dying from abortions. One such celebrated case was that of Dr. Andre L. Stapler. Stapler may have been responsible for as many as ten deaths of women for whom he performed abortions. The deaths were covered in the press but not sensationally, the way botched abortions had been previously. The press waited for the police to intercede.[21]

The decades of the 1920s and 1930s saw Sanger move to a more global approach in which she worked hard against overpopulation. She gained international fame until the Second World War provided one compelling argument why birth control in Western countries might not be an unmixed blessing. Once papers began reporting on how often German naval boats were sinking ships of the Allied forces, the idea of birth control for whatever reason fell to the back pages of the public press, if it was covered at all. While extremely successful in her cause, she was not always the easiest person to deal with. When fellow pro-choice activist Mary Coffin Ware Dennett challenged her, Sanger replied, "The more I see the acts of the person in question, the more I am inclined to believe that a sanitarium is the proper place for her."[22]

Sanger made international trips, engaging in debate well into her seventies. When the phrase "family planning" replaced birth control in the press, she opined loudly, "What were they planning, vacations?" Given her lifelong campaign for birth control, it is no surprise that she was bothered that her own son had six children. She contended, however, that it was fine since he could afford them all.[23] She died in Tucson, Arizona, in 1966. Her place in history as one of the preeminent figures on the pro-choice side remains intact. Clearly, without Margaret Sanger, the pro-choice movement would not be where it is today.

EMMA GOLDMAN

Emma Goldman (1869–1940) was cut from the same cloth as Sanger.[24] Goldman struck fear in the hearts of most of her opponents, and no wonder: she fought an all-or-nothing revolution. Goldman was born in 1869 in a Jewish ghetto in Kovno, Lithuania, and after a brief stint in St. Petersburg, emigrated with her sister to Rochester, New York. The rest of her family soon followed. The Haymarket Square bomb set by anarchists (who were later executed) strongly influenced her and she later became one of the most controversial and celebrated anarchists. Goldman strongly advocated for birth control instead of abortion. Marriage and prostitution were the same, she said, but women received better pay under prostitution.[25] She often held rallies, speeches, and other events purposely on Yom Kippur, the holiest of Jewish holy days, in order to make the point that she was not bound by any law but her own. Oddly, however, she did question abortion on moral grounds. Nevertheless, her work greatly benefited the pro-choice cause.

THE VOLUME INCREASES: MARY COFFIN WARE DENNETT

At the same time that Sanger was making news all over the world, another, competing figure made her own abortion contributions, so much so that Sanger and she nearly came to blows to settle it. Mary Coffin Ware Dennett (1872–1947) came from a different class of women than Sanger. If Sanger's beginnings seemed humble, Dennett's seemed aristocratic in comparison.[26] Born in Worcester, Massachusetts, Dennett studied in private schools, then at the Boston Museum of Fine Arts (a later Dennett design would resurrect an old art form). Dennett began as a suffragist, incorporating her children into the fray as often as herself. But before she began to gain publicity for her views, she first had to suffer the humiliation (her words) of a very celebrated, very public divorce. Dennett fell under the spell of Freud and Ellis and advocated their principles but not their "free love" principles, especially when her own husband became involved with another woman.[27] Her home, like Sanger's, became a hangout for the activist-minded. While active in the movement before her divorce, it may have been her divorce that eventually spurred her to more public, political battles.

Dennett served in the National American Women's Suffrage Association (NAWSA). Her association with the organization lasted only five years. She had a falling out with the organization because of what she viewed as the group's political timidity, a charge Sanger would later level at Dennett herself. After the First World War broke out, she joined a peace activist organization to protest U.S. involvement. Sanger and Dennett crossed swords over Sanger's commitment to what Dennett viewed as political activist rabble-rousing; Dennett felt that approach hurt the birth control cause. Later, when Dennett published her pamphlet, "The Sex Side of Life," she and Sanger would disagree over tactics. Sanger wanted a "doctors' only" approach, while Dennett wanted to place knowledge in the hands of every woman. Dennett resigned rather than give in to Sanger, whose doctor's-only position eventually carried the day. Although Dennett tried several times to repair the rift, Sanger would have none of it.

Dennett helped to establish the National Birth Control League and it is there that she had her brush with the law and with abortion. Dennett and Sanger never worked in tandem. Separately, they both worked hard to repeal the Comstock Law. Dennett's pamphlet fell under the Comstock Law using the Hicklin Test as the measure of prosecution. (In English law, *Regina v Hicklin* found that if the most susceptible person could take offense to any material in part or in whole, then all of the material was obscene.) The Hicklin rule established Dennett's pamphlet as obscene. Compared to others of the time, the pamphlet was actually more tame than most.[28] But its graphic drawings of both male and female reproductive organs proved too much for the times. Dennett's advocacy of individual rights led her to fall out of favor with some groups. Even close friends abandoned her when she sounded the alarm against eugenics movements, a favorite of Sanger's. She touted sex education and birth control but never agreed to lend her name to the calls for limiting family size or coercive attempts to accomplish that goal.

Given the movement's penchant not only for the big headlines but also for Sanger's take-no-prisoners politics, Dennett did not last long in the movement. Dennett had already distanced herself from what she viewed as the more pro-lesbian aspects of the birth control and eugenics movements. When she lost Sanger's support (which she actually never had) and that of Goldman, who had eyed her suspiciously from the beginning, Dennett knew to bow out altogether. The break came when Sanger and Dennett appeared at the same rally, and a former friend of Dennett's all but threw her to the ground in disgust.[29]

Dennett advanced the cause of abortion, not by advocating it per se, the way Sanger had, but *de facto,* by advocacy that the Ellis-Freud philosophy allowed.[30] Dennett's protestations against the Victorian place of women, her dismissal of religion, and her strong advocacy of sex education coupled with birth control, met with protest, of course, given the times, but already the country's views on these subjects was changing. Like so many other women in the abortion battle, Dennett pushed, as did Pelletier and Sanger before her, too hard and too fast, and became a victim of her own machinations. Interestingly, like Sanger and Pelletier, Dennett believed that the fundamental tenet of capitalism—private property—created the world's greatest unhappiness.

Dennett's case is important in the pro-choice/pro-life debate for it is here that change in the laws began. The press provided Dennett's best defense as it headlined her as the "grandmother" charged with pornography. Dennett did have gray hair, as much from her own personal stress as anything else. Although convicted, the public outcry could not have been louder, aided and abetted by a press that picked and chose what it wanted the people to know. When public sentiment grew so loud that it was heard by political leaders, politicians made the change. The Hicklin Test was dropped, though the Comstock Law itself remained, but in greatly modified form.[31]

EMMELINE PANKHURST: PRO-CHOICE DECIBELS

Emmeline Pankhurst blustered advocacy in a different manner than either Sanger or Dennett.[32] Although more like Restell than Sanger, Pankhurst, an

Englishwoman, achieved something lasting for the pro-choice movement. Pankhurst (1858–1928) mirrored Dennett's behavior in England as the leading women's suffrage figure. Like Sanger, she embraced militant, law-changing means to achieve her ends, means that landed her in prison and, by her own choice, on a thirty-day hunger strike. Like Dennett, her abortion views remained less *de jure* than *de facto*. But her embrace of the full women's movement, including civil disobedience, pushed the abortion debate from the closet of back alleys to the forefront of everyday life. Unlike her predecessors, Pankhurst had a very happy marriage that ended only when death took the love of her life away. The circumstances of life forced her to fend for herself and her children. The potential poverty she faced forged her strong feminism into a feminism for all women. Her visits to America did not go unnoticed by Dennett, who tried to learn from her, and Sanger, who tried to upstage her.

Sanger, Goldman, Dennett, and Pankhurst all made significant contributions to the abortion cause. What is more intriguing is that these women made their contributions in what is often called the "silent era" of the abortion crusade.[33] Stories would appear here and there about the pro-abortion cause but the press ignored or remained mute about it for most of this time. When abortion was covered in the press, it was generally in stories that expressed outrage over politicians' lack of effort to make them safe.

About the time Dennett went to prison, convicted of obscenity in America, England made a very significant and long-lasting change in its law, the Infant Life (Preservation) Act of 1929. On May 10 of that year, England made the destruction of a viable fetus unlawful. What makes this important in the history of abortion, however, is not the law itself, but the exceptions it enters into the criminal code. Section 2, "Prosecution of Offenses," lays the proper groundwork:

Where upon the trial of any person for the murder or manslaughter of any child, or for infanticide or for an offense under section fifty-eight of the Offenses against the Person Act 1861 (which relates to administering drugs or using instruments to procure abortion), the jury are of the opinion that the person charged is not guilty of murder, manslaughter or infanticide, or of an offense of the said section fifty-eight, as the case may be, but that he is shown by the evidence to be guilty of the felony of child destruction, the jury may find him guilty of that felony, and thereupon the person convicted shall be liable to be punished as if he had been convicted upon an indictment for child destruction.[34]

Although this is a book about America's struggle with the abortion debate, this English law is very important to the American effort. The change decriminalized abortions performed in good faith to protect the life of the woman. Some scholars have argued, and compellingly, that the law merely placed more emphasis on the doctor and the woman finding the narrow way between necessity and good faith than it did on providing a means of escape. The law did make a provision that established the physician's preeminence in the matter of abortion. And here we may see the wisdom, for pro-choice advocates, of Sanger's "doctor's only" stratagem. By establishing, as she did, the physician's central role in the abortion equation (often in direct opposition to those who supported her), she laid the foundation for what would later prove to be the deciding factor in *Roe v Wade*. Nearly a half-century would elapse before physicians would take precedence in the debate. But their role would soon figure in a most commanding way from this moment on. Even stories that denigrated the profit to be made in abortion still argued that "abortion cannot be wished out of existence.... [W]omen resort to abortion, year in and year out, and will continue to do so unless some remedy for their predicament is supplied."[35]

The death of Goldman in 1940 marked a change in the way abortion stories were covered in the press. Out of nowhere, the New York *Daily News* published a story about an "outstanding physician" who also performed a few abortions in his spare time. The story portrayed the doctor as sympathetic and altruistic. The story indicated that there could be both bad abortionists—who should be punished—and good ones—who should be praised.[36] Other city papers followed suit. While newspapers continued to run stories that criticized abortionists, especially those who were making fantastic sums of money (more than $3 million annually in today's dollars), editors talked out of both sides of their mouths.

Another, much more important event occurred in 1940 to aid the pro-choice movement: the introduction of penicillin. Penicillin alone reduced the number of abortion-related deaths by 90 percent![37] Here at last was a way to perform abortions in a safe manner, protect the life of the mother-to-be, and yet still remove the "offending problem."

The two decades that followed Goldman's death in 1940 witnessed an increase not only in the number of abortions but also in the propagandizing about them. Conference after conference extolled abortion not only as a right but as an inalienable right of women. Abortion opponents, however, had learned a good lesson from Sanger. If physicians could be won over, perhaps other groups could be too. So they targeted groups who opposed abortion most: theologians and lawyers.[38] In the mid-1930s, Justice McCardie had made a judicial pronouncement at the Leeds Assizes where, following his advocacy of active propaganda of contraceptive methods, he urged that "the law of abortion should be amended. As it stands it does more harm than good."[39] By 1934, the *New Republic* was printing articles like one by Helena Huntington Smith in which she stated that too many mothers were dying as a result of abortion and yet the country remained mute. She urged better training for physicians, and more widespread knowledge about contraception.[40] Intellectuals began teaming up all over the country to speak "common sense" about abortion to the common man. Abortion killed mothers for no good reason. A change in attitude with respect to abortion must come, a change that all civilized minds understood and urged. The discovery of penicillin underscored this common sense.

RUTH BARNETT: ILLEGAL ABORTIONS AND POLITICS

Ruth Barnett (1895–1969) provides the portrait of an early abortionist in the middle of an era fraught with peril. Most of her work came to her from referrals when physicians in her Portland, Oregon, area were too afraid to perform them. But Barnett saw a need and tried to respond to it, becoming for many women of her practicing life (1918–1968) the only hope for an unwanted pregnancy.[41] Together with Dr. Robert Spencer in Ashland, Pennsylvania, Sophie Miller in St. Louis, and Laura Miner (also in Oregon), Barnett and these three were perhaps the only known abortionists who did not pursue the practice for mercenary reasons alone, although that charge was leveled against her.[42] Barnett provides a striking contrast to Restell. Barnett practiced under the worst of conditions, too, for she knew she provided a service that Oregon had criminalized and then strengthened in the late 1800s. Nevertheless, Barnett knew her trade well, and wanted to provide a service that women could use without fear of any recriminations or death. Apparently, neither the law, nor the reputation of abortionists at the time, made any difference to her.[43] Her work was not without penalty, however: Barnett holds the dubious distinction as the oldest woman ever imprisoned by the state of Oregon. She was released only a few months before she died of cancer.

PHYSICIANS OF CONSCIENCE

Barnett was not alone. A number of physicians came forward just prior to the passage of *Roe*.[44] Jane Hodgson, an obstetrician/gynecologist in St. Paul, Minnesota, earned the distinction of being the only physician in this country to be convicted of performing an abortion in a hospital. Hodgson allowed herself to be used as a test case in the early 1970s, knowing full well that not only might she face imprisonment, but the loss of her license to practice as well. L. Cottrell Timanus, based in the Washington-Baltimore area, became one of the best-known abortionists prior to *Roe*. Robert Spencer, mentioned above, was also well-known for his work in helping to change U.S. law. Timanus and Spencer teamed up at an early Planned Parenthood conference to discuss abortion procedures.[45] Peter Smith, Ethel Bloom, Sheldon Roth-stein, Joe Davidson, and Thomas Darrow, all before *Roe,* would occasionally perform abortions when needed. Daniel Fieldstone, Simon Ross, Irving Goodman, David Bennett, and Henry Morgentaler (in Canada) were all reg-ular "rule-breakers."[46]

THE CONTROVERSY HEATS UP

As debates concerning abortion arose, both sides were sometimes less than truthful. Abortion proponents made claims that had no basis in fact about the number of illegal abortions being performed. Extrapolated figures ap-peared from which no sense could be made. While estimates as high as 1.3 million illegal abortions were quoted, it's likely these were not accurate. Even some pro-choice writers today have revised those numbers downward (closer to the 100,000 to 200,000 range).[47] But these revisions came many years later. At the time of the allegations, the pro-choice argument had been se-cured. The point of the arguments, numbers, and pro-choice portrayals did the work that could not have been done before because now all this came be-fore a receptive populace. Couple this with the 1959 revision of the American Law Institute's Model Penal Code that changed the homicide status of abor-tion, making it "an offense against the family," and the spadework had been readied for *Roe v Wade.*[48] The advent of thalidomide in the late 1950s, and the outbreak of German measles in the early 1960s, left the door wide open for a change in the abortion laws in America.

Thalidomide, a drug given to alleviate the "morning sickness" that often accompanied the early stages of pregnancy, turned out to be a horror story. The drug, while curbing morning sickness, also, in many cases, severely mal-formed fetuses, especially their arms and legs. Children whose mothers had taken thalidomide oftentimes delivered babies born with "flippers" instead of arms and stumps where their legs should have been. Because the science of prosthetics—artificial limbs—was still developing, and virtually no prosthe-ses had been perfected for infants, these babies often looked like something out of nightmares to the unsuspecting public, with wildly mechanical arms and weirdly unstable legs.

German measles (rubella) is rare today because of vaccines, but before vac-cines, when a pregnant woman contracted this disease during the first three months of her pregnancy, the resulting child was often born blind, with se-vere heart defects, deafness, or mental retardation. Even today, a woman who contracts German measles is often counseled by her obstetrician to have an abortion.[49] When thalidomide babies and babies whose mothers had con-tracted German measles during their pregnancies delivered these children, public sentiment began to change. No mother, it was argued, should have to live with the fear of delivering such children into the world. One of the most celebrated cases of either, a thalidomide case that turned the tide for the pro-choice side, has its roots in the children's show, *Romper Room.*

ROMPER ROOM AIDS THE PRO-CHOICE CAUSE

In the case of Thalidomide, one celebrated event stands out vividly. Now an icon on the pro-choice side, Sherri Chessen Finkbine, an Arizona mother of four, learned in the late 1950s of the possible birth defects to her unborn child because of exposure to the drug thalidomide.[50] Finkbine had been taking doctor-prescribed tranquilizers early in her pregnancy to reduce stress-induced chest pains. When these ran out, she took thirty or forty pills her husband Bob, a schoolteacher, had picked up while in England. When the *Arizona Republic* ran stories on thalidomide, Finkbine took her pills to her doctor and learned that she had in fact been taking the drug between the twenty-eighth and forty-second days of her pregnancy. Her doctor explained that she had at least a 50/50 chance of delivering a baby suffering from some form of phocomelia, a horrible birth defect. Already responsible for tragic birth defects in England, Germany, and Canada, thalidomide had come under increasing scrutiny in this country. Understandably, Finkbine panicked. Her doctor advised her to terminate her pregnancy and try again later under better conditions.

Under the condition of anonymity, Finkbine talked to a reporter in an attempt to warn others of the possible side effects on the day before her abortion. While any ordinary housewife might have been given equal press coverage, Finkbine was none other than the star of the Phoenix, Arizona, version of the nursery school show, *Romper Room.* The story made national headlines and the hospital then refused to perform the abortion without prior judicial approval. Getting none, it canceled Finkbine's abortion. Her attorney requested a court order to allow the abortion to proceed, and suddenly the debate fell into the national spotlight. Finkbine fled to Sweden (she had originally planned on Japan but could not get clearance) where she secured her abortion, but even there the procurement was difficult. The doctor explained that her unborn child was so severely deformed it would never have survived anyway.

When the Finkbines returned to Arizona, some of Bob's high school students requested transfers out of his classes, and Sherri herself never hosted *Romper Room* again. The Reverend Thurston N. Davis, editor of the Jesuit weekly *America,* summed up the feelings of the pro-life majority on the Finkbine case: "No matter how praiseworthy the motives that inspire abortion the answer must always be no. To deliberately terminate the life of an innocent being...is, in one word, murder."[51]

While it would doubtless have been wiser to wait until after her abortion to go public, Finkbine's public attempt to secure an abortion left those who supported her legally exposed with little alternative. But her case, which gained widespread publicity, provided a growing impetus to the pro-choice movement rapidly gaining ground among Americans. The decision by the American Law Institute, alluded to earlier, coupled with Finkbine's case, made some form of legalized abortion inevitable. True, the Finkbine case polarized individuals. But for the first time, pro-choice advocates had a case that nearly evenly divided the public. Not only was she a mother, but Finkbine was also obviously very good with children. Further, Finkbine's case helped defuse arguments made by such notable figures as Nicholas J. Eastman, who argued in *Expectant Motherhood* (1963) that abortion "constituted murder" unless the mother herself was dying. Finkbine had no fear of dying, but she gained great sympathy anyway. Alan Guttmacher, of later facility-fame, argued that abortion was a "medical-legal disease" and that "every town or hamlet" had an abortionist; its people just didn't know him.

Finkbine proved the perfect role-model. As a star of *Romper Room,* her status with mothers could not be shaken. Newspapers further vouchsafed this image by showing her being kissed by a young child, perhaps her son. Further, her case came to public attention during the turbulent 1960s. Moreover, she provided every stay-at-home mother free day care for their children for a few hours each morning. Furthermore, the press jumped on the story of a mother—Finkbine already had four children whom she obviously loved and cared for—who saw abortion as the only alternative for an intractable problem. Finkbine's advocacy really had little to do with abortion per se (or so it seemed at the time) but with quality-of-life issues. All opponents had to do was look at some of those awful pictures (and the pictures were indeed frightening) of deformed children who *did* survive thalidomide.

Today, our view of the differently abled has changed. But any parent during the 1960s, who had raised a child with anything remotely resembling the multiple handicaps that thalidomide promised children subjected to it, would almost certainly have felt sympathy for the Finkbines.

BETTY FRIEDAN: FREEDOM FIGHTER

The following year saw yet another major media event that further pushed the debate to the center of both family life and political discussion. Betty Friedan (1921–) has been called the "mother" of the modern feminist movement. The title is well-deserved. Until 1963, Friedan enjoyed a life very *un-*

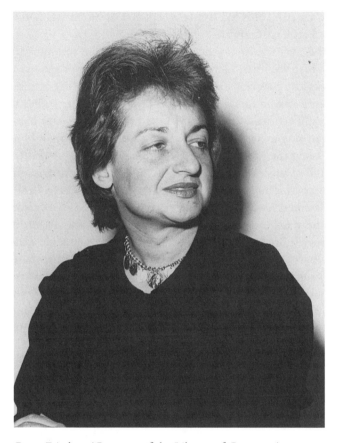

Betty Friedan. (Courtesy of the Library of Congress.)

like that of most women in America, and not at all like what she wrote about. Born Betty Naomi Goldman, Friedan enjoyed one of those idyllic upbringings that most only dream about. Raised in Peoria, Illinois, Friedan found her feminist voice as a result of the discrimination she experienced in the Midwest for being Jewish. Her father owned a jewelry store and her mother was a quiet and unassuming woman. Neither could understand why their eldest daughter read so much or found life so problematic. Because Friedan grew up on the right side of the tracks, however, she did not experience the mind-numbing discrimination that others did.

"You're in, but you're not, and you grow up an observer," she complained once in an interview to the New York *Post*'s Judy Michaelson.[52] School was not a terrible experience for her, either. She established herself as a literary figure even in high school, founding a literary magazine and graduating as her class's valedictorian. This led to her acceptance at an exclusive women's college on the East Coast, Smith.

There she majored in psychology and during the summers interned in nearby psychiatric clinics. Her literary aspirations did not grow cold. As editor of the Smith newspaper, she won a literary prize for her biting editorials. She graduated *summa cum laude* and went on to graduate studies at Berkeley in California. Eventually she married Carl Friedan, who later became a successful advertising executive. Her life seemed perfect, living in Queens, New York, and being the mother of three children. Not long thereafter, her husband became so successful that they bought a huge Victorian house (eleven rooms, three baths, and a stunning view of the Hudson River) and, for most women, life could not have been more complete. But Friedan was not only unhappy, she was borderline depressed. Too many cocktail parties with famous people left her feeling useless and something akin to a lost soul. After a series of mistarts, she wrote a piece for *Good Housekeeping* (September 1960) titled "Women are People Too!" The article proved an instant success and Friedan realized that she had tapped into a silent majority of women. She took all she had learned at those cocktail parties with the rich and famous, drew on her own rather unrepresentative past, and shut herself up while she wrote the blockbuster book of the year, *The Feminine Mystique.*

The book became an instant best-seller. After its appearance, excerpts appeared everywhere: *Saturday Review, Mademoiselle,* and *McCall's.* Before all the hoopla was over, *The Feminine Mystique* had sold literally millions of copies (the Dell paperback sold over a million copies alone) and has since been translated into thirteen languages. Friedan had become a feminist icon of bigger-than-life dimensions.

The book's theme comes from its title. According to Friedan, there is a "feminine mystique" that, like a siren song, woos women to give up their search for identity and find fulfillment in what their husbands do. This comes about over a series of years in which their achievements are not measured by what they accomplish, but by what they do: raise children, clean house, and deaden their minds with endless trivia. The book proved a scathing excoriation of housewifery: women became housewives because they had listened to the siren song of this "feminine mystique" and could do nothing else. According to Friedan, women had much more worth than as "mere" housewives.

The book struck a chord with women whose lives had been circumscribed in this way. But what Friedan had not counted on was the presence of so many women who had purposely sought this life for themselves. Twenty years after the publication of *The Feminine Mystique,* housewives struck back and Friedan's book has been buried under an avalanche of invective and anger because Friedan discounted the fact that housewives do, in fact, "work."

Underlying this becoming-a-housewife-is-not-a-real-job thesis was, of course, the liberation it gave to women to have abortions. Friedan later became a strong advocate not only for the rights of women, represented by the National Organization of Women (NOW), but also for those women who chose to exercise their reproductive rights after the fact. Friedan relied heavily on the work of Margaret Mead, Alfred Kinsey, and Bruno Bettelhiem, three scholars whose work in recent years has come under heavy attack and even academic pillorying.[53] The argument today raises the question of whether or not such a philosophy has any validity when its very foundations have been proved to be untrue.[54] Friedan's reliance on suspect sources, such as Kinsey's sex study, raises the question of just how widespread the problem outlined in *The Feminine Mystique* really was. But these arguments were too little and too late. Friedan made her case and made it eloquently. In the end, some women burned bras, left their husbands, and had abortions whenever they felt their rights had been overshadowed by forces beyond their control. Today, however, Friedan has abandoned her "superwoman" stance as a fallacy. Speaking at a Smith College commencement recently, she revealed that having it all and being a "superwoman," two ideas she popularized, have been cruel illusions. "Women have been spared petty prejudice only to be met with personal catastrophe. For the first time in American history, women work far harder than their mothers. And they miscarry more, are divorced more, abandoned more, abused more, and fall into poverty more."[55] Furthermore, Friedan's new book, *The Second Stage,* like her feminist sister Germaine Greer's new opus, *The Change: Women, Aging, and the Menopause,* virtually takes back half of what she decried thirty years ago in *The Feminine Mystique.*

HENRIE V GRIFFITH: VICTORY IN DEFEAT

Hard on the heels of this new gauntlet for pro-choice advocacy came a single court case that, though decided in favor of the pro-life side, did as much to harm it as anything else. With the whole country now moving in a pro-choice direction, Oklahoma stepped in to muddy the waters. In *Henrie v Griffith* (1964 OK 215; 395 P. 2d 809), the Griffith estate brought a wrongful death suit against Grove, Oklahoma, physician J. Bryan Henrie. The Court laid the case out in black and white:

In action for wrongful death against a party (Henrie) performing an illegal abortion upon a decedent (Griffith) who consented to such operation, as a result of which the decedent suffered an infection, allegations of the petition that after said operation the decedent suffered serious complications resulting from the operation and defendant failed to give her ordinary and proper care and completely abandoned her without informing the family of her condition, as a direct and proximate cause of said negligent acts the decedent died, held sufficient to state a cause of action against a general demurrer.

Derrell H. Griffith came to the clinic in Grove, Oklahoma on March 10, 1962, and died as a result of complications on March 25 of the same year. Griffith left behind a husband and three minor children. Henrie served his two years in prison and then became a celebrity, touring the country "to save the honor and respect of many women," as he put it. Few histories have pointed out the obvious: Dr. Henrie was a Doctor of Osteopathy, not a doctor of obstetrics or gynecology.

GRISWOLD AND A PRO-CHOICE VICTORY AT LAST

Friedan's best-selling book and the organization it spawned (NOW) were quickly followed by yet another nail in the coffin of the pro-life forces. Two years after the storm of *The Feminine Mystique* came *Griswold v Connecticut.* Justice William O. Douglas delivered the opinion of the Court in 1965. Estelle T. Griswold, the salaried executive director of the Planned Parenthood League of Connecticut, and C. Lee Buxton, a licensed physician and professor at the Yale Medical School who had served as medical director for the League at its center in New Haven, were arrested. They had been operating the center since 1961. The charge stemmed from the fact that they supplied married persons with medical advice, both written and verbal, about how to prevent pregnancy. This, by itself, would probably not have been enough to result in arrest. But Griswold and Buxton also charged fees. Although some married couples got the information free of charge, others paid for it. Like many organizations operating at the time, those who could pay fees often made up the difference for those who could not.

The two were charged under Sections 53–32 and 54–196 of the General Statutes of Connecticut. Section 53–32 provides that "Any person who uses any drug, medicinal article or instrument for the purpose of preventing conception shall be fined not less than fifty dollars or imprisoned not less than sixty days nor more than one year, or be both fined and imprisoned." Section 54–196 states that any person who "aids and abets, counsels, causes, hires or commands" someone to commit an offense may be prosecuted and punished as if he were the offender. In his opinion, Douglas argued that association is not mentioned in the Constitution or the Bill of Rights but quickly pointed out that certain "peripheral rights" are present and must be made secure. In what has now become a famous line, Douglas asserted that "The foregoing cases [Henrie and others] suggest that specific guarantees in the Bill of Rights have penumbras [shadows], formed by emanations [rays, as from the sun] from those guarantees that help give them life and substance." In other words, Douglas admitted that the case had no real grounds in the Constitution or the Bill of Rights, the documents heretofore used to frame law in America.

Rather, for Douglas what became more important, or at least equally important, were these "penumbras" with their "emanations." Earlier, Douglas had asserted that the "First Amendment has a penumbra where privacy is protected from governmental intrusion." It proved as radical as saying that the moon's "own" light (actually reflected light from the sun) was equally as important as the sun's.

While Douglas found penumbras and emanations in the Constitution, others focused on what the Constitution did say. Madison and Hamilton, in *The Federalist Papers* numbers 45 and 17, argued that the federal government should never overtake rights not outlined in the Bill of Rights. For these two Founding Fathers, the Constitution provided very limited power to centralized or federalized government. Douglas didn't see it that way.

Further, Douglas's insistence on those "penumbras" and "emanations" he found in the Constitution did not sit well with virtually any legal mind of that time or this. Because Douglas very rarely allowed clerks in his office to influence his opinion, the "penumbras" or shadows were all his. Common opinion had it that clerks drafted the opinions and the Justices edited them for clarity and accuracy. Not so with Douglas. Clerks in Justice Arthur J. Goldberg's chambers expressed shock at the weakness of the *Griswold* opinion. Douglas clerk Jim Campbell remembered, "No one who read it liked it," particularly the "emanations" and "penumbras," which "attracted the giggles of other clerks."[56]

Did the Justices understand that *Griswold* would have this chilling effect? Clearly they saw abortion as a "right" (I place the word in quotes for it was not until after *Roe v Wade* that abortion gained this status). But the states never would have seen abortion as a right, at least not most of them. For more than a hundred years, laws against abortion remained on the books in various states without change, or with very minor changes only. *Griswold,* by opening the door of one Amendment to include privacy between doctor and patient on one matter when none could be seen, opened the door for the same Amendment to be used later to guarantee privacy between doctor and patient for any other related matter. For more than 150 years, privacy as a right had not been located in the Constitution or any of Amendments by the Court. Justice Douglas saw privacy as part and parcel of those penumbras emanating from the First, Third, Fourth, Fifth, and Ninth Amendments, each one creating, Douglas said, "zones of privacy." Had Justice Douglas invented a precedent in the Constitution? Most legal observers think so. Original intent—trying to interpret the Constitution's meaning as set forth by those who had written it—gave way to viewing the Constitution as a living document, capable of being interpreted by the times in which it now existed.

Justices Goldberg, Brennan, Harlan, and White (Mr. Douglas delivered the opinion of the court) concurred, arguing that the Connecticut statute "unconstitutionally intruded" upon the "right" of marital privacy. Goldberg and Brennan also cited similar Amendments for the protection of privacy. Justices Black and Stewart, however, argued that no such privacy protection existed anywhere in the Constitution. In fact, Justice Black complained that the "right of privacy" in the Fourth Amendment was so open and vague, so unbounded, as to make the Amendment meaningless. Black further stated that, "The adoption of such loose, flexible, uncontrolled standards for holding laws unconstitutional, if ever it is finally achieved, will amount to a great unconstitutional shifting of power to the courts which I believe and am constrained to say will be bad for the courts and worse for the country."

Black's dissent sparked a heated debate among constitutional scholars, many of whom sided with Black's understanding of federalism and the Constitution. Black's words proved prophetic: for over the last thirty-five years since *Griswold*, the change in how the Constitution is interpreted has bedeviled both the courts and the country. This change meant that the Supreme Court Justices, whoever they happened to be—and not the Constitution— now determined U.S. law.

Griswold struck down at least fifty of the one hundred years of anti-abortion law in this country. A change in public sentiment had already been evolving. *Griswold* made its case by punning, not once but twice, on the word "privacy," a point both sides have referred to, for different reasons.[57]

Another momentous factor for abortion in America occurred in the late 1960s and focused on the group calling itself "Jane."[58] Organized as a grass-roots group referring women to underground abortion providers, Jane acted illegally and behind the scenes from the late 1960s until *Roe v Wade* was decided in 1973. Loosely formed, the group helped women secure abortions, many of which were done in Chicago. Jane was the contact name for what was, in fact, the Abortion Counseling Service of Women's Liberation. Activist-minded and feminist-driven, Jane often acted without regard for the law, running from police, disguising its whereabouts to opponents, and lying under oath. It did not take either side long to figure out that when you hold law in contempt, civil disobedience may be the only solution: on the pro-choice side, there was Jane; on the pro-life side, as we shall see, there was Operation Rescue.

Jane's proponents disrupted legislative hearings, held teach-ins, testified to their own illegal abortions, and actively sought out abortionists and made them well-known to women seeking them, as well as demanding that women "take control" of their reproductive selves. Jane's recruitment brochures were straightforward and to the point:

We are women whose ultimate goal is the liberation of women in society. One important way we are working toward that goal is by helping any woman who wants an abortion to get one as safely and as cheaply as possible under existing conditions.... [C]urrent abortion laws are a symbol of the sometimes subtle, but often blatant, oppression of women in society.... Only a woman who is pregnant can determine whether she has enough resources—economic, physical and emotional—at a given time to bear and rear a child.... [59]

For some, the Jane language may sound outrageous. It must be remembered, however, that this occurred during the late 1960s, a turbulent time in the United States, often marked by various groups making sweeping and, at times, outrageous claims.

The philosophical change in the United States is easier to grasp when one understands just how many physicians performed abortions prior to 1967. "It is a tremendous under-appreciated part of the history of this issue," writes David Garrow, "just how many fully credentialed and well-respected doctors were, 'under the table,' so to speak, providing abortions prior to 1967 for women patients whom they knew or who were referred by mutual acquaintances."[60] We cannot know who all these physicians were for their work was kept secret, by and large, because it was illegal. Another reason for the philosophical change may be seen in the clergy's change of heart on the question.

The first clergy group to recognize the "moral imperative" of Jane was the New York Clergy Consultation Service on Abortion, founded by Howard Moody, a Baptist minister. Moody's group, along with countless others, served notice that times were changing. No longer could pro-life advocates rely on the law. No longer could they rely on physicians to make their case. Pro-life advocates now discovered that they could not count on theologians to uphold their arguments. Clergy groups not only provided women with a safe haven for abortion counseling, but sought abortionists for them, in addition to paying their fees. By the end of 1969, abortion on demand would not be far off. Jane took advantage of the times and parlayed the changing attitudes into securing illegal abortions immediately with the hope of securing legal ones ultimately. Ironically, though one of the more compelling arguments of *Roe v Wade* was that it would put an end to "back-alley abortions," meaning those done by untrained personnel, Jane itself did not employ a bona fide physician, something that it never really addressed to the satisfaction even of its own members.[61]

The story of Jane was replicated, though hardly as publicly, in other states. Missouri had one such group. By this time, however, certified doctors were performing more and more illegal abortions, though few were gynecologists or obstetricians. Many physicians brought in their patients and, with full hospital knowledge, performed abortions under different names, most often as hysterectomies. This service was not available, however, to everyone, the final goal of pro-choice forces. Women with financial means could secure an abortion in nearly any state they chose (and at any time in this history). Women without means but with connections (through nursing students, friends of physicians, or through the various still-illegal networks that had formed) were essentially acquiring abortion on demand, too. Many physicians did not like this arrangement, and none of the pro-choice forces were satisfied with what was at the time an abortion version of "Don't Ask, Don't Tell."

As Jane and other similar groups provided abortion on demand for their clients, Colorado's liberal abortion law went into effect in April of 1967. Although many thought Colorado would become the "abortion mecca of the United States," by the late 1960s pro-choice advocates thought abortions were still difficult to secure. While Colorado's new law allowed for abortions "when the pregnancy seriously threatens the life or physical well-being of the mother," many pro-choice advocates found that the law did not go far enough.[62] When the law went into effect, however, a flood of requests came from Pittsburgh, New York, Cleveland, and elsewhere. Most had gleaned the names of physicians from the Denver Yellow Pages. During its first year, Denver's abortion rate tripled. Moreover, though advocates had sold the new law to the Colorado legislature as a way of reducing illegal abortions, Denver's illegal abortion rate did not decrease. By the end of the decade, more than twenty-eight states had sought to change, or had changed, their abortion laws.

THREE FINAL CASES

Three further cases remain to close out this period: *The People v Belous* (71 Cal. 2d 954, September 5, 1969), *Eisenstadt v Baird* (405 U.S. 438; S. Ct 1029, March 1, 1971), and *The United States v Vuitch* (402 U.S. 62; 91 S. Ct. 1294, April 21, 1971). In the first case, the California Supreme Court by a narrow one-vote majority, declared the state's abortion laws to be unconstitutional and exonerated Dr. Leon Belous. Belous had been charged with performing an abortion as well as conspiracy to perform abortion. Belous had been a physician in good standing since 1931 and specialized at the time of the trial in obstetrics and gynecology. A young woman and her husband approached the doctor seeking to terminate a pregnancy. They explained that they would have the abortion "one way or another," even if it meant driving to Tijuana. At this point, Belous interceded and explained to them the dangers of illegal abortions in general, and those in Tijuana in particular. He then agreed to send them to a friend of his, Laitrus, who performed safe abortions in Mexico.

The case records the facts clearly, including Belous's activist work in securing illegal abortions. It should have been an open-and-shut case according to California statutes. Laitrus pled guilty. In what would have a significant impact on the *Roe v Wade* decision, the California Supreme Court found that, "The fundamental right of a woman to choose whether to bear children follows from the Supreme Court's and this court's repeated acknowledgment of a 'right of privacy' or 'liberty' in matters related to marriage, family and sex." Even though California law saw "a child conceived, but not yet born" as an existing person, and, further, that the Penal Code specifically prevented execution of a pregnant woman in deference to the unborn but real child, the court still favored Belous. This was the first such decision that overturned abortion laws at the state level. Just two months later, the U.S. District Court for the District of Columbia exonerated Dr. Milan Vuitch (see below) by declaring the District's abortion laws unconstitutional. Dr. Vuitch reaped the dividend by opening a clinic within walking distance of the White House, performing hundreds of abortions weekly. At any rate, *Belous* opened the door to a national abortion law.

In *Eisenstadt v Baird* the Supreme Court ruled that Massachusetts' law regarding crimes against chastity was unconstitutional. Baird, after delivering a lecture on overpopulation and contraception, asked members of his audience to come to the stage and help themselves to contraceptives. Baird personally handed a young woman a package of contraceptive foam. He was convicted in Massachusetts under a statute that made it a crime to sell, lend, or give away any contraceptive drug, medicine or instrument, or article, except to married persons. Baird was neither a physician nor a pharmacist, two loopholes through which he could have skirted the Massachusetts' law and conviction. Although the law was directed at single people, it served to overturn any barrier for single persons seeking contraceptives. "There is no ground of difference," the Justices found, "that rationally explains the different treatment accorded married and unmarried persons" under the state statute. The Court went on to cite as unconstitutional the law's violation of the equal protection clause of the Fourteenth Amendment. The Court cited *Griswold's* finding of a "fundament human right" significant. But not all the Justices followed suit. Warren G. Burger, dissenting, wrote,

The appellee (Baird) has succeeded, it seems, in cloaking his activities in some new permutation of the First Amendment although his conviction rests in fact and law on dispensing a medical substance without a license. I am constrained to suggest that if the Constitution can be strained to invalidate the Massachusetts' Statute underlying the appellee's conviction, we could quite as easily employ it for the protection of a "cornerstone" quack reminiscent of the "witch doctor" of times past who attracted a crowd of the curious with a soapbox lecture and then plied them with "free samples" of some unproven remedy.

One attorney assigned to the *Belous* case was Abby Soven. She had been seeking a way to address the issue of reproductive rights ever since *Griswold*. *Belous* now provided her that opportunity. Soven helped build the case around the Court's "vagueness" issuance. Matters could be overturned owing only to vagueness about the law in question. Soven jumped at the chance to pursue her goal: "This is the opportunity," she said later. "I had just graduated from law school. I'm a woman. I'm a liberal. And *this is the issue*. This is the opportunity to say...that a woman has a fundamental right and the state can't impinge upon it."[63] The case virtually settled the fact that contraceptives would become a staple of life.

From this moment on, unmarried individuals gained access to birth control at will. On the face of it, this does not seem to be a very strong case for the pro-choice side. But as we shall see in the next chapter, *Eisenstadt* provided a strong precedent for the Supreme Court. The Justices now had in their hands a number of very important cases. Beginning with *Griswold*, the Court had controlling influence for an activist precedent. Cases in California and Washington, D.C., provided further ammunition for the case to be made on the grounds of privacy. With "penumbras" now at hand, and cases on the books declaring several state laws to be unconstitutional, the stage was set for the Supreme Court to act. This, as much as anything, explains the rise of the two opposing camps, as both NOW and the Right to Life established "beachheads" of protective interests for their constituencies. Once *Roe v Wade* was established (ironically, by a woman who later came to side with the Right to Life movement and today speaks as its voice against her own case), overturning every remaining state law in the country, the two camps would spend the remainder of the next three decades trying to garner support for their opposing positions.

While the *Belous* case unfolded in California, *Vuitch* took place in the District of Columbia. By now, all such cases followed the same general pattern. A licensed physician (Milan Vuitch) was indicted for performing or attempting to perform abortions, a direct violation of a provision in the District of Columbia Code. The Code criminalized the performance or attempted performance of an abortion unless undertaken "as necessary for the preservation

U.S. Supreme Court building, Washington, D.C. (Courtesy of the
Library of Congress.)

of the mother's life or health." The abortion still had to be performed by a licensed physician. The U.S. District Court dismissed the case on the grounds
that the abortion statute was unconstitutionally vague, since "health" could
not be determined to mean mental as well as physical health, and since the
burden was on the physician to show that the abortion was necessary under
these "vague" provisions. Justice Hugo Black found that the state's law was indeed constitutional, and that "health" in this case did provide for both the
physical and mental health of the woman. He further found no real ambiguity. What made this case a win for the pro-choice side was the insistence by
Black that the prosecution had to prove that the abortion was performed
when the mother's health was *not* in danger. Justice Byron White further

strengthened the case by arguing that the unambiguous statute put everyone on notice that the health of the mother was now the governing standard. Justice Potter Stewart, while dissenting, argued that the "abortion statute, properly construed, a licensed physician, exercising his judgment in favor of performing an abortion as necessary to preserve a patient's life or health, did not violate the statute and was immune from prosecution."

The Court further found a number of important planks that would remain as the scaffolding of Roe. The statute, the Court said "does not outlaw all abortions, but only those which are not performed under the direction of a competent, licensed physician, and those not necessary to the mother's life or health." This last phrase is critical, because the country was forced to believe that 1.5 million abortions annually (as occurred after Roe) were in fact owing to the mother's "health." With this understanding, no abortion could be prosecuted. It did not outlaw all abortions; rather it made all of them that were performed in a hospital or clinic, under the supervision of a licensed physician, legal for whatever reason, as long as the mother's "health" was cited. In another sentence, the Court confirmed Sanger's war for "physicians only" rule once more, while, if not overturning, certainly weakening all that Mary Coffin Ware Dennett had hoped to accomplish.

The Justices found that the state and the Supreme Court did not want to intercede between the woman and her doctor, since that arrangement is made on the premise of privacy. The Court, in other words, was loath to second-guess the doctor. Further, health could not be considered vague since the very definition meant "sound in body and mind." Finally, the Court settled two major points. First, "that it would be highly anomalous for a legislature to authorize abortions necessary for life or health and then to demand that a doctor, upon pain of one to ten years imprisonment, bear the burden of proving that an abortion he performed fell within that category." Second, it found that "We are unable to believe that Congress intended that a physician be required to prove his innocence," and placed the burden on the prosecution.

If attorneys were looking for a map to make all abortions legal, Vuitch provided it. If the District of Columbia's statute, asserting that the "health and the life of the mother" was not only not unconstitutionally vague, but crystal clear, then any state without such a law either interfered with the privacy between a woman and her physician, or defined health in a peculiar manner.

During the turbulent year of 1969, Texas attorneys Linda Coffee and Sarah Weddington met a woman by the name of Norma McCorvey, a pregnant, single mother who complained that another child would create an undue hardship on her and her children. Both attorneys had recently graduated from the University of Texas and saw the chance to challenge Texas' restrictive abortion laws. They promised McCorvey anonymity by referring to her as Jane Roe. Later a physician by the name of James Hubert Hallford was granted permission to add his name as a plaintiff. Hallford faced prosecution for performing abortions in his medical office. Three weeks after the original complaints were filed, the case would come to be known as *Roe v Wade.*

CONCLUSION

Before turning to the pivotal case in this history, a moment's reflection on these nearly two hundred years of pro-life/pro-choice debate is in order. At the beginning of the period, we saw the Marquis de Sade making bold attempts to create a new sexual awareness among the populace in France. While he did not fully and successfully make that case, he planted a strong seed that sex should not be limited to procreation alone. Once this view was accepted, there *had* to be a way to limit unwanted offspring from pleasurable unions. In the end Sade failed because his work was so outrageous, and because most of the deaths resulting from his work were purposeful ones to women who sought sex for its own sake. Curiously, Sade's work retains a tincture of respectability among the intellectual class. At the very least, Sade's uncompromising view that sex-as-pleasure alone, not for purposes of procreation, would figure pivotally in the discussion later on. While his name may have been lost, his philosophy remained.

The next fifty years marked a slow progression from a country foursquare on the side of the pro-life debate, to a country lost in a fog of conflicting rights and constitutional protections. This came about through a series of very colorful characters. From the scandalous Restell, to the outspoken Pelletier, to activists like Sanger and Pankhurst, to the demurring Dennett, the pro-choice side of the debate would have what amounted to a continuous line of defense (as opposed to offense) on its side, taking on the pro-life side at every turn. For its part, the pro-life side had only a handful of voices, Storer being its strongest. But the pro-life side also held as *fait accompli* the voices of the entire medical profession, the entire legal system, and all the clergy. It was, of course, this powerful threesome that the pro-choice side attacked, chipping away the arguments, one by one, until the majority in the legal, medical, and clerical professions became divided on the question. The division may never have become 50/50 because it didn't have to. Once the door opened but a little, the pro-life advocates holding it shut continued to lose allies, one by one, leaning against their side of the door.

With the Protestant clergy pretty well divided on the question, only the Roman Catholic Church remained staunchly in the pro-life column. As late as 1960, Catholics in this country were still not accorded a comfortable place in the public square. President John F. Kennedy felt it necessary during his presidential campaign to reassure the American public that his Catholicism would have no bearing on his presidency. He further added that the executive branch of the U.S. government would most definitely *not* be influenced by the Vatican. This marginalized the Roman Catholic argument to the extent that most voters discounted it. Nevertheless, the Catholic Church fought tirelessly against pro-choice advocates. Only a small band within the Protestant denominations would come to aid the Catholic Church. It proved too little, too late. After *Roe,* this union of pro-life Evangelical Protestants and Roman Catholics would still retain enough clout to bedevil the courts, winning some cases, while losing most.

It is important, too, not to underestimate the importance of the Finkbine case. Here a mother of four, the star of *Romper Room,* a show designed to entertain young children, faced an impossible decision: carry to term what was in all likelihood a deformed child, or seek an abortion. The horrors that thalidomide had already wrought in the mind of the American public proved too ubiquitous to discount. Should a mother be *forced* to carry to term a child that might be horribly deformed, cost tens of thousands of dollars to raise, and take her away from the four young children she had cared for splendidly and clearly loved? At the very least, this provided the American public with a clear case in which abortion could be seen as a viable choice by everyone except for the most pro-life of pro-lifers.

The remaining years of this period witnessed the country's about-face on the abortion question. Clearly, a nonpartisan look at the cases reveals that the judges of various states, followed by the Supreme Court Justices, moved toward a much different way of interpreting the Constitution. Pro-life advocates would argue that the Justices made law; pro-choice advocates claimed that they viewed the Constitution correctly, as a living document.

As a result of all these judicial rulings and shifts in public opinion, the clergy, once solidly on the pro-life side, saw some among its members begin breaking ranks to join forces with pro-choice advocates. At the end of the 1960s the air was full of anticipation and change. So many non–abortion-related factors came into play. The Vietnam War was raging, President Kennedy had been assassinated, and student unrest was roiling just about every college or university campus in America. Anyone who flouted authority became an instant celebrity. Calling into question medical, legal, and theological authorities proved the best of all possible worlds for pro-choice advocates. Meanwhile, women demanded their rights as equal citizens. If ever a theater for change existed, here was the stage. And the proscenium for change occurred just as the 1970s began.

NOTES

1. "Criminal Abortions," *Boston Medical and Surgical Journal* 30, no. 15 (May 15, 1844): 302–303, also quoted in Mohr, 87. "Procuring Abortions," *Boston Medical and Surgical Journal* 51, no. 10 (October 4, 1854): 224–205 (the pages are obviously misnumbered).

2. Patricia Knight, "Women and Abortion in Edwardian England," *History Workshop Journal* (1977): 62.

3. Angus McLaren, "Abortion in France and the Regulation of Family Size: 1800–1914," *French History Studies* 10, no. 3 (1978): 481.

4. Rachel G. Fuchs, "Public Power and Women's Bodies: Abortion, Infanticide, and the Penal Code in the Nineteenth Century," *Proceedings of the Annual Meeting of the Western Society for French History* 18 (1991): 567–577.

5. Fuchs, 570ff.

6. Joan Wallach Scott, *Only Paradoxes to Offer: French Feminists and the Rights of Man* (Cambridge, Mass.: Harvard University Press, 1996), 125–160. See also Felicia Gordon, "Reproductive Rights: The Early Twentieth Century European Debate," *Gender & History* 4, no. 3 (1992): 387–399.

7. Ibid., 134.

8. Ibid., 135.

9. Ibid., 137.

10. See, for example, Gordon, 390ff. See also Charles Sowerwine, "Socialism, Feminism, and Violence: The Analysis of Madeleine Pelletier," *Proceedings of the Annual Meeting of the Western Society for French History,* 8 (1980): 415–422. Sowerwine believes the rescue as a feminist has been vouchsafed and attempts to rescue her as a "militant Socialist."

11. Scott, 155.

12. See Scott. Also see Madeleine Pelletier, "Feminism and the Family: The Right to Abortion," trans. Marilyn J. Boxer, *French-American Review* 6, no. 1 (1982): 3–26.

13. Knight, 60–61.

14. Olasky, "Victorian Secrets," 33.

15. Most of the biographical material that follows comes from Esther Katz, "Sanger, Margaret," *American National Biography* 19 (1999): 264–267; David M. Kennedy, "Sanger, Margaret," *Dictionary of American Biography,* Supplement Eight, 1966–1970 (New York: Scribner's, 1988): 567–570; "Sanger, Margaret," *National Cyclopedia of American Biography,* vol. 52 (New York: James T. White & Company, 1970), 325–326; and Ellen Chesler, *Woman of Valor: Margaret Sanger and the Birth Control Movement in America.* (New York: Doubleday, 1993).

16. Chesler even believes this, and her biography is mostly hagiography.

17. Craig L. LaMay, "America's Censor: Anthony Comstock and Free Speech," *Communications and the Law* 19, no. 3 (September 1997): 22.

18. Constance M. Chen, *The Sex Side of Life: Mary Ware Dennett's Pioneering Battle for Birth Control and Sex Education* (New York: New Press, 1996). Interestingly, Chen contends that this particular pamphlet was filled with mistakes and outright wrong information. Dennett tried to point this out to Sanger, who would have none of it.

19. Olasky, *The Press and Abortion, 1838–1988,* 45.

20. Ibid., 57.

21. Ibid., 59.

22. Chen, *The Sex Side of Life,* 221.

23. Chesler, 404–405.

24. For more on Goldman, see Alice Wexler, "Goldman, Emma," *American National Biography,* ed. John A. Garraty and Mark C. Carnes, vol. 9. (Oxford: Oxford University Press, 1999), 191–194; Candace Falk, "Editor's Introductory Essay: Reconstructing the Documentary History of a Vibrant Life," http://sunsite.berkeley. edu/Goldman/Guide/introduction.html. Accessed Fall 2000.

25. Wexler, 192.

26. Much of what follows comes from Robyn L. Rosen, "Dennett, Mary Coffin Ware," *American National Biography,* 435–437; and Chen, *The Sex Side of Life.*

27. See Chen, *The Sex Side of Life.* The trial never really determined if sexual infidelity had occurred on his part but in all likelihood it did.

28. For example, it contained a section on masturbation. And while Dennett did not argue against it, she did warn that its repeated performance *could* result in insanity. This mimics Sanger's treatise in which the facts of her early pamphlets were medically incorrect, especially when it came to pessaries and other abortifacients. Dennett did not know better; Sanger did but refused to correct her earlier mistakes.

29. Chen, pp. 220–221.

30. Henry Havelock Ellis (1859–1939) befriended both Dennett and Sanger. He believed in free love and was a member of the Fabian Society, a political group, many of whose members believed in and supported the sexual liberation of both men and women. Ellis's book, *The Erotic Rights of Women* (London: Battley Brothers, 1918) was widely acclaimed and often criticized. His six-volume work, *Studies in the Psychology of Sex (1897–1910)* (New York: Random House, 1936) is still read today. Both books have stirred up controversy and been banned.

31. Although not a part of this study, pornography as a business is indeed lucrative. In the mid-1990s, it grossed more than ABC, CBS, NBC, ESPN, and CNN combined.

32. A brief but intriguing account of her life appears in W. L. Grant, "Pankhurst, Emmeline," *The Dictionary of National Biography,* ed. J.R.H. Weaver, 1922–1930 (1937) (London: Oxford University Press, 1917), some of which is repeated here.

33. So called by Olasky, *Press,* 58.

34. "Infant Life (Preservation) Act 1929 (c34)," http://members.aol.com/ abtrng/ilpa.htm. Accessed Fall 2000.

35. A. J. Rongy, "Abortion: The $100,000,000 Racket." *American Mercury* 40 (February 1937): 145–150.

36. Olasky, *The Press and Abortion,* 80.

37. Ibid, 82.

38. Ibid, 85.

39. L. A. Parry, "Criminal Abortion," *Living Age* 342 (April 1932): 174.

40. Helena Huntington Smith, "Wasting Women's Lives," *The New Republic* 78 (March 28, 1934): 178–180.

41. Rickie Solinger, *The Abortionist: A Woman Against the Law* (New York: Free Press, 1994). The Barnett material in the paragraph comes from this book.

42. Ibid., 53. Early in her career, from 1945 to 1952, Barnett raked in over $200,000, a huge amount for the time.

43. Ibid., 37.

44. Carole E. Joffe, *Doctors of Conscience: The Struggle to Provide Abortion Before and After* Roe v. Wade (Boston: Beacon Press, 1995). I am indebted to NARAL for directing me to this source.

45. Ibid., 39–41.

46. Ibid., 70–107.

47. Olasky, *The Press and Abortion*, 90.

48. Nina C. Leibman, "The Way We Weren't: Abortion 1950s Style in *Blue Denim* and *Our Time*," *The Velvet Light Trap* 29 (Spring 1992): 32.

49. See, for example, www.drreddy.com/shots/measles.html. Accessed Fall 2000.

50. James Risen, and Judy L. Thomas, *Wrath of Angels: The American Abortion Wars* (New York: Basic Books, 1998), 11–15; "Abortion: Mercy or Murder?" *Newsweek* (August 13, 1962): 54.

51. Risen, 11–15.

52. *New York Post* (November 26, 1966): 25.

53. See, for example, Derek Freeman, *Margaret Mead and Samoa: The Making and Unmaking of an Anthropological Myth* (Cambridge, Mass.: Harvard University Press, 1983); E. Fuller Torrey, *Freudian Fraud: The Malignant Effect of Freud's Theory on American Thought and Culture* (N.Y. HarperCollins, 1992); Hans J. Eysenck, *Decline and Fall of the Freudian Empire* (Washington, D.C.: Scott-Townsend Publishers, 1990); Judith A. Reisman, *Kinsey, Sex, and Fraud: The Indoctrination of a People, an Investigation into the Human Sexuality Research of Alfred C. Kinsey, Wardell B. Pomeroy, Clyde E. Martin, and Paul H. Gebhard* (Lafayette, La.: Huntington House Publishers, 1990); and James H. Jones, *Alfred C. Kinsey: A Public/Private Life* (N.Y. W.W. Norton, 1997).

54. For example, see Adam Wolfe, "The Mystique of Betty Friedan," *Atlantic Monthly* 284, no. 2 (September 1999): 98ff; Hal Colebatch, "Dumbing Down Sarah," *Quadrant* 43, no. 9 (September 1999): 63ff; Jerome Zeifman, "The Feminine Mystique of the Feminist New Left," *Insight on the News* 15, no. 25 (July 5, 1999): 28ff; and Daniel Horowitz, *Betty Friedan and the Making of the Feminine Mystique: The American Left, the Cold War, and Modern Feminism (Culture, Politics, and the Cold War)* (Amherst, Mass.: University of Massachusetts Press, 1998). The argument will doubtless be made that because all four of the cited sources were written by men that they cannot be trusted. Be that as it may, their arguments have not been well rebutted by those supporting the other side.

55. Quoted in Paige Comstock Cunningham and Clarke D. Forsythe, "Is Abortion the 'First Right' for Women?: Some Consequences of Legal Abortion," in J. Douglas Butler and David F. Walbert, eds., *Abortion, Medicine and the Law*, 4th ed., (New York: Facts on File, 1992), 115.

56. David J. Garrow, *Liberty and Sexuality: The Right to Privacy and the Making of Roe v. Wade.* (New York: Macmillan, 1994), 249.

57. Hyman Gross, "Concept of Privacy," *New York University Law Review* 42 (1967): 41–42.

58. For more on this, see Laura Kaplan, *The Story of Jane: The Legendary Feminist Abortion Service* (Chicago: University of Chicago Press, 1995).

59. Ibid., 28.

60. David Garrow, "Abortion Before and After *Roe v. Wade:* An Historical Perspective," 62 *Albany Law Review* 83(3) accessed via Lexis-Nexis database, 2.

61. Kaplan, 28–32.

62. "Not in the Yellow Pages," *Newsweek* (October 9, 1967): 94–95.

63. Cynthia Gorney, *Articles of Faith: A Frontline History of the Abortion Wars* (New York: Simon & Schuster, 1998), 132.

4

Firebrand: January 22, 1973, *Roe v Wade*

The *Roe v Wade* decision has been a controversial one; some would say the High Court's most controversial decision. What is little known, however, is how controversial the decision was *inside* the Supreme Court itself. Beginning with *Griswold*, the Justices set legal precedents since no pro-choice decision has been made before then. John Ely, a clerk in Justice Earl Warren's office before taking a position at Harvard University where he became one of the strongest pro-choice legal scholars, told Warren before *Griswold* came down, "This opinion incorporates an approach to the Constitution so dangerous that you should not join it."[1] He was not the only one, either. The very left-of-center and almost always pro-choice *New Republic* cited Rehnquist's dissent in *Roe* as the right decision.[2] Even Ruth Bader Ginsberg, former President Bill Clinton's nominee to the High Court and today a devout defender of the pro-choice argument, stated at the time *Roe* was handed down that while she liked the outcome, she disliked its legal reasoning. Indeed, in some very surprising twists in this history we find many odd occurrences. Senator Edward Kennedy (D–MA), a long-time pro-choice supporter, wrote to his constituents the following in 1971, one year before *Roe:* "[T]he legalization of abortion is not in accordance with the values which our civilization places on human life."[3]

Further, the Kinsey Institute pointed out that abortions prior to *Roe* were being done by the clumsy and the ill-trained. Statistics show, however, that 85 percent were being done by licensed physicians under sanitary conditions.[4] Laura Kaplan points out that the group called Jane, a pro-choice group before *Roe* (see chapter 3), did not have an obstetrician on staff, and at one point, did not even have a physician. When this was discovered, members of the Jane collective found it "disturbing."[5] Additionally, then–Yale Law School Dean Harry H. Wellington, and widely respected legal scholars Alexander Bickel and Alan Wright, found parts or all of the *Roe* decision not well argued and a dangerous precedent for the country.

Many women were said to be dying from back-alley abortions, or so the claim was often made. While illegal abortions did cause death often up to 1940, it was increasingly less true afterwards. The main reason was the invention of penicillin by Scottish bacteriologist Alexander Fleming.[6] Although discovered in 1928, penicillin did not come into wide use until after 1940. In fact, most pro-choice scholars agree that bringing a halt to back-alley abortions was not the right argument to make in favor of *Roe*. "The proverbial 'back-alley butcher' story of abortion," Leslie Reagan points out, "overemphasizes fatalities and limits our understanding of the history of illegal abortion."[7] "A related myth," writes Rickie Solinger, "is that before [abortion] legislation abortionists were dirty and dangerous back-alley butchers.... [H]istorical evidence does not support such claims."[8] But back-alley arguments as a reason for *Roe* have yet to disappear. When Robert Bork was nominated to the High Court by George H. W. Bush, Senator Edward Kennedy and others rushed to the foreground, warning about a return to "back-alley abortions" if Bork were confirmed. He was not.

So, if all this opposition was present, how in the world did *Roe* come about? The most obvious reason, of course, is that the Supreme Court decided in favor of *Roe*. Another reason were the number of abortion "home remedies" that ranged from harmless to deadly: hot sitz baths, doses of aloes, straining exercises, walking, horseback riding, and jumping. The more dangerous included running a current of electricity through the thighs.[9] Add to this teeth-pulling (which occurred often in the nineteenth century), which left most women toothless before they were forty, and the stage for something to be done begins to emerge. That is, without a legal precedent to control abortions by legalizing them, women resorted to whatever methods were at hand. These methods often ended in death for both the mother and the unborn.

Too, while the Justices had *Griswold* and other cases to refer to, the Court also had in hand the American Law Institute's Model Penal Code (MPC). The MPC also had the persuasive endorsement of the powerful American Medical Association. Louis B. Schwartz, a University of Pennsylvania law professor who penned the Code, made this clear.

A licensed physician is justified terminating a pregnancy he believes [contains] substantial risk that the continuance of the pregnancy would gravely impair the physical or mental health of the mother or that the child would be born with grave physical

or mental defect, or that the pregnancy resulted from rape, incest or felonious intercourse.[10]

The Model Penal Code helped to establish the concept of legal "therapeutic" abortions (coupled with the Finkbine case) and paved the way for public
opinion and judicial decision-making. The Code looked like a blueprint for
legal abortion, and also had the advantage of having already influenced at
least half a dozen state laws since its inception.[11]

Just prior to *Roe* the nation had experienced an outbreak of rubella or the
German measles. Pregnant women who contracted the disease had given
birth to more than 14,000 children, many with everything from blindness to
severe mental retardation. By 1972, more than a dozen states had legalized
what were called "therapeutic" abortions. In 1970, Alaska, Washington, and
New York were already offering what amounted to abortion on demand.

So, the country was already moving in the direction of *Roe* when the case
came before the Court. What made *Roe* necessary from a legal standpoint was
the inequality of states offering abortions. Women in states where therapeutic abortions were legal had little complaint; those living in states without any
abortion law had no recourse at all. For example, if you lived in or around a
major city in the Northeast or on the West Coast, chances were good that you
could secure an abortion before *Roe* was decided. On the other hand, if you
lived in the South, the Midwest, or in small towns, the likelihood of finding
an abortion was so small as to be almost impossible.[12] Abortion came to the
Court under these conditions. Although *Roe* has received the most attention,
it has been estimated that there were at least seventy criminal and civil cases
in twenty states that the Justices could have chosen from to hear the abortion
question. Of that number they chose two, *Roe* and *Doe v Bolton.* To better understand why abortion went from unlawful to lawful literally overnight nationwide, both *Roe* and *Doe* will be discussed.

ROE V WADE

The Justices (Justice Harry Blackmun delivered the opinion of the Court)
for their part understood the matter as carefully as anyone. They wrote:

We forthwith acknowledge our awareness of the sensitive and emotional nature of the
abortion controversy, of the vigorous opposing views, even among physicians, and of
the deep and seemingly absolute convictions that the subject inspires. One's philosophy, one's experiences, one's exposure to the raw edges of human existence, one's religious training, one's attitudes toward life and family and their values, and the moral
standards one establishes and seeks to observe, are all likely to influence and to color
one's thinking and conclusions about abortion.

The Justices certainly understood from this that they knew they were entering new and uncharted waters. They continued:

Our task, of course, is to resolve the issue by constitutional measurement, free of emotion and predilection. We seek earnestly to do this, and, because we do, we have inquired into, and in this opinion place some emphasis upon, medical and medical-legal history and what history reveals about man's attitudes toward the abortion procedure over the centuries. We bear in mind, too, Mr. Justice Holmes' admonition in his now-vindicated dissent in *Lochner v New York,* 198 U.S. 45, 76 (1905): [The Constitution] is made for people of fundamentally differing views, and the accident of our finding certain opinions natural and familiar or novel and even shocking ought not to conclude our judgment upon the question whether statutes embodying them conflict with the Constitution of the United States.

By citing medical evidence as the decisive point, the Justices sought to couch the decision in legal, medical, and moral reasons as well. The American Medical Association had changed its view regarding abortion just a few years before *Roe.* Under the Fourth, Fifth, Ninth, and Fourteenth Amendments, "Jane Roe" (an alias for Norma McCorvey) argued that she was entitled to an abortion based on economic hardship. By the time Jane Roe appeared before the Court, her pregnancy had been terminated so the case was also brought "on behalf of [Jane Roe] and all other women." As Justice Blackmun pointed out, "The usual rule in federal cases is that an actual controversy must exist at stages of appellate or certiorari review, and not simply at the date the action is initiated." This was set aside because the normal human gestation of 266 days for a baby to be born is too short for the judicial process to be completed.

"Jane Roe" attacked the Texas statutes against abortion because they "improperly invade a right said to be possessed by a pregnant woman, to choose to terminate her pregnancy." The right is "discovered" wrote Blackmun, in the concept of personal liberty embodied in the Fourteenth Amendment's due process clause, "or in personal, marital, familial, and sexual privacy said to be protected by the Bill of Rights or its penumbras." This is the key sentence in *Roe,* for it is here that the case was decided.

Before deciding the case, however, the Justices reviewed the history of abortion. Blackmun concluded that the church had no real consensus opinion, since proponents could be found on both sides. *Roe* then summed up the history of abortion in what occupied several pages of the case: that anti-abortion statutes are of recent vintage; that "quickening" figured into most of the laws prior to this one; that Lord Ellenborough's Act was the first criminal abortion statute; and then taking note of the Hippocratic Oath, common law, English and American laws, and so on. The Justices argued that criminal

Norma McCorvey, left, who was "Jane Roe" in the 1973 *Roe v Wade* Supreme Court case, walks with attorney Gloria Allred. (Photograph by J. Scott Applewhite. AP/Wide World Photos.)

abortion laws evolved for three reasons: Victorian concerns to discourage illicit sexual conduct; abortion as a [haphazard] medical procedure; and the state's interest in protecting prenatal life.

"The Constitution does not explicitly mention any right of privacy," Blackmun argued, but the "Court has recognized that a right of personal privacy, or a guarantee of certain areas or zones of privacy, does exist under the Constitution." After this finding, the Court admits, "The privacy right involved, therefore, cannot be said to be absolute," and further argues that while this penumbra is indeed present, it cannot be extended without limits. Wrote Blackmun, "We, therefore, conclude that the right of personal privacy includes the abortion decision, but that this right is not unqualified and must be considered against important state interests in regulation."

What troubled, and troubles, pro-life advocates about *Roe* may be stated simply: the Court could not find a right so it, in their view, created or invented one as an emanation from another right. Pro-life advocates argue that the Justices in *Roe* acted as if the Constitution were some celestial body emanating rays of goodwill, which allowed the Justices to find whatever they wanted. Further, they argued that Roe v Wade allowed for too many types of abortions without assessing the danger (Table 4.1).

Pro-choice advocates, on the other hand, argued that the privacy rights were implied in the Constitution. In the end, the argument over *Roe* came down, and comes down, to how one sees the Constitution. Either it is a code that doesn't change or it is a "living document" that changes as society changes.

But *Roe* was not completed yet. The Justices still had to address the state's "duty" to protect persons under its jurisdiction.

The Court began:

The Constitution does not define "person" in so many words. Section 1 of the Fourteenth Amendment contains three references to "person." The first, in defining "citizens," speaks of "persons born or naturalized in the United States." The word also appears both in the Due Process Clause and in the Equal Protection Clause. "Person" is used in other places in the Constitution: in the listing of qualifications for Representatives and Senators; in the Apportionment Clause; in the Migration and Importation provision; in the Emolument Clause.... But in nearly all these instances, the use of the word is such that it has application only postnatally. None indicates, with any assurances, that it has any possible pre-natal application.

Pro-life advocates have since argued that if *person* means everyone *but* the most defenseless among us, what good is its meaning? Shouldn't the Constitution protect, as it clearly does in every nonabortion case before or since, the most unprotected? Pro-choice partisans counter that no one knows when life begins and so personhood cannot be determined until after birth, when it is obvious to all. The Justices, as if sensing this coming controversy, added, "This conclusion, however, does not of itself fully answer contentions raised by Texas, and we pass on to other considerations."

After dissecting abortion history and indicating the wide divergence of views regarding when life begins, the Justices conceded that science sees life as a "process." Near the close of this section, the concurring Justices did limit abortion, a matter that has since been lost in the shuffle of so many conflicting claims and counterclaims. During the first trimester, the abortion is a matter between the pregnant mother and her physician. During this first trimester, the state is perfectly within its rights to interfere between the mother and the physician and "if it chooses, regulate the abortion procedure in ways that are reasonably related to maternal health." For any stage "subsequent to viability, the state... may, if it chooses, regulate, and even proscribe [limit], abortion except where it is necessary, in appropriate medical judgment, for the preservation of the life or health of the mother." After this, the Justices claimed that the Texas statute (Article 1196) "must fall."

This section is very important in the abortion debate for the Justices were concerned that allowing abortion did not mean allowing any abortion whatever. Justice Burger tried to answer this by adding his statement in favor of abortion: "I do not read the Court's holdings today as having the sweeping consequences attributed to them by the dissenting Justices.... Plainly, the Court today rejects any claim that the Constitution requires abortion on demand." In the seven years following *Roe* (1973–1979), the abortion rate doubled.[13]

The dissenting Justices were equally confident in their dissent. Justice Byron White summed up his disagreements by arguing,

At the heart of the controversy in these cases are those recurring pregnancies that pose no danger whatsoever to the life or health of the mother but are, nevertheless, unwanted for any one or more of a variety of reasons—convenience, family planning, economics, dislike of children, the embarrassment of illegitimacy and etc. The common claim before us is that for any one of such reasons, or for no reason at all, and without asserting or claiming any threat to life or health, any woman is entitled to an abortion at her request if she is able to find a medical advisor willing to undertake the procedure.

Table 4.1
Types of Abortions Granted by *Roe*

Type of abortion	When Performed	Possible Side Effects
Suction-aspiration	First trimester	Torn uterus
Dilation & Curettage (D & C)	First trimester	Severe bleeding
Mifepristone (RU-486)	First trimester	Bleeding, vomiting
Methotrexate	First trimester	Liver, lung damage, nausea, diarrhea
Dilation & Evacuation (D & E)	Second trimester	Surgical procedure complications
Saline amniocentesis	Second trimester	Diarrhea
Urea abortion	Second trimester	Diarrhea
Digoxin	Second trimester	Diarrhea, nausea,
Hysterotomy	Second & third trimesters	C-Section surgery
Intact Dilation & Extraction (Partial birth or late term)	After 20 weeks	Vomiting, severe bleeding, possible death

White goes on to say that "The Court simply fashions and announces a new constitutional right for pregnant mothers and, with scarcely any reason or authority for its actions, invests that right with sufficient substance to override most existing state abortion statutes." White was hardly through. He called the decision "raw judicial power" and further found it to be "an improvident and extravagant exercise of the power of judicial review that the Constitution extends to this Court."

Justice Rehnquist was even more unrestrained. He argued that,

The Court eschews the history of the Fourteenth Amendment in its reliance on the "compelling state interest" test. But the Court adds a new wrinkle to this test by transposing it from the legal considerations associated with the Equal Protection Clause of the Fourteenth Amendment to the case arising under the Due Process Clause of the Fourteenth Amendment. Unless I misapprehend the consequences of this transplanting of the "compelling state interest test," *the Court's opinion will accomplish the seemingly impossible feat of leaving this area of the law more confused than it found it.* [emphases added]

Whether Rehnquist was right in his understanding of the decision is a matter of debate. But in this last portion he was exactly right: the Court *did* leave the abortion question more confused than ever!

Rehnquist went on to argue that the Court had found "within the scope of the Fourteenth Amendment a right that was apparently completely unknown to the drafters of the Amendment." On the surface, this would appear to be stating the obvious: if the Constitution was a "living document," of course they didn't see it. But Rehnquist was quick to point out that by 1868, after the Fourteen Amendment had been adopted, thirty-six laws enacted by the states and territorial legislatures had limited abortion. His argument had a compelling ratiocinative power: if those who lived at the time of the Constitution's drafting missed it, how could the Justices be so certain they saw it now? What Rehnquist opposed was not *Roe* and the allowance of abortion so much as it was the allowance *Roe* gave the Court to overturn the states' power to legislate.

For most then and now, this legal intellectual argument was lost, but not on scholars. As much as we like to tout our "democracy," Rehnquist knew we lived in a Republic and in a Republic, the states retain all the power, not a centralized government. Rehnquist was also quick to point out what has been alluded before: the *Roe* decision struck down the Texas statute prohibiting abortion while at the same time it allowed that under certain trimesters the state *does* have a right to prevent abortion. No wonder Rehnquist said that *Roe* left the matter more confused than it found it!

Lest we be quick to argue that politics determined *Roe* entirely it may be useful to refer to Tables 4.2 and 4.3. President Richard Nixon, considered a

Table 4.2
Supreme Court Justices and the Presidents Who Appointed Them

Name of Justice	When Appointed	President Who Appointed
Harry Blackmon	1970	Richard M. Nixon
William Brennan	1956	Dwight D. Eisenhower
Warren Burger	1969	Richard M. Nixon
William Douglas	1939	Franklin D. Roosevelt
Thurgood Marshall	1967	Lyndon B. Johnson
Lewis Powell	1972	Richard M. Nixon
William Rehnquist	1971	Richard M. Nixon
Potter Stewart	1958	Dwight D. Eisenhower
Byron White	1962	John F. Kennedy

conservative, had appointed the lion's share of Justices sitting on the Court in 1973, and yet Blackmun, who wrote the concurring opinion, sided with *Roe*. Burger, who of course sided with *Roe*, was liberal President Franklin D. Roosevelt's appointment but stated baldly that whatever else the Court decided in *Roe*, it did not decide in favor of abortion on demand. President Dwight D. Eisenhower, on the other hand, clearly the most conservative of all presidents here named, appointed Potter Stewart and William J. Brennan, while the second most liberal of presidents, John F. Kennedy (Bill Clinton was the most liberal president), appointed the chief dissenter in the case, Byron White. With respect to appointments anyway, clearly the politics of the president making the appointments did not predict the outcome.

Roe then provides a most curious quilt of everything that has made this debate so fierce: politics, faulty reasoning, passion, and emotion. The point is not perhaps that *Roe* should not have been decided but that what both pro-life and pro-choice legal scholars consider a poor case should have been used as the basis of so momentous a decision.

DOE V BOLTON

On January 22, 1973, the Justices also handed down a decision in another very similar case that need not detain us too long. This case spoke to Georgia's criminal abortion law's constitutionality. Mary Doe, the pseudonym for Sandra Race Cano, alleged that when she was a twenty-two-year-old Georgia resident, married, nine weeks' pregnant, and the mother of three living children, this fourth child would present an economic hardship. Two of her older children had already been placed in foster homes owing to her inability to care for them. Her youngest child had been put up for adoption when her husband left her, forcing her to move in with her parents and their eight children. By the time her case arrived on the Supreme Court docket, Cano and her husband had reconciled. She was unemployed, and he worked only when construction work was available. At one time, she had been a mental patient in the Georgia State Hospital.

The Georgia law had been changed just prior to Cano's attempt to procure an abortion. The new law superseded an abortion law that had been in effect for nearly one hundred years. The new law had been modeled on the American Law Institute's Model Penal Code, allowing for therapeutic abortion if the mother's life or health were at risk, the unborn child she carried would "very likely" be born with "grave, permanent and irremediable mental or physical defect," or the pregnancy was the result of forcible rape. When Cano applied for her "therapeutic" abortion in 1970, it was denied since it did not fall under one of the three proscribed provisions. She sued on "her own behalf and on behalf of those similarly situated."

The Court (with Blackmun again writing the opinion for the majority) concluded that *Roe* applied in this case and chose not to restate the matter, save by pointing out that "a pregnant woman does not have an absolute constitutional right to an abortion on her demand." Health is extended in this case to refer to "all factors—physical, emotional, psychological, familial, and the woman's age" as relevant to what constitutes "health." Next, the Court found fault that the Georgia statute should demand that the abortion be performed in a hospital accredited by the Joint Commission on Accreditation of Hospitals (JCAH), that the procedure be approved by the hospital staff's abortion committee, and that the physician's judgment be confirmed by two other licensed practitioners.

Because the JCAH is not a governmental body and requires a hospital to be in operation at least a year before it can apply for accreditation, the Court rejected the requirement that a hospital be JCAH accredited as unconstitutional. The Court then added, "This is not to say that Georgia may not, or should not, from and after the end of the first trimester, adopt standards for licensing all facilities where abortions may be performed so long as those standards are legitimately related to the objective the State seeks to accomplish." The committee requirement was likewise rejected, even though Doe's arguments against it were found by the Court to be insulting to physicians. Because the two other licensed physicians brought to a total of six required by the statute, the Court struck that requirement down as unconstitutional as well. Six were too many; one was more than enough. Finally, the residency requirement (that the pregnant woman had to be a resident of Georgia) was also struck down, even though "A requirement of this kind...could be deemed to have some relationship to the availability of the post-procedural medical care for the aborted patient."

It what has become one of the most celebrated passages of this decision, the Court concluded that the Georgia statute did not adequately protect a woman's right. What the Court said stunned nearly everyone, pro-life and pro-choice alike, because of the sweeping nature of the decision. Medical reasons had been enlarged to include emotional stability, while "therapeutic" had been extended to encompass economic considerations. The Court agreed with Doe "[B]ecause it would be physically and emotionally damaging to Doe to bring a child into her poor 'fatherless' family, and because advances in medical techniques have made it safer for a woman to have a medically induced abortion than for her to bear a child." Under these circumstances, pro-life forces could not see where any abortion could ever be prohibited.

What further angered pro-life advocates about both these cases was the Court's attempt to have it both ways: to allow for abortion under every circumstance but not in every trimester. They felt the Court had determined a right even when no right could be found. How could arguments be made against the right when the right itself could not be located in the Constitution by the Court's own admission? Lastly, while the Court claimed that it did not provide abortion on demand, how would it be possible to prevent it since *health* could be defined in any manner the woman and her physician required? Legal scholars lined up complaining that the Court had "just invented for the states, one rule for the first-trimester abortions, another for second-trimester, another for those 'subsequent to viability.'"[14] Even if you put aside the chorus of questions those directives quickly inspired (Why trimesters? Who defines viability? Why didn't the Court just go ahead and write the obligatory legislation itself?), you had to read *Doe v Bolton,* the second case, to see the very large loophole in *Roe's* option.[15]

If all of this was not enough to galvanize pro-life forces to take up the gauntlet *Roe* and *Doe* had thrown down, the aftermath of both decisions certainly did. After *Roe* and *Doe,* abortion clinics sprang up all over the country, and the practice proved very lucrative. Even before *Roe,* abortionists were making $2,000 a day. After both cases, the figures skyrocketed. Of course, heart surgery was also lucrative, but this argument was not employed in that case. Countering this were the number of physicians (their numbers are hard to determine precisely) who performed (and doubtless still perform) abortions for free, or performed them because women found themselves in impossible circumstances.

Perhaps the Court's own confusion may be summed up by a poll taken by Louis Harris and Associates three months after the *Roe* decision. When asked to respond to the following statement, "It's against God's will to destroy any human life, especially that of an unborn baby," 63 percent agreed while 28 percent disagreed. When rephrased as, "So long as a doctor has to be consulted, the matter of an abortion is only a question of a woman's decision with her doctor's professional advice," 68 percent agreed and 23 percent disagreed. Apparently, most Americans were both pro-life and pro-choice, and the Court's apparent determination to adjudicate the case both ways reflected this sentiment.[16]

In some ways, the pro-choice movement created the distrust among pro-life advocates. Some pro-life advocates were not only willing to entertain abortion law with exceptions but even worked for passage of this kind of legislation. When the Model Penal Code was released, it essentially added conditions under which abortion could take place. What it specifically did not do, however, was allow for therapeutic abortions, however that term was defined. As we have seen, the American Law Institute was unsure about a proposal that provided for abortion on demand. The pro-choice movement used the legislation provided by the ALI's Model Penal Code in over a dozen states to push for more conditions for abortions.[17] Lawyers such as Susan Grossman and Sybille Fritsche, ACLU attorneys in Illinois, along with others in Missouri, Georgia, and Texas, were working for nothing less than the total repeal of the abortion laws. By using the Court's own cases against them, Grossman, Fritsche, and others were able to influence the Court to decide *Roe* as it did. From this, pro-life advocates concluded that any help to the pro-choice side backfired against their own.

In all fairness to the Court, the matter had really been decided before the Justices got around to making the case in favor of *Roe*. Pro-choice forces had effectively worked a full court press on all fronts, as pointed out in the previous chapter. The medical profession was already on board via the American Medical Association but only by the hardest arguments. Even as late as 1970, the AMA was still holding out against requiring any physician to perform "any act violative of personally held moral principles."

Roe did not put an end to abortion-related deaths. For example, it has been argued that legal abortions in the first trimester are nine times more safe than carrying a child to term.[18] While this may be true, what is equally clear is that the reporting of deaths following abortions changed after *Roe*. Although deaths following abortions have occurred as little as four days after an abortion up to eleven months after, the cause of death has usually been listed as suicide, homicide, or accidental. Unless further research is done, the number of abortion-related deaths will remain a question. While it is unquestionably true that abortion-related deaths will never again equal those before the advent of penicillin, it is also equally clear that abortion-related deaths are not as low as is often reported.[19]

The grounds for *Roe,* the right to privacy, also created its own problems. When Blackmun cited the Fourteenth Amendment, he was citing the right of privacy:

As recently as last Term, in *Eisenstadt v Baird* (1972) we recognized "the right of the *individual*, married or single, to be free from unwarranted governmental intrusion into matters so fundamentally affecting a person as the decision whether to bear or beget a child." That right necessarily included the right of a woman to decide whether or not to terminate her pregnancy. "Certainly the interests of a woman in giving her physical and emotional self during pregnancy and the interests that will be affected throughout her life by the birth and raising of a child are of a far greater degree of significance and personal intimacy than the right to send a child to a private school protected in *Pierce v Society of Sisters* (1925), or the right to teach a child a foreign language…. Clearly, therefore, the Court today is correct in holding that the right asserted by Jane Roe is embraced within the personal liberty protected by the Due Process Clause of the Fourteenth Amendment. It is evident that the Texas abortion statute infringes that right directly.

But it is against this same right that Rehnquist dissented:

I would reach a conclusion opposite to that reached by the Court. I have difficulty in concluding, as the Court does, that the right of "privacy" is involved in this case. Texas, by the statute here challenged, bars the performance of medical abortion by a licensed physician on a plaintiff such as Roe. A transaction resulting in an operation such as this is not "private" in the ordinary usage of that word. Nor is the "privacy" that the Court finds here even a distant relative of the freedom from searches and seizures protected by the Fourteenth Amendment of the Constitution, which the Court has referred to as embodying a right to privacy.

The point here is that the Court *could* have made its case without reference to the Fourteenth Amendment but did not.[20] This made the legal reasoning all the more unstable.[21] Furthermore, Rehnquist pointed out that if *Roe* stood, it would overturn summarily the abortion laws in twenty-one states, most of which had been on the books for a century or more. How could matters have so changed in 1973 that laws in twenty-one states were now, without fanfare, dismissed as unconstitutional?

All this points to what could be seen as a weakness in *Roe*. It would be revisited time and again in subsequent cases. It is also this weakness that eventually led to the *Casey* decision that scared most pro-choice advocates into thinking that *Roe* could eventually be overturned. Because so many individuals had criticized the decision itself, if not its outcome, many knew, or secretly feared, that the day would come when the decision and its outcome would be reconsidered.

Circumstances surrounding *Roe* were not the best. Norma McCorvey (the "Jane Roe" in *Roe*) did not have the best of stories. Sarah Weddington and Linda Coffee, the two lawyers who took on her case, claimed she had been gang-raped. Later she admitted to an intimate but brief liaison. Further, just prior to the case coming to trial, she admitted to being a lesbian.[22] All of this did not come out until later, and its impact was felt only after the fact. But it did give the argument mounted against *Roe* more credibility than it would have otherwise. Even Weddington later admitted that had she known this particular case would have made it to the Supreme Court, she would most likely have changed her mind about pursuing it.[23]

PRO-LIFE FORCES SLOW TO RESPOND TO *ROE*

Lethargic best describes the pro-life reaction to *Roe*. Catholics, who made up more than three-fourths of the early dissenters, mounted the most sustained dissent. Only later were they joined by Protestant and Protestant Evangelical forces. Although Congress had Human Life Amendments on the "table" in late 1973, none of these ever reached a floor vote. Indeed, by the end of 1973, more than a dozen such bills had been introduced. In short, pro-life forces had been caught flat-footed. Even pro-choice forces, while elated, were shocked by the decision, though not even all of them were fully impressed by *Roe*. Though the Sanger contingent had won the day by making abortion a medical matter, the Dennett forces within the movement felt that the case effectively removed the decision from the hands of pregnant women and placed it in the hands of medical personnel and the state. The point is that both the Sanger argument and the Dennett argument were needed to bring *Roe* about.

The emergence of the Evangelical forces in the pro-life mix (what some scholars have termed "the New Right") galvanized the movement. They also nearly killed it. Even with their entrance into politics, they were unable to change the Court substantially when 6 of the 8 appointments made, were made by presidents favorable to the pro-life cause (see Table 4.3). While Catholic forces used a nonviolent approach, often spending long hours praying for the unborn, first in private, then in church, and finally on the street corners near abortion clinics, Evangelical forces wanted to see something happen—now. After years when nothing significant happened, when they saw just one or two women turn away from the clinics compared to the liter-

Table 4.3
Justices Appointed Since *Roe*

Justice	When Appointed	President Appointing
Stephen Breyer	1994	William Jefferson Clinton
Ruth Bader Ginsburg	1993	William Jefferson Clinton
Anthony Kennedy	1988	Ronald Reagan
Sandra Day O'Connor	1981	Ronald Reagan
Antonin Scalia	1986	Ronald Reagan
David Souter	1990	George H. W. Bush
John Paul Stevens	1975	Gerald R. Ford
Clarence Thomas	1991	George H. W. Bush

ally hundreds who went through with the procedure, Evangelical pro-life groups began to call for more obvious, more activist-minded approaches that would bring a swift end to what they viewed as "murder."

Pro-life forces viewed what had taken place in *Roe* as nothing less than an assault on revealed moral truth.[24] This was, they argued, a "Christian nation" or, in a phrase they often liked to cite, "one nation under God," and the presence of abortion on demand flew in the face of such arguments.[25] Abortion took the country much too far afield from its moral moorings. America was, they argued, still by and large "a nation with a soul of a church." Moreover, the *Roe* ruling, they complained, voided the restrictive laws in more than two dozen states and required revisions in another fifteen.[26] And one axiom of the pro-life forces proved true: whatever the Court subsidizes in law it is bound to get more of. In the case of *Roe,* the Court paved the way for increases in the number of abortions and they were, as we have seen, immediate. Since *Roe* there have been over 1 million abortions annually.

The *Roe* decision also made for rather odd bedfellows. Jews and Christians, Catholics and Baptists began to unite on a single political cause.[27] It even turned up a very odd advocate in Christopher Hitchens, the liberal essayist *par excellence.*[28] Hitchens, writing in the liberal magazine *Nation,* said abortion was horrific and called for a compromise. Later the FFL emerged, Feminists for Life in America. FFL consisted of feminists who staunchly defended the pro-life side of the debate. Mary Ann Glendon, on the opposite side politically as Hitchens, argued for pro-lifers to take their marching orders from England and other countries that appeared to have "settled" the debate amicably. Meanwhile, Conservative columnist George Will asked for both sides to "split" their differences. Switches such as these, where those normally associated with a liberal or conservative position took an opposite one on abortion, further confused the issue. No longer was it easy to peg one as an advocate or a foe. It also made for potential political suicide for politicians to "assume" positions on either side. With the battle lines blurred, the battlegrounds often became seemingly unrelated to the cause. The first had to do with third-party consent (*Planned Parenthood v Danforth*) and the second with Medicaid (*Beal v Doe*).

PLANNED PARENTHOOD V DANFORTH

One such early battleground was *Planned Parenthood v Danforth,* adjudicated in the summer of 1976. The issue began in June of 1974, about a year after *Roe* and *Doe.* The second session of Missouri 77th General Assembly enacted House Committee Substitute for House Bill No. 1211. The Act sought to impose a structure on the control and regulation of abortions in Missouri during all stages of abortions, a right seemingly granted the state legislature by the implied conditions set forth in *Roe*. Just three days after the Act was adopted, this case was challenged in the U.S. District Court for the Eastern District of Missouri.

Planned Parenthood brought the case "on behalf of the entire class consisting of licensed physicians and surgeons presently performing or desiring to perform the terminations of pregnancy, all within the State of Missouri." Planned Parenthood argued that the Act prevented citizens from exercising their constitutional rights, including "the right to privacy in the physician-patient relationship." In a 6–3 decision, the U.S. Supreme Court said states could not give a husband veto power over his pregnant wife, if the wife decided to have an abortion. By a 5–4 vote, the Court held that parents of unwed, underage girls could not have absolute veto power over sought-after abortions.

The case led the Court first into a definition of *viability* because the Act itself attempted to define that term. The Court found the definition in the Missouri Act to be consistent with *Roe*. With respect to the Act's requirement of a woman's consent, even a written one, the Court found that the Act did not allow for adequate provision. "We would not say that a requirement imposed by the State that a prior written consent for any surgery would be unconstitutional." But the Court did find unconstitutional *spousal consent:* "We now hold that the State may not constitutionally require the consent of the spouse..." It also found parental consent to be unconstitutional. Wrote Blackmun, who wrote the Court's opinion, "We agree...that the State may not impose a blanket provision...as a condition for abortion." Blackmun went on to further decide the case by writing, "The State does not have the constitutional authority to give a third party an absolute, and possibly arbitrary, veto over the decision of the physician and his patient to terminate the patient's pregnancy, regardless of the reason for withholding the consent."

While on the surface, the case appeared to be a victory for pro-choice advocates, the Court continued to cloud the issue by finding some aspects of the Missouri Act constitutional and some aspects not. The Court chose to decide the case in the manner it did, because it saw the Act as of one cloth. This hardly helped matters since it decided, again, for both sides. Some things the states chose to do were constitutional; others were not. What the states were to do, however, was anyone's guess. Were they supposed to pass a series of acts, each one dealing with only one aspect of the abortion argument, and watch to see which ones passed muster with the Court and which ones didn't? It seemed so, but such an approach was neither practical nor reasonable. Nevertheless, this appeared to mean what, in fact, the Court was trying

Planned Parenthood poster. (Courtesy of the Library of Congress.)

to say. *Danforth* was decided 5–4, with newcomer John Paul Stevens and Warren Burger, a *Roe* proponent, siding with the minority. *Roe* had been decided by a clear majority, 7–2. *Danforth,* however, changed all that. Now neither side could read the Court. Burger had switched sides. The "balance" of *Roe* was neither stable nor sure.

BEAL V DOE

While not the last case during the 1970s, *Beal v Doe* proved to be one of the more pivotal. The issue before the Court in *Beal* had to do with whether Title XIX of the Social Security Act required that states participate in the Medicaid program to fund nontherapeutic abortions. Title XIX established the Medicaid program, under which states fund medical services for indigent persons. The Act covers five areas of medical funding and does not require that medical treatment in all five areas be funded, but it does require states to establish "reasonable standards" under Title XIX.

The Doe in this case was an indigent person who qualified under Title XIX but was denied funds for a nontherapeutic abortion in Pennsylvania. Pennsylvania had been allowing abortions under clauses for the health of the mother but refused, in effect, abortions on demand. Doe alleged that the state practice was unconstitutional on the grounds that it denied her equal protection under the Fourteenth Amendment.

Justice Lewis Powell, who wrote the Court's opinion, found the Pennsylvania law *not* to be unconstitutional. "We therefore hold that Pennsylvania's refusal to extend Medicaid coverage to non-therapeutic abortions is not inconsistent with Title XIX. We make clear, however, that the federal statute leaves a State free to provide such coverage if it so desires." Joining Powell in this decision were justices Burger, Stewart, White, Rehnquist, and Stevens. Dissenting Justices were Brennan, Marshall, and Blackmun.

The deciding factor proved to be the statute itself. Title XIX did not make mandatory all medical procedures, especially those desired but not required. Thus, an indigent person may have wanted breast augmentation or a nose job, but could not have gotten either under Title XIX. Since the issue before the Court was a *nontherapeutic* abortion, that is, one not required for any reason other than that it was desired, the Court found Pennsylvania's actions to be consistent with the law and with the Constitution.

Marshall's dissent bordered on the political:

Since efforts to overturn [*Roe* and *Doe*] have been unsuccessful, the opponents of abortion have attempted every imaginable means to circumvent the commands of the Constitution and impose their moral choices upon the rest of society. The present cases involve the most vicious attacks yet devised. The impact of the regulations here falls tragically upon those among the least able to help or defend themselves. As the Court well knows, these regulations inevitably will have the practical effects of preventing nearly all poor women from obtaining safe and legal abortions.

What pro-life forces rebutted, however, was that the Court had already "imposed" its moral decision on all fifty states. Further, they argued that abortion on demand was not what *Roe* decided, and if every abortion fell under the Constitution (what Marshall seemed to be arguing), then *Roe* in fact granted abortion on demand.

Powell had attempted to make this clear in his own opinion:

Roe did not declare an unqualified "constitutional right to an abortion." ...Rather, the right protects the woman from unduly burdensome interference with her freedom to decide whether to terminate her pregnancy. It implies no limitation on the authority of a State to make a value judgment favoring childbirth over abortion, and to implement that judgment by the allocation of public funds.

While the ruling delighted pro-life forces, the Court's makeup provided little guidance as to where the issue of abortion in American life was headed. Tables 4.2 and 4.3 make this clear. If pro-life and pro-choice forces were seeking a quick guide to how to predict which way a ruling would go, *Beal* did not give much more evidence than *Roe, Doe,* or *Danforth.* What it did show, however, was that pro-life forces could, by and large, "count" on Rehnquist and White.

Once this was determined, both sides began to pay a great deal more attention to both the party of each presidential candidate and how many Justices he would be likely to appoint. This, in turn, led to a more pervasive examination, not only of Supreme Court Justices, but of all federal court nominees. Eventually, this led to the famous "litmus test" cases in the 1980s, in which presidential candidates were grilled over whether they would require a vote for or against *Roe* to determine how they would appoint Justices to the Supreme Court and the lower federal courts.[29]

If anything, these cases tell us that abortion, even for Supreme Court Justices, was not an easy matter. Although the Justices claim impartiality, claim independence from the political process, claim not to be making moral judgments, each case represented their struggle with the question with which the rest of the country was struggling: what is right, and fair, and good? Advocates at the extremes—those who say no abortion under any circumstance is good; those who say no denial of any abortion for any reason is fair—are of little help in discussing this question. Those who remain are, as the Justices have been and continue to be, conflicted about where the "happy medium" resides.

CONCLUSION

In *Roe,* the Justices acknowledged that the state had an "important and legitimate interest in potential life" but nowhere defined that interest as a moral one. *Roe* gave the United States the most liberal code regarding abortion of any industrialized country on earth.[30] The result has been that the courts and the country remain unable to arrive at any abortion policy agreeable to both sides in the debate. Already the issue of abortion is indelibly imprinted on the minds of many. Susan Estrich, former President Bill Clinton's aide during his first term, wrote, "By definition, [the woman's] right is to control her bodily autonomy *even at the expense of partial human life.*"[31] As these early decisions have shown, both the courts and the country will be mired in decisions that at once favor both sides.

Inherent in legal decision-making following *Roe* are the ingredients to make the abortion debate go on endlessly. As the old legal saying goes, hard cases make for bad law. And unless and until the Justices find the right case to clear up these matters, the two sides will forever be presenting their arguments to a divided judiciary. Perhaps in the end that simply reflects this country's divided mind on this most critical matter.

NOTES

1. David J. Garrow, *Liberty and Sexuality: The Right to Privacy and the Making of Roe v. Wade* (New York: Macmillan, 1994), 248.

2. Ibid., 607. Also Bickel and Wright below.

3. Richard John Neuhaus, "While We're At It," *First Things,* no. 119 (January 2002): 83.

4. Olasky, *The Press and Abortion, 1838–1988,* 90. This was not the first time the Kinsey Institute, long a staple of the press for sexual matters, was wrong. See Judith A. Reisman, *Kinsey, Sex and Fraud: An Investigation into the Human Sexuality Research of Alfred C. Kinsey, Wardell B. Pomeroy, Clyde E. Martin and Paul H. Gebhard* (Lafayette, LA: Huntington House Publishers, 1990); and James H. Jones, *Alfred C. Kinsey: A Public/Private Life* (New York: W. W. Norton, 1997). Kinsey's research is filled with errors and bad research models.

5. Laura, Kaplan, "Beyond Safe and Legal: The Lessons of Jane," in *Abortion Wars: A Half Century of Struggle, 1950–2000,* ed. Rickie Solinger (Berkeley, Calif.: University of California Press, 1998), 35.

6. Olasky, *The Press and Abortion,* 82.

7. Leslie Reagan, *When Abortion Was a Crime: Women, Medicine, and Law in the United States, 1867–1973* (Berkeley, Calif.: University of California Press, 1997), 133.

8. Rickie Solinger, *Abortion Wars: A Half Century of Struggle, 1950–2000* (Berkeley: University of California Press, 1998), 4.

9. Jeffrey Rieman, *Abortion and the Ways We Value Human Life* (New York: Roman & Littlefield, 1999), 24.

10. See http://members.aol.com/abtrbng/mpca.htm. Accessed Spring 2001.

11. Cynthia Gorney, *Articles of Faith: A Frontline History of the Abortion Wars* (New York: Simon & Schuster, 1998).

12. For more about this, see Leslie, *When Abortion Was a Crime;* and Garrow, *Liberty and Sexuality.*

13. Maureen Harrison and Steve Gilbert, eds., *Abortion Decisions of the United States Supreme Court: The 1970s* (Beverly Hills, Calif.: Excellent Books, 1993), v–vi.

14. Gorney, 164 and *sic passim.*

15. Gorney, 164.

16. Everett Carll Ladd, and Karlyn H. Boman, *Public Opinion about Abortion,* 2d ed. (Washington, D.C.: American Enterprise Institute Press, 1999), 2–3.

17. Reagan, 237–239.

18. James D. Shelton, and Albert K. Schoenbucher, "Deaths after Legally Induced Abortion," *Public Health Reports,* 93, no. 4 (1978): 375–378.

19. Shelton and Schoenbucher, 377.

20. This point and the one before it are addressed by Jeffrey Reiman, *Abortion and the Ways We Value Human Life* (New York: Rowman & Littlefield Publishers, 1999), specifically 19–22 and 40–41.

21. Regan, 235–236.

22. "Roe vs. Roe," at www.frameline.org/festival/22nd/programs/roe_vs._roe.html. Accessed Spring 2001.

23. Garrow, *Liberty and Sexuality,* 404, 436–437.

24. See, for example, Paul Grimley Kuntz, "The Ten Commandments on Schoolroom Walls? Why Did the Supreme Court Reject the 1978 Kentucky Statute (*Stone v. Graham*)? Could Such a Law Succeed?" *Florida Journal of Law and Public Policy* 9, no. 1 (1995): 19–22.

25. Some have argued that the phrase "one nation under God" does not refer to the Judeo-Christian God. But the phrase was added in 1954 after a campaign by the Catholic group, the Knights of Columbus. For more see, www.vineyard.net/history/pledge.htm, accessed Spring 2001. After the phrase was added, then-President Dwight D. Eisenhower said, "In this way we are reaffirming the transcendence of religious faith in America's heritage and future. . . ." See also www.usflag.org.pledge.of.allegiance.html, accessed Spring 2001. Of course, today many who say it may not be thinking of the Judeo-Christian God, but that is an individual change, not a historic one.

26. "Abortion and the Law," *Newsweek* (March 3, 1975): 18.

27. Michele Dillion, "Religion and the Culture in Tension: The Abortion Discourses of the U.S. Catholic Bishops and the Southern Baptist Convention," *Religion and American Culture* 5, no. 2 (1995): 159–163.

28. See the "outrage," Ruth Rosen, "The Abortion Struggle: Summer 1989: Historically Compromised," *Tikkun* 4, no. 4 (1989): 20–21.

29. The term "litmus test" refers to a familiar test in chemistry. Litmus paper is used to determine the acidity (or lack thereof) of a compound. In this case, the question about abortion asked of a president's judicial appointee was the "litmus test."

30. Mary Ann Glendon, *Abortion and Divorce in Western Law* (Cambridge, Mass.: Harvard University Press, 1987).

31. Susan Estrich, and Kathleen M. Sullivan, "Abortion Politics: Writing for an Audience of One," *University of Pennsylvania Law Review* 138 (November 1989): 146.

5

Backlash: Old Right, New Right

Roe, Doe, and other similar decisions of the early to mid-1970s galvanized pro-life forces. Heretofore, these advocates were content to make their case, say prayers, hold vigils, and engage in debate, but only when necessary. The Catholic Church stood virtually alone actively fighting the pro-choice side on a day-to-day basis. Evangelicals, by and large, did not think their religion called them to political activism.[1] To many of them, politics foreshadowed a wholly secular business that had little or nothing to do with worship, the church, or one's faith and practice. The *Roe* decision caught them flat-footed and they had to mobilize quickly. Five pivotal events marked this decade following *Roe* that moved Evangelicals into pro-life political activism.

First, Pope Paul VI's *Humanae Vitae* (which really occurred four years prior to *Roe* but helped to galvanize the pro-life debate) alerted Catholics and Protestants alike that something was amiss in the culture. Second, what are variously known as the Human Life Amendments were approved by Congress. Third was the rise of the Moral Majority, which constituted a formidable group that might be mobilized for pro-life activism. Fourth were the rise *and fall* of Randall Terry and Operation Rescue. And fifth was what is generally referred to as "the New Right," a political force that became so formidable it would later have to be reckoned with.

All five influenced the pro-life/pro-choice debate in various ways. And at least three of the five continue to influence the ongoing debate. Along the way we will also examine various court cases that helped to encourage or energize either side of this controversy.

Pope Paul VI. (Courtesy of the Library of Congress.)

HUMANAE VITAE

It has been argued that *Humanae Vitae* is really a birth control document and therefore inappropriate in a book focusing on abortion. But such is not the case. While *Humanae Vitae* is the Roman Catholic Church's teaching on birth control and contraception per se, it is also a document that reveals that church's position on a number of other issues, abortion included. Though the word "abortion" does not appear often in the document, the teaching is nevertheless clear, as *Humanae Vitae* warns the world that *any* interruption of the natural procreative process is wrong-headed and destined to human failure. Indeed, Pope Paul VI argues that "every contraceptive act is intrinsically evil." The encyclical "more specifically forbids the artificial regulation of birth by direct abortion, direct sterilization...as contrary to natural law and thus to the will of God."[2]

Pope Paul VI's warning in the form of *Humanae Vitae* (hereinafter *HV*) came on July 25, 1968. It is important to let the document speak for itself, for it is one of the early, persuasive, and compelling documents on the pro-life side. If *Roe* shouted the clarion call for the pro-choice side, *HV* is a similar shout for the pro-life side.

Almost from the beginning, *HV* warns in no uncertain language:

The transmission of human life is a most serious role in which married people collaborate freely and responsibly with God the Creator.... The...recent course of human society and the concomitant changes have provoked new questions. The Church cannot ignore these questions, for they concern matters intimately connected with life and happiness of human beings. (1)

At once, Pope Paul argues that not only is this a moment in which the behavior of human agents coincides with the creative aspects of divinity, but also that the "recent course" of events has sparked new questions. While many pro-choice advocates (some of them Catholics) saw the document as so much meddling in private affairs, the document begins by pointing out that this matter of privacy, so later celebrated in *Roe,* is viewed by the Magisterium as private *only* between God and humanity. It is too important a matter, *HV* argues, to be decided by a judiciary divided on the most fundamental of questions: what is humanity?[3]

The document proceeds to take into account the nature of the debate: it is faith versus modernity; the Scriptures versus the philosophies of men; God's commandments versus the easy allowances of the courts. *HV* outlined a reassessment of what these new challenges to social mores meant for the church and society. *HV* appeared to the world at a time when its contents would surely be ridiculed (even by those who would later embrace it) as being out of touch, out of focus with the times. Reading its words over three decades later, however, it is easy to be impartial about it: if anything, *HV* spoke to the events head-on and without flinching. Indeed, it even sees itself as a "sign of contradiction" in a modern age (*HV*, 17).

HV does not underestimate the role of marriage, observing that it can only be accomplished "with the gravest difficulty, sometimes only with heroic effort.... " (*HV*, 3). First, *HV* calls for marriage to be "exclusive...and this until death." (*HV*, 9). It goes on to call for mutual agreement about sexual relations, calling on husbands, especially, to be loving to their wives, and considerate in the marital union. It warns against using contraceptives and engaging in sexual relations for their own sake, lawful and unlawful therapeutic unions, and, staggeringly, the limits of human power. Staggering, because the 1960s can be seen as a period when people turned away from religion and toward an embrace of human power and understanding. *HV* stands amid the currents of history with challenging claims. *HV* concludes that humankind must be limited in its power because "These limits are expressly imposed... reverence due to the whole human organism and its natural functions, in the light of [Christian] principles...."

What makes *HV* so interesting in this debate is not that it "dictates" to men and women moral behavior but that it treats men and women as moral adults, not children who are slaves to caprice and whimsical pleasure. On the contrary, it treats them as extraordinary creatures, as thinking men and women who have important choices to make. Great pains were taken to make sure readers understood how hard *HV* knew these choices to be. *HV* sees the choices as monumentally difficult, but to be made by those of great intellect and discrimination.

From the pro-choice side of things, *HV*'s history is not without problems, and not just from the obvious one that argues against abortion. *HV* has a conspiratorial tone to it, or so some have claimed.[4] The Papal Commission on Birth Control had been in place under Pope John XXIII in the 1960s. When Pope John XXIII died, Pope Paul VI would continue it until the publication of *HV*. *HV* caught many inside the Church off-guard. Those seeking the aggiornamento (updating, modernizing) of the church, especially pro-choice leaders, were left breathless. Vatican II had signaled what they interpreted to be a loosening up, a modernization of church teachings. *HV* they thought, moved it backwards. Tom Burns, then editor of the (Catholic) London *Tablet,* said that *HV* proved "the greatest challenge that came my way. Never in the 150 years of the [*Tablet's*] existence had an editor... been presented with a problem of conscience and policy so great as that which confronted me with the publication of *Humanae Vitae.*"[5] In the end, *HV* created debate both within and outside of the Church.

Nevertheless, *HV* has been embraced by the longest-living pontiff in modern times, Pope John Paul, Karol Wojtyla. This pope, coming from one of the harshest of communist countries, and wildly popular among both Catholics and Protestants, has made *HV* central to his teaching.[6] No other pope in modern history has been more uncompromising on abortion, and no other pope in modern times has clung more tenaciously to the teaching of *HV* and connected it to abortion.

In many ways, while addressing the issue of birth control as the church rebounded from the fallout from "the Pill," *HV* also spoke out against abortion. As a document, it is perhaps not read as often as it once was. But for many, the call to sanctity of life even in sexual relationships proved important. Within the Catholic side of the pro-life movement, there can be no doubting

that *HV* ranks as one of the church's most important teachings on modern social issues. *HV* has also become something of a litmus test for Episcopal appointments.[7] If anything, Pope John Paul has encouraged this. In his own
encyclical, *Evangelium Vitae,* the Pope's support is without qualification:

By the authority which Christ conferred upon Peter and his successors, and in commission with the bishops of the Catholic Church, I confirm that the direct and voluntary killing of an innocent human being is always gravely immoral.... I declare
that direct abortion, that is abortion willed as an end or as a means, always constitutes
a grave moral disorder, since it is the deliberate killing of an innocent human being.[8]

HV viewed all abortions, including therapeutic ones, as strictly prohibited.
While many in the church would doubtless wish to qualify this, it remained
the church's position and led to the mounting opposition against abortion
following *Roe*. One would not want to attribute to *HV* more than its due.
Clearly, however, in the years following *Roe, HV* proved to be a sustaining
document, both for its eloquence and for its uncompromising posture with
respect to modern social issues and the tendency of pluralism and its coun-
terpart, secularism, to weaken the resolve of church dogma.

HYDE, BUCKLEY, AND "HUMAN LIFE" AMENDMENTS

Following *Roe,* pro-life advocates quickly began to make up for lost time.
If *Roe* caught them flat-footed, they determined that no other bill or law
would catch them unawares. For example, in 1974, just a year following *Roe,*
eighteen proposed constitutional amendments came to the floor to protect
the unborn. Though few of these ever reached a final vote, they nevertheless
proved effective in bringing public attention to the forces of resistance to *Roe*.
    One early effort in this process was the Hyde Amendment (1977) and
named after Senator Henry Hyde (R–IL). This legislation cut off funding for
abortions for the poor. In other words, Medicare and Medicaid funding could
not be used by those availing themselves of it for abortions unless a physician
indicated that the mother's health was seriously at risk if she carried the unborn to term. This had predictable results, depending on which side of the
debate one talked to first. Pro-choice forces had seen their chances of getting
any sort of pro-abortion legislation thwarted, so they moved to the judiciary
branch of government to secure what they could not obtain legislatively. In
response, the pro-life side moved quickly to Congress to secure what the High
Court had, in their eyes, abandoned.
    While the Justices debated *Beal v Doe,* discussed in the previous chapter,
Congress enacted what became an annual position in the form of the Hyde

Amendment.[9] While the 1977 version of the amendment specified the mother's health only, the 1979 version added, "severe and long-lasting physical health damage affecting the child." By 1980, the Hyde amendment included both rape and incest if either were reported promptly to a law enforcement agency or public health services.[10]

The amendment had a long reach. By 1979, the president forbade the U.S. International Development and Cooperation Agency, via the Agency for International Development (AID), to provide funds under the Foreign Assistance Act of 1961 to foreign nongovernmental organizations that performed or promoted abortions, even if that objective was accomplished through separate funds.[11] This, too, was challenged in court but later upheld. Planned Parenthood's argument that its right to free speech was abridged, failed. In *Rust v Sullivan* (1990), as we shall see later, this took the form of essentially allowing the executive branch of government to proscribe an organization from offering any advice concerning abortion if the organization received federal funding.

While the Hyde amendment broke new ground for the pro-life forces and gave them a measure of encouragement, Hyde was not the only one working hard for their cause. Prior to the passed legislation of the Hyde amendment, Senator Jesse Helms (R–NC) proposed Senate Joint Resolution 178.[12] The Helms resolution granted personhood to every human being from the moment of fertilization, thereby granting "to any human being, from the moment of conception, within its jurisdiction, the equal protection of the laws." The effect of the resolution would have been to overturn *Roe*. The resolution eventually failed and another was not put forward until 1983. This signaled pro-life advocates that the votes in Congress were not yet in their favor, though they were increasing. The movement then pushed to restrict funding, which led to Hyde.

Senator James Buckley (R–NY), brother of the well-known conservative pundit William F. Buckley, Jr., proposed yet another amendment in 1976. Buckley's amendment sought to extend the definition of the word *person* to include the unborn, specifying that *persons* were "human beings including their unborn offspring at every stage of their biological development, irrespective of age, health, function or condition of dependency."[13] The Buckley amendment also allowed for certain medical exigencies when the term *person* would not apply. "This article shall not apply in an emergency when a reasonable medical certainty exists that continuation of the pregnancy will cause the death of the mother." The amendment also allowed that the states would have the power to enforce it in "their respective jurisdictions."

The Buckley amendment tried to meet pro-choice advocates part way by allowing for abortion in cases where the life of the mother was at risk, a point lost in later pro-life legal forays. On the one hand, the reluctance of pro-life advocates to make such allowances today may be mere stubbornness. On the other hand, it could also be the result of failures such as the Buckley amendment to make any sort of headway at all. Pro-life advocates may have reasoned that because the Buckley amendment failed, rape, incest, and the other allowances were really only a smokescreen for pro-choice compromises that would never come to pass.

Others, such as the amendment proposed by Lawrence Hogan (R–MD) in 1974, sought to bring the due process clause of the Fourteenth Amendment to bear from the moment of conception. Hogan argued that if the Fourteenth Amendment allowed for due process, and all American citizens were entitled to due process, then certainly this would cover the unborn. The problem arose when other members of Congress argued that the Fourteenth Amendment did protect every American citizen, but only after those citizens were *citizens,* that is, persons. When did the unborn reach personhood? And so the debate returned to familiar territory: pro-life advocates arguing that personhood began at the moment of conception, pro-choice adherents arguing that it was impossible to know when life began and that even science had not offered any guidance on the question until after birth.

Of course, it certainly helped to spur on the Republican party when it saw that political hay could be made in this process. The Democratic party had made its own hay by representing the already-born as downtrodden if poor. A sizable minority (estimates ranged as high as 15 million) were, during this time, unrepresented in the political process. Republicans jumped on the pro-life bandwagon and reaped its now-considerable political rewards. It did not hurt, either, that since *Roe,* pro-life rallies began attracting (depending on the source cited) between 25,000 and 500,000 protestors *and* potential voters. Since each protestor represented as many as five other voters, the mathematics of pro-life politics looked inviting.

Pro-life groups working furiously for a Human Life Amendment via the Buckley, Helms, and Hogan efforts were early ventures. That Buckley could muster six other senators to support his amendment so soon after *Roe* spoke to the sizable opposition that awaited *Roe* supporters. But the failure of all such efforts, while discouraging, did not end pro-life activism. If anything, it spurred it onward. Because *some* support appeared evident, pro-life advocates realized that *Roe* could not be viewed as a door that had been slammed in their faces, locked, and bolted, but an obstacle that could be overcome. Any slip-up by the pro-choice side, they reasoned, would mean an advantage, however slight, in their favor.

One such slip-up occurred very soon. The case of Dr. Kenneth Edelin in 1975 garnered public attention, not to mention public outcry. In the face of the Hyde and Human Life amendments, the case proved both pivotal and important to the pro-life side. Edelin was charged with manslaughter when he did not attempt to preserve the life of an unborn child he removed from a teenager during a hysterotomy, a procedure used in later-term abortions wherein the uterus is cut open, caesareanlike, but without regard to the unborn. Partial-birth, or late-term, abortions had not yet been perfected so this procedure, while rare, was nevertheless being used.

Other doctors working with Edelin also worked with a team of researchers who had been studying the effects of antibiotic drugs on the unborn by giving antibiotics to women about to have abortions. The unborn corpses were then examined following the abortion.[14] This datum would prove important in the case. From a pro-choice view, this was nothing more than good, investigative science. From a pro-life view, this looked like scientific meddling and useless experimentation. The case, *Commonwealth of Massachusetts v Kenneth Edelin* (1976), came to the Massachusetts Supreme Court after *Roe*. Doctors were divided about the gestation time of her term, some putting her at twenty-four weeks, others, including Edelin, at twenty-one to twenty-two weeks.

The difficulties began when the introduction of a 20 percent sodium chloride solution was attempted. When the needle was inserted into the amniotic sac, the tap was bloody, indicating that it had not penetrated the amniotic wall. The procedure was halted and attempted the next day, when it also failed. When the hysterotomy was finally performed, the unborn baby was removed and Dr. Edelin checked, according to testimony, for heartbeat by placing his hand on the baby's chest. Finding none, he cast the baby into a metal basin for examination by a pathologist. The autopsy later revealed partial expansion of air into the lungs. This occurred in one of three ways: either intrauterine (before the hysterotomy), when the uterus was cut open, or before expiring after the procedure, suggesting a live birth.[15] Massachusetts found Edelin guilty of manslaughter. He appealed to the Massachusetts Supreme Court and won on appeal. At stake here was, of course, the issue of personhood. In the judge's charge to the jury, the issue of personhood was made clear:

Let me first discuss the word "Person." I do this at the very beginning because if there had been no "person" as such in this case there could not be any conviction of the crime of manslaughter. That is so because one of the essential elements of the crime of manslaughter, of course, is the death of a person.[16]

The judge went on to point out that the Constitution does not define *person* but all of its oblique references are postnatal ones and so a fetus cannot be considered a person. The judge's words were seen by some as leading the jury to a predetermined conclusion, but the jury found Edelin guilty anyway. The four companion researchers were also charged with illegal dissection under an

1814 state statute (originally designed to prevent grave-robbing) but were never tried.

Pro-choice advocates saw this case as an attempt to overturn *Roe* early on, and to prevent fetal tissue research. The historical record remains unclear. It appeared that the baby born to the seventeen-year-old died *after* the hysterotomy, in pro-life terminology, "tossed aside to die." Such an event was bound to occur sooner rather than later, given *Roe* and its allowance of abortion on demand. Since *Roe,* about 90 percent of all abortions have not been for physical or health-related reasons.[17] Given this high percentage, it was inevitable that the rush to abort for any reason would lead to unpleasant, if unintended, consequences. With respect to the second charge, illegal fetal research, the matter remains unresolved to this day.

The case did bring light to bear on the process of abortion, however, and served, if in a small way, to fuel the fires of the pro-life side of the argument. Abortionists would have to take more care in the process of abortion, predict gestation better, and abstain from innovating beyond what the law allowed. If anything, the Edelin case did give some impetus to state legislatures to provide for possible unpredictable outcomes. Babies born alive after abortions now become wards of the state in some locales.

Ever since the Hyde and Buckley amendments, the Republican National Convention Platform has sought to incorporate a human life amendment. Its platform supports a human life amendment but does not specify any language for that amendment.[18] Opponents have called this amendment the equivalent of a constitutional ban, but such charges are hyperbolic. If successful, the amendment would merely return the matter to the states. It's unlikely that such an amendment will ever become law. In addition to the failure of the early Buckley and Hyde amendments, the Hatch and Eagleton amendments, the Federalism amendment, and the Federal Rights amendment have all met similar fates. The division is predictable enough down party lines: Democrats, nearly without exception, vote against the amendments; Republicans, again nearly without dissent, vote in favor of them.

Lately Republicans have had more difficulties inside their party. In the 2000 election, pro-choice Republicans took center stage within the party.[19] For at least the last three elections, the Democratic party has struggled with dissent of its own, particularly in the very public form of the late Pennsylvania governor, Robert Casey. As a pro-life Democrat, Casey was refused a place on the party's platform, or even a hearing at its convention.

Early or late, these pro-life efforts have not been futile ones, though they surely may have seemed so at the time. When they gained national attention, they brought more individuals into the pro-life movement. The larger numbers meant more funding, and the increases in funding meant increases in political power. If pro-life supporters were part of the vast Silent Majority, a phrase coined by the Nixon Administration (and one often used by a later well-known pro-lifer, Patrick Buchanan), then perhaps, pro-life advocates reasoned, some attenuation of *Roe* might be possible. The sleeping, silent giant may not have been awakened fully, but he was at least partially aroused by what came to be known as the Moral Majority.[20]

THE MORAL MAJORITY

The scope of this book cannot provide adequate background on the Moral Majority, nor is it meant to. But some treatment of the Moral Majority is in order since its impact on the abortion question has been both profound and long-lasting. On the surface, the likelihood that a man by the name of Jerry Falwell would turn Thomas Road Baptist Church in Lynchburg, Virginia, a congregation of nearly three-dozen members, into a force of more than 22,000 in less than a decade seemed nil, but that is precisely what he did.[21] The Old Time Gospel Hour, which at its height transmitted to 34 million homes on Ted Turner's WTBS cable-TV station every Sunday night, showcased what is generally referred to as religious fundamentalism, the taking of Scriptures as literally as possible.[22] Media treatments of the Moral Majority focused on what reporters saw as the lockstep mentality of its (presumably) poorly educated followers. Such is not the full story, as research as recent as July 2000 makes plain. The new research contends that the Christian Right is more diverse than was originally believed.[23]

The Moral Majority (the name was suggested to Falwell by Paul Weyrich, another formidable Conservative in the pro-life cause) is made up of a widely diverse group of individuals from all walks of life, from all levels of education, from numerous races, but with one unifying goal: to return Western tradition to its more moral historical moorings.[24] Indeed, today Falwell, with the Moral Majority now defunct, meets with gays and lesbians, writes affectionate blurbs for Alan Dershowitz's books (a self-proclaimed pro-choice leftist) and is good friends with Geraldo Rivera—hardly the picture of what many once called Falwell: "the most hated man in America."[25]

The Moral Majority gained its political compass in the 1970s and found its political voice in the 1980s. While the name of Jerry Falwell was most frequently associated with it, it also included many other individuals. The late Evangelical theologian Francis Schaeffer was as much a part of the Moral Majority as political pundit Richard John Neuhaus, at least when it came to the question of abortion. And though Falwell, the late Schaeffer, and Neuhaus would differ considerably on other political issues (in addition to the manner in which the abortion debate was engaged), all were united under the pro-life banner.

The Rev. Jerry Falwell. (Photograph by Jerry Laizure. AP/Wide World Photos.)

Falwell developed and controlled the entity known as the Moral Majority for a few years. He was aided and abetted by Pat Robertson and his *700 Club*. Robertson's *700 Club* made its way into 30 million homes and mixed charismatic Evangelicalism with politics on a regular basis. Between the two of them, Falwell and Robertson added more than 8 million new voters to the pro-life cause.[26] (Schaeffer and Neuhaus may be said to have supplied the intellectual content of the pro-life debate.) As a political force, the Moral Majority was at one time as powerful as any pro-choice group, and more powerful than most. Without its evolution and eventual development, the pro-life side would not have had nearly as many victories as it did, and would certainly have been far less influential politically, judicially, and socially. Once Falwell and his Moral Majority broke the ice, so to speak, in the public forum, many others were more ready to speak out and be accounted for.

Falwell and the Moral Majority's voter's guides influenced the abortion political process in many ways. At the very least, it forced would-be political candidates to come out on one side of the issue or the other. No longer was it possible to be vague, indecisive, or diffident about it. Individuals who wanted to run for office, for example, would not only be quizzed by the Moral Majority on abortion and other social issues, but their views would be widely disseminated for many would-be constituents to read and decide for themselves whether they favored the candidate's positions or not. For years pro-choice devotees had made known candidates' positions on abortion. Where the Moral Majority made its presence felt was in the widespread publication of all candidates' views on abortion, pro or con.

Falwell did not limit his influence to politics alone. He also established Save-A-Baby centers for pregnant mothers who gave their children up for adoption. Then there was his new $30 million church and Liberty University, with enrollments between eight thousand and ten thousand.[27] It's hard to assess just how important this has been, but Falwell's work—coupled with Weyrich's Free Congress Foundation, Robertson's *700 Club*, and a half-dozen other right-of-center organizations—served to make certain abortion remained (and remains) a key ingredient in political discussions. Pro-life intellectuals are in agreement that Falwell's work has been pivotal in turning the tide from a pro-choice ascendency to a pro-life resurgence.

Falwell's Moral Majority took center stage in 1979. With Ronald Reagan in the White House for eight years, Falwell, Robertson, Weyrich, and others took important roles in shaping Republican policy on all social issues. During the two terms of the Reagan administration, Falwell and his cohorts had access not only to virtually every policy-making committee in the Republican administration and party, but also to the president himself. Indeed, Reagan saw the group as part and parcel of his administration.[28]

What made the Moral Majority so important in the history of abortion is that it kept alive the pro-life side of the abortion debate even when ending abortion was not the first or even the second priority on the nation-wide agenda. Falwell did this through his Old Time Gospel Hour. That is, after he made the case through Moral Majority publications and through the other avenues open to him through the millions of viewers of the Gospel Hour. With the completion of Moral Majority publications and the appeals through the Gospel Hour, he made further appeals to the Moral Majority membership. Abortion always remained a key or central issue for the Moral Majority, a claim agreed on even by its critics.[29] What Falwell and the Moral Majority accomplished was to take the theoretical arguments of the pro-life side and turn them into palpable ideas average Americans could relate to.

Falwell enlisted every weapon in his arsenal. Articles addressed to his membership called abortion "murder" and compared it to the practices of the Nazi regime. Francis Schaeffer wrote pieces for the membership. Analogies not only to Nazi death camps but to the murder of slaves in the antebellum South also appeared. Interlarded in all of this were calls to the membership to write, call, and visit local, state, and federal politicians.

Had the Moral Majority kept to this course, it would doubtless have seen more victories. In its haste, however, it made one tactical mistake: Falwell and the Moral Majority did not fully appreciate that incendiary rhetoric can have explosive results. One huge, tactical mistake proved to be one man by the name of Randall Terry.

OPERATION RESCUE AND RANDALL TERRY

If Jerry Falwell seemed unlikely as a leader of one of the largest pro-life groups in America, Randall A. Terry seemed impossible as the leader of any group, much less of a group that at one time wielded the single-largest measure of pro-life power of any organization in North America. Randall Terry was not the only figure in the rescue operation, indeed not even its first, but he was certainly its most public.

Before Randall Terry there was John O'Keefe.[30] John O'Keefe was the father of the rescue movement. His work began just prior to the *Roe* decision and from the beginning was marked by O'Keefe's quiet and unassuming ways. O'Keefe summed up his views in his *Peaceful Presence,* a pamphlet that became something of an early *locus classicus* of the pro-life movement. O'Keefe wrote, "Any movement that sets out to change society has to provide a picture of a world that is an ideal, that is convincing, so you can compare what is going on with what ought to be, and so you can be prepared to struggle for it."[31] O'Keefe meant what he said. He advocated a nonviolent movement to wage war against abortion and even evoked the memory of Martin Luther King, Jr., to sharpen his rhetoric.

With Reverend Martin Luther King Jr., we must come to believe that unearned suffering is somehow redemptive. A change of heart will not occur without suffering, and we have to ask ourselves whether we are willing to suffer ourselves or only ask others to suffer.... It is not enough to change people's minds; we are engaged in a struggle to change people's hearts. We are engaged in a process of metanoia—conversion, repentance.[32]

O'Keefe urged sit-ins to show solidarity with the unborn. "To be a presence before the world that would say to the world, 'Yes, we can perform safe abortions.' That's not the point. The point is that we can do it but that we should not be doing it at all," he argued. O'Keefe, as much as anyone, set for himself the arduous task of involving Protestants in his peaceful, nonviolent cause, and he did it very well.[33]

Joseph Scheidler, founder of the Pro-Life Action League in Chicago, caught wind of O'Keefe's ideas and tactics. He adopted the nonviolent tactics of going limp when removed by police and began adding new twists and turns for his group. He took under his wing an energetic protégé, Randall Terry, and coined the word "rescue" for their efforts. Much later, however, even O'Keefe would bow to activist pressure. Although he never endorsed violence, he offered excuses for it. His nonviolent tactics, some of which involved active resistance rather than nonviolent compliance, though effective, were never as effective as Randall Terry thought they should be.

RANDALL TERRY AND THE INFLUENCE OF FRANCIS A. SCHAEFFER

Terry may not have been aware of all these influences but one he was not only aware of, but fully enamored with: Francis August Schaeffer. The name perhaps does not resonate with anyone outside the pro-life movement. Certainly on the surface, Schaeffer did not *look* the part. Weary of the humdrum life of a minister, Schaeffer took his family to Switzerland, to a remote place in the Swiss Alps "to think." He told his wife he wanted to think about his life and his work. If ministry was not for him, he would return to the States and become a shoe salesman.

Luckily, Schaeffer found his epiphany in a Swiss resort he later called *L'Abri* (meaning "shelter"). Here Schaeffer took up a ministry for wayward young people who wanted to question everything about their faith. Schaeffer would listen to their questions and answer them. Drawing on the enormous intellectual background of Reformed thinkers from Augustine through John Calvin, Schaeffer taught more than he preached. "Students" who came to *L'Abri*, many of whom were searching for something to believe in, were given room and board in return for menial work. Work was prayer in a sense (a new twist on *ora et labore*, "prayer and work") and these students, many from affluent families back in the States, took on assigned duties that included anything from cleaning out latrines to making bread.

In what became the Evangelical version of *Roots*, Schaeffer penned what many consider his best book, *How Should We Then Live?: The Rise and Decline of Western Thought and Culture*. Its title taken from Ezekiel 33:10, the book is in some ways a Christian precursor to Sister Wendy Beckett's *The Story of Painting*. Schaeffer's book differs from Beckett's because it encompasses all art, culture, and philosophy, and spins Christian themes at every juncture. The book begins with Ancient Rome and recounts the movement of God's hand in history through modern existentialism. The book itself was a block-buster, runaway best-seller.

More important than this or any of his books, however, were the accompanying five one-hour videotapes (based on *How Should We Then Live?*) that were shown in thousands of churches in the late 1970s and early 1980s. Suddenly churches all over America whose congregations had never heard of Jean-Paul Sartre, sat in pews on Sunday nights discussing his *No Exit.* The book and the videotapes had a profound, long-lasting impact.

Whatever Happened to the Human Race?, another book and five-tape videotape series, quickly followed *How Should We Then Live?* Coauthored with C. Everett Koop, a born-again Philadelphia pediatric surgeon who had cared for Schaeffer's children, the 1979 book galvanized huge numbers of once-quiescent Evangelicals. In it, Schaeffer said, "Of all the subjects relating to the

Former U.S. Surgeon General C. Everett Koop. (Photograph by Toby Talbot. AP/Wide World Photos.)

erosion of the sanctity of human life, abortion is the keystone."[34] At one point
in the video series, Schaeffer stands on the shores of the Dead Sea as thousands of plastic babies wash up in the tide. This, he tells viewers, is the legacy
of the *Roe* decision. What will be the legacy of Christians? Koop, later the
Surgeon General of the United States under Reagan, and Schaeffer made a
twenty-city tour, lecturing and answering questions about "this human
tragedy."

While *How Should We Then Live?* had been well-received, Evangelicals and
other church leaders did not take to *Whatever Happened to the Human Race?*
In Jackson, Mississippi, for example, major Baptist and Episcopal churches
arranged mandatory religious services to prevent members from going to the
lecture series. At Wheaton College in Chicago, a school known for its Evangelical ties, administrators scheduled a mandatory worship service to prevent
students from going to hear Schaeffer and Koop.[35] It didn't matter. In most
big cities, the pair drew between 2,500 and 3,000 people. In one of those
crowds sat Randall Terry, and he "got" all that Schaeffer was trying to say.

While Koop withdrew by and large to become Reagan's Surgeon General,
Schaeffer penned his most effective, and most acerbic book to date, *A Christian Manifesto.* Published just three years before Schaeffer's death from cancer,
the book called on Christians to take a stand for what they believed. While it
focused on abortion, and perhaps abortion could be said to be its galvanizing
issue, it touched on a number of other issues that contributed to what Schaeffer described as the decline of the West. *A Christian Manifesto* encouraged
Christians to become more than pew-warmers. It encouraged them to become involved, to become activists for the Kingdom's sake.

This is precisely what Randall Terry found in *A Christian Manifesto.* Before
he read the book, he was content, if restless, with nonviolent sit-ins at abortion clinics. After he read it, he took his nonviolent protest to the next level.
Terry was not alone. Pat Robertson of the *700 Club* was telling his millions of
viewers that Schaeffer was calling Christians to active civil disobedience and
radical action as one possible solution. Schaeffer did not live to see what his
book wrought and it is entirely unclear whether he would have given his consent to Terry's extreme approach to abortion. There can, however, be no
doubt of the influence of Schaeffer's books on Randall Terry.

Until 1984, Randall Terry looked like any number of anonymous young
men struggling to find his voice after college. Born in 1959, Terry grew up in
the rock-and-rumble era of his generation. Indeed, Terry claims to have been
"delivered from the whole rock-n-roll culture" for God's work.[36] Terry proved
an excellent student as long as he remained in school. The problem began
when, as an accelerated honors student, he dropped out of high school just
four months shy of graduation.[37] While he later earned his GED, he spent the

next few months hitchhiking across the country. It occurred to him that if there were a "dark side" to humankind, there must also be a God to deliver them.

He eventually returned to Henrietta, New York, literally with a Gideon Bible in hand, which he had lifted from a motel room. While working in an ice cream parlor, he met a minister from the Elim Bible Institute, an Evangelical missionary training school in Lima, New York. The two men hit it off famously, and Terry's amorphous revelation became his complete conversion in the fall of 1976.

Two years after his conversion, he enrolled in the Lima school and studied more carefully the writings of Francis Schaeffer and especially his *A Christian Manifesto*. Terry remarked to an interviewer, "You have to read Schaeffer's *A Christian Manifesto* if you want to understand Operation Rescue."[38]

As he became more involved in the abortion debate, Terry wanted to do more, so he began picketing abortion clinics and offering what he called "sidewalk counseling." Sidewalk counseling involved confronting pregnant women going into an abortion clinic with the hope of talking them out of it. The movement grew, as Terry wrote:

In the midst of this harassment and discouragement, the brothers and sisters at our home church—the Church at Pierce Creek—rallied around us. We organized a picket-making session and made pro-life signs. Then one morning to the astonishment of the clinic personnel, we showed up with thirty other people who were picketing, singing, praying and standing with us.[39]

Suddenly the media took a very keen interest in these individuals. Though few understood it at that moment, this was the birth of a very powerful and, eventually, a very violent organization.

Although, from the beginning, Operation Rescue had been strongly influenced by the language of Martin Luther King Jr., and his nonviolent approach to civil disobedience, Terry's own words often evoke martial imagery.[40] He regarded the abortion struggle as "the fiercest battle in a war of ideologies and allegiances" that must be "waged" on many fronts, abortion being at once the most public and most virulent. Terry viewed the battle as one of life and death. Using war imagery and war language, it did not take long before Operation Rescue members—dissatisfied with the time it took to change the law, and disappointed in the numbers of women they could turn away (only five at his first event)—began bombing abortion clinics and shooting physicians who performed abortions. Terry tried to deflect attention from Operation Rescue's role in the attacks on clinics and physicians by saying, "I believe in the use of force. But, I think to destroy abortion facilities at this time is counterproductive because the American public has an adverse reaction to what it sees as a virtue."[41] Although he always pointed out that abortionists had killed more than 20 million during the same time as his attacks on abortion clinics, he failed to mention that his acts of violence against abortion physicians and clinics resulted in 1,712 deaths between 1977 and 1995.[42] Of course, Terry was not responsible for these in the technical sense. Violence as a means of stopping abortions in clinics did not become policy until 1983. But he clearly did everything to escalate the level of violence against abortion providers.

In the late 1990s, the Nuremberg Files web site sprang up listing the names and addresses of doctors performing abortions in the form of "wanted" posters.[43] The Web site claimed First Amendment protection. It listed the names of physicians who performed abortions and invited readers to send in the names, addresses, license plate numbers, and even the names of these doctors' children. Three doctors whose names appeared on the site's "top ten" list were eventually fatally gunned down, one by sniper fire outside his home in Buffalo, New York. After their deaths, their names appeared on the Web site with a line stricken through them. Although the $100 million verdict against the site proved only symbolic (all assets had been transferred to make them "verdict-proof" and the case was dropped in 2000), it did send a message that such behavior would no longer be tolerated.

Terry's personal difficulties in the 1990s are now well-documented and these contributed further to the failure of Operation Rescue. His marriage of eighteen years failed amid charges of adultery on his part. His own pastor in Binghamton, New York, censured him in November of 1999. His radio debut in 1995, *Randall Terry Live,* was canceled after airing only a few times.[44]

The end of the 1990s saw most Christian groups divorced from Operation Rescue. It still staged a number of important blockades, but it had not distanced itself from the killings soon enough. Legal orders against it made picketing more difficult. Fines for violating the "safe zones" around abortion clinics established by the Clinton administration made it financially devastat-

Table 5.1
Executions by Pro-Life Attackers (Wounded Not Listed)

When	Shooter	Victim
March 1993	Michael Griffin	David Gunn
1993	At large	Dr. Wayne Patterson
July 1994	Paul Hill	Dr. John Britton, James & June Barrett
December 1994	John Salvi	Shannon Lowney, Leanne Nichols
January 1998	At Large (Reward for Eric Rudolph)	Officer Robert Sanderson
October 1998	At Large	Dr. Barnett Slepian

ing to cross into the safe zones (some fines were $100,000 for the first offense, higher for subsequent offenses).

As the bad publicity for Operation Rescue mounted, the pro-life movement realized that it would have to find a new spokesperson far removed from Terry and Operation Rescue. If rebuilding were to take place, it would have to begin from scratch. What was needed was a new O'Keefe, a new spokesperson not given to violence and willing to work through the system, a spokesperson devoid of warfare and battle imagery. As it turned out, it was not a man or a woman, but the New Right of the Republican Party.

THE NEW RIGHT AND THE REPUBLICAN PARTY

The exact name of this group varies with each author who describes it. There's the New Right, the New Christian Right, the Christian Right, the Neo-Conservative Right, and one or two other names. There is some difference among the names. For example, the Neo-Conservative Right is best represented in the magazine the *Weekly Standard* and pundits William Kristol Jr., and John Podhoretz. It embraces, by and large, many of the same positions as the New Right or the New Christian Right; only the emphasis differs from topic to topic. Of course, Kristol and Podhoretz are Jewish. The New Christian Right was for a time best represented by Ralph Reed and the Christian Coalition, at least until Reed formed his own political agency for candidates of widely varying degrees of conservatism. The New Right may best be exemplified by Newt Gingrich and a cadre of politicians who flooded into office in 1992–1994 and assumed control of both the House and Senate.

While each one of these groups took center stage for a time, they are all really one group with different spokespersons. For the pro-life coalition to survive Randall Terry, its members (who are essentially the same individuals embracing slightly different causes) will need to fashion a cohesive message and send it consistently to Washington.

The membership of these groups has always been "there," mostly in the Republican party, at least for the last two decades. The difference today is that they have more vocal members in Congress helping to deliver their message. Pro-life intellectuals have a number of magazines of opinion from which to choose (such as *First Things,* the *Weekly Standard,* the *National Review,* and the oldest conservative magazine, *Human Events*); and Evangelical Christians have the New Christian Right to draw upon. What these groups have done, however, is bring sophistication to the delivery of this message, especially as it touches upon pro-life themes, to the general public and to those in Congress.

The New Christian Right, for example, moved away from Pat Robertson to Ralph Reed's Christian Coalition and grass-roots politics. When Falwell pulled out in the late 1980s, and Randall Terry had all but decimated the pro-life movement, many pundits wrote off the Christian Right.[45] By 1992, Reed had reorganized the Christian Coalition, won numerous local and state elections for candidates, and helped Gingrich bring to Congress new and energetic blood for renewed battles against the Old Left. They urged members to focus on broad-based, win-win politics, and remained loyal to Republican politicians at almost any cost, even accepting compromise, something they had avoided at all costs in the past.[46]

The importance of this change, especially at a time when Terry had marginalized everyone who disagreed with him, cannot be underestimated. Reed developed in a masterful way the grass-roots organizations that supported local politicians who embraced the key elements of the Coalition. Gingrich, meanwhile, took the elected politicians and framed for them an agenda that resonated with most middle-class Americans. Gingrich stressed classical liberalism, with its emphasis on freedom and citizenship, interlarded with a social message.[47] Gingrich also focused on economic development as an overarching theme. Quoting Friedrich Hayek and wearing Adam Smith ties, the New Right in Washington no longer sounded like a one-issue special-interest group. The New Right also stressed moral conservatism, but did not leave pro-life expression alone. Rather, it took a broader scope and made inroads into the welfare state, education, and even entertainment.[48]

The New Right also created an awareness of what it referred to as the Culture Wars. This involved everything from abortion to teen pregnancies, to secular humanism in the schools, to the welfare state.[49] What all this means for the pro-life movement remains to be seen. By the close of the twentieth century, the pro-life movement had all but abandoned Terry and Operation Rescue and had embraced a large quilt of conservative and neo-conservative positions. But the endgame for the pro-life movement is still very much anyone's guess.

The 1996 elections saw many departures from the norm. For example, drawing on the "big tent" philosophy espoused of late, the *Weekly Standard* all but abandoned the necessity of a pro-life presidential candidate, and even called for the removal of the human life amendment from the Republican Platform.[50] Pro-life warrior Bill Bennett sent a letter to pro-life activist James Dobson, indicating his willingness to accept a pro-choice presidential candidate.[51] This new tactic did not succeed within the Republican party but it did stir up enough debate to serve as a warning within the party that "pro-life only" candidates may not be given exclusive rights to vie for the nation's highest office. Bennett's softening of his position is important, for it had been Bennett who had earlier campaigned vigorously to keep the "pro-life plank" in the party's platform. While it did not stir much imagination to point to a small group within the GOP who wanted the pro-life platform removed (they were, after all, highly vocal and very publicly pro-choice), many were amazed to hear Bennett's claim that he could endorse a pro-choice candidate.

Whether this dissension will lead to the eventual fragmentation of pro-life forces is not clear. Certainly, within the party it did not go far. Bob Dole's candidacy against Bill Clinton in 1996 ended disastrously for the Republican party. Further, it is important to keep all this in perspective: the pro-life plank in the party's platform remains. But times are changing and pro-life advocates will have to continue to work hard to keep the issue on the front burner. Clearly, the loss of this voting bloc would mean disaster for any Republican candidate.[52]

As far as politics is concerned, for now anyway, pro-life advocacy is still well situated within the Republican party. The Republicans are not the only political party with difficulties. While the Republicans have in recent years attempted to appear more mainstream, the Democrats have worked hard to drop the "radical" posture that has dogged them for the last two decades. Indeed, Bill Clinton campaigned as a "New Democrat," presumably in con-tradistinction to the Old Democrat persona. As far as abortion was con-cerned, Clinton still supported the pro-choice side, as all the "Old Democrats" had done. While pro-choice Republicans sought to get a hearing for the pro-choice side within their party, the Democrats did not openly sup-port the pro-life position of campaigners within its ranks. For the time being anyway, it would appear that neither party will countenance too public a plat-form for dissenters on the pro-life or pro-choice side. Even with George W. Bush's 2000 election, pro-life issues were not, according to his White House spokesperson, "a priority issue."

With the advent of partial-birth abortion now in the mix, it is unlikely that pro-life advocacy will diminish. While abortion per se is somewhat easy for a majority to tolerate, partial-birth abortion is more troubling. If Randall Terry was the Achilles heel for the pro-life side, partial-birth abortion may be it for the pro-choice side.

CONCLUSION

The rise of each of the groups cited in this chapter as a response to *Roe* helped to solidify the pro-life cause in American politics. Both the pro-life and pro-choice sides, however, are beginning to show some fragmentation. Still, it isn't easy for a major political movement to recover from the publicity of cold-blooded murders of physicians practicing abortions or clinics being blown up. While most Americans understand holding fast to a philosophy, most are not ready to tolerate any organization taking the law into its own hands. For the pro-life side to fully recover in the twenty-first century and make any additional political gains in its favor, it must continue to distance itself from a once-large group that took vigilantism to the extreme.

NOTES

1. Although many consider Evangelicals to be a new type of believer within the church, they appear rather as young believers brought up in the church who were convinced that practical faith meant activist expression. Doubtless many have turned out to be once-left-of-center radicals who found a new revolution: belief.

2. John A. Thiel, "Tradition and Authoritative Reasoning: A Nonfoundationalist Perspective," *Theological Studies* 5, no. 4 (December 1995), accessed via InfoTrac database.

3. See Gary Wills, *Papal Sin: Structures of Deceit* (New York: Doubleday, 2000). Wills, himself a Catholic (some Catholics would argue the point), takes the document to task in chapter 5 and 6, calling it one of the worst and most deceitful documents in the history of the papacy.

4. This is the view throughout Robert McClory, *Turning Point: The Inside Story of the Papal Birth Control Commission and How Humanae Vitae Changed the Life of Pat Crowley and the Future of the Church* (New York: Crossroads, 1995).

5. Richard McCormick, "*Humanae Vitate* 25 Years Later," *America* 169, no. 2 (July 17, 1993): 1, accessed via InfoTrac database.

6. George Weigel, *Witness to Hope: The Biography of Pope John Paul II* (New York: Cliff Street Books, 1999), 206–210.

7. McCormick, 4.

8. "Pope's 'Culture of Death' Assessment Gets Agreement, with Reservations," *National Catholic Reporter* 31, no. 24 (April 14, 1995): 3.

9. J. George Jr., "State Legislatures versus the Supreme Court: Abortion Legislation into the 1990s," in *Abortion, Medicine and the Law,* ed. J. Douglas Butler and David F. Walbert, 4th ed., (New York: Facts on File), 67.

10. Pub Law no. 98–139, section 204, 97 Stat. 871, 887 (1983).

11. George, 72, note 512.

12. Senator Bob Packwood, "The Rise and Fall of the Right-to-Life Movement in Congress: Response to the *Roe* Decision, 1973–1983," in Butler and Walbert, eds., *Abortion, Medicine and the Law,* 636–39.

13. Eva R. Rubin, *Abortion, Politics, and the Courts: Roe v Wade and Its Aftermath* (Westport, Conn.: Greenwood Press, 1982), 117. (See also www.elca.org/jle/alc/alc.abortion(5).html.)

14. Ibid., 118–120.

15. In addition to Rubin, *Abortion, Politics, and the Courts,* other accounts can be found in Eva R. Rubin, *The Abortion Controversy: A Documentary History* (Westport, Conn.: Greenwood Press, 1994), 186–188; and Fred M. Frohock, *Abortion: A Case Study in Law and Morals* (Westport, Conn.: Greenwood Press, 1983), 86–88.

16. *Commonwealth of Mass. v Kenneth Edelin.* No. 81823 (Mass. Super. Ct. 1974), 93rd Congress, 2nd Session. Also quoted in Rubin, *The Abortion Controversy,* 187.

17. "Issues in Brief: The Limitations of U.S. Statistics on Abortion," www.agi-usa.org/pubs/ib14.html, accessed Spring 2002. Also see any annual issue of *Statistical Abstracts of the United States.*

18. Clarke Forsythe, "The Missing Abortion Amendment," *The Human Life Review* 22, no. 3 (Summer 1996): 119–122, accessed via InfoTrac's Expanded Academic ASAP database.

19. David Bowermaster, "The GOP's Abortion Battle: Family Feud," *U.S. News and World Report* 120, no. 19 (May 13, 1996): 32, accessed via InfoTrac's Expanded Academic ASAP database. See also Rameshk Ponnuru, "Abort, Retry, Fail?" *National Review* 48, no. 1 (January 29, 1996): 21–23, accessed via InfoTrac's Expanded Academic ASAP database; Lee A. Casey, "Pragmatic Abortion Foes Won't Mind Altering Plank," *Insight on the News* 12, no. 17 (May 6, 1996): 28–30, accessed via InfoTrac's Expanded Academic ASAP database; Fred Barnes, "Try Again," *New Republic* 210, no. 24 (June 13, 1994): 9–11, accessed via InfoTrac's Expanded Academic ASAP database.

20. The evolution of the Silent Majority into the Moral Majority is also chronicled by Sidney Blumenthal in his think-piece, "The Righteous Empire: A Short History of the End of History, and Maybe Even of the G.O.P.," *The New Republic* 191 (October 22, 1984): 18–24, accessed via InfoTrac database.

21. Edward Gilbreath, "The Jerry We Never Knew," *Christianity Today* (April 24, 2000): 113–116, accessed via InfoTrac database.

22. Richard N. Ostling, "Jerry Falwell's Crusade: Fundamentalist Legions Seek to Remake Church and Society," *Time* 127 (September 2, 1985): 48–54, accessed via InfoTrac database.

23. D. W. Miller, "Striving to Understand the Christian Right," *Chronicle of Higher Education* 46, no. 43 (June 30, 2000): A17–A18.

24. Paul Weyrich, "The Moral Minority," *Christianity Today* (September 6, 1999): 44–46, accessed via InfoTrac database.

25. Gilbreath, 114–115.

26. Ostling, "Falwell's Crusade," page 5 of the electronic version.

27. Richard N. Ostling, "A Jerry-Built Coalition Regroups: Falwell's Exit Changes the Landscape of the Religious Right," *Time* 20, no. 20 (November 16, 1987): 68–70, accessed via InfoTrac database.

28. Matthew C. Moen, "From Revolution to Evolution: The Changing Nature of the Christian Right," *Sociology of Religion* 55, no. 3 (Fall 1994): 345–358.

29. See, for example, David Snowball, *Continuity and Change in the Rhetoric of the Moral Majority* (New York: Praeger, 1991), 111–114.

30. James Risen and Judy L. Thomas, *The Wrath of Angels: The American Abortion War* (New York: BasicBooks: 1998).

31. Risen and Thomas, 66.

32. Ibid.

33. Ibid., 65–66.

34. Francis A. Schaeffer, *Whatever Happened to the Human Race?* (Old Tappan, N.J.: Fleming H. Revell Company), 31. The quote attributed to Schaeffer in Risen and Thomas, 124, is really by Noonan. See Schaeffer, 32.

35. Risen and Thomas, 125.

36. "Randall A. Terry," *Current Biography Yearbook 1994,* Judith Graham, ed. (New York: H. W. Wilson, 1994), 590–593. All biographical notations are from this source unless otherwise noted.

37. Garry Wills, "Evangels of Abortion," *New York Review of Books* 36, no. 10 (June 15, 1989): 15.

38. Ibid.

39. Randall A. Terry, *Operation Rescue* (Springdale, Penn.: Whitaker House, 1988), 16.

40. Wills, "Evangels," 19.

41. Quoted in Barbara Hinkson Craig and David M. O'Brien, *Abortion and American Politics* (Chatham, N.J.: Chatham House, 1993), 58.

42. Charles S. Clark, "Abortion Clinic Protests," *The CQ Researcher* 5, no. 13 (April 7, 1995): 297ff.

43. Lauren Dodge, "Jury Slaps Anti-Abortion Website: $100 Million Verdict in FACE Case," *The Legal Intelligencer* (February 3, 1999), accessed via Lexis-Nexis database. The site appealed the verdict but lost on appeal in May 2002 when the 9th Circuit Court of Appeals found the site liable for illegal threats in a 6–5 vote.

44. Dana Kennedy, "Abortion, Inc.," *George* 5, no. 10 (2000), 101.

45. Mark Rozell and Clyde Wilcox, "Joining the Mainstream: The New Christian Right in Virginia," *Spectrum: The Journal of State Government* 69, no. 1 (winter 1996): 26–33, accessed via InfoTrac's Expanded Academic ASAP database.

46. Ibid., 3–4.

47. Timothy J. Gaffaney, "Citizens of the Market: The Un-Political Theory of the New Right," *Polity* 32, no. 2 (Winter 1999): 79–89.

48. Rosen and Wilcox, 8–10.

49. Micaela de Leonardo, "Patterns of Culture Wars: The Right's Attack on 'Cultural Relativism' as Synecdoche for All That Ails Us," *The Nation* 262, no. 14 (April 8, 1996): 25–30, accessed via InfoTrac's Expanded Academic ASAP database.

50. See, for example, "Abortion Rights GOP Want Platform Changed," *Congress Daily/ A.M.* (March 8, 2000), accessed via InfoTrac's Expanded Academic ASAP database.

51. "The Right's New Abortion Fight," *Harper's Magazine* 292, no. 1748 (January 1996): 22–23, accessed via InfoTrac's Expanded Academic ASAP database.

52. For example, it is estimated that more than 4 million of these voters did not vote at all in the 2000 election, helping to create the Gore-Bush stalemate in Florida.

6

Morning After Bills: After *Roe*, before *Casey*

Of the "morning after" bills, three stand out most prominently, one from the 1980s, and two from the 1990s: *Webster v Reproductive Health Services* (July 3, 1989), came in conventional fashion to the Supreme Court and proffered more to pro-life advocates than it actually delivered. On the surface, pro-life enthusiasm for the decision was not unwarranted. But a close reading provides a clearer picture of what the then-constituted Court had in mind (at least for as long as it was so constituted). The other case treated here is *Rust v Sullivan* (May 23, 1991). (*Casey*, the case that focused on informed consent for parents, husbands, and guardians, and challenged *Roe* on its most fundamental point, will be examined in the next chapter.) *Rust*, too, provided the proverbial light at the end of the tunnel for pro-life activists. Only *after Casey* did pro-lifers realize the light was from an onrushing *Roe* train that showed no chance of derailment then, or in the near future.

Webster, Rust, and *Casey* provide the most dramatic of backdrops to this ten-year period, roughly 1983–1992. But other cases, and issues, are equally important. Three other decisions occurred before *Webster* and made fodder for the disputatious 1980s complete: *Akron v Akron Center* (decided on June 15, 1983), *Planned Parenthood v Ashcroft* (June 15, 1983), and *Thornburgh v American College of Obstetricians and Gynecologists* (June 11, 1986). *Rust* was decided early in the 1990s, just prior to *Casey*.

Before examining *Webster* in detail, we will delve into each of these others in turn to see what light they shed on the later *Webster* decision. Of course, other important decisions were rendered at this time as well. For example,

Demonstrators march in front of St. Patrick's Cathedral in New York City, protesting the Roman Catholic Church's fight to change the New York State abortion law. (Courtesy of the Library of Congress.)

consider the Medicaid decision in *Harris v McRae* (which held that an indigent woman could not be reimbursed for an abortion while she could be reimbursed for expenses related to childbirth). For those fighting these battles on the front lines, *all* court decisions seemed important. These five provide an ample backdrop to the *Webster* decision. Two ancillary issues, *The Silent Scream* video and the so-called "abortion pill," RU-486, bookend this time period even down to 2003.

The interminable abortion debate escalated in the 1980s over the pivotal 5–4 decision in *Webster v Reproductive Health Services,* a case that focused on when life begins, the protection of the unborn under the Constitution, the prohibition of *any* abortions after twenty weeks, and the denial of federal funds to encourage or secure an abortion. Pro-choice advocates saw it as an ominous sign of the beginning of the end of *Roe,* though, it will be recalled, *Roe* itself allowed states to restrict abortion after the first trimester. Clearly, pro-life advocates felt encouraged by the decision. For the first time since *Roe,* the Supreme Court appeared in its 5–4 decision to signal observers that it might be willing to reconsider *Roe.*

In the aftermath, the *Webster* decision provided the Justices only an opportunity to vent spleen over the *Roe* decision but little else. Perhaps pro-life advocates saw *Webster* as more than it was. While the decision ceded a little ground to the pro-life side, it took away much more than it granted. Meanwhile, the pro-choice side used the perceived "loss" to galvanize public opinion in its favor; it gave pro-choice advocates a chance to voice their concerns about *Webster* to the public.

AKRON V AKRON CENTER

By the time *Akron* came before the High Court in June of 1982, the makeup of the Court had changed considerably. Justices Warren Burger, William Brennan, Byron White, Thurgood Marshall, Harry Blackmun, and Lewis Powell remained in place. William Rehnquist also remained, as did his pro-life stance on abortion. Endowed with a keen intellect, Rehnquist came into his own during the 1980s, and this case catapulted him to further prominence. Justices John Paul Stevens (a Ford appointee) and Sandra Day O'Connor, the first female Justice and a Reagan appointee, joined Rehnquist. Justices White, Rehnquist, and O'Connor would form the minority opposed to *Akron,* which nevertheless held the day with six justices in agreement on the decision.

At issue in this case was Akron Ordinance no. 160–1978, titled "Regulation of Abortions." As Powell pointed out in his opening remarks on the case, the provision of *Roe* that allowed states to exercise *some* regulation of abortion created this mare's nest. As *Roe* supposedly provided, the Akron ordinance regulated abortions performed after the first trimester. After the first trimester, abortions had to be performed in a hospital. Parental notification had to be obtained for unmarried minors. An attending physician had to make certain specified statements "to insure that the consent for the abortion is truly informed consent." There had to be a twenty-four-hour waiting period, and "fetal remains" had to be "disposed of in a humane and sanitary manner." Twelve other regulations appeared in the Akron ordinance but did not come under the Court's scrutiny at this time.[1]

On April 19, 1978, a lawsuit challenged virtually all seventeen of the ordinance's provisions. Three abortion clinics in Akron and one physicians' clinic came before the Court as the plaintiffs. Three Akron city officials were named as the defendants. The District Court preliminarily enjoined (i.e., stopped) the enforcement of the ordinance eight days after the lawsuit was filed. In

August of the same year, the District Court invalidated parental consent, parental notice, disposal of fetal remains, and disclosure of certain facts about the pregnant woman. It left intact hospitalizations, informed consent about risks for the pregnant woman after the first trimester, and the twenty-four-hour waiting period.

Although *Roe* allowed that at the end of the first trimester the state had a right to regulate abortion, the Court in deciding *Akron* found the hospitalization requirement to be unconstitutional. Even though *Roe* granted that the state had a compelling interest (and scientific evidence showed that complications were more numerous after the first trimester), the Court still found that this compelling health interest "is only the beginning of the inquiry." The Court found it reasonable "only if…designed to further that state interest." The Court concluded that hospitalization posed a significant obstacle to abortion which, apparently, proved the key ingredient to *Roe* (79, 81).

The Court then turned to parental consent for abortions performed on minors under the age of fifteen. The Court found that *Akron* may "not make a blanket determination that *all* minors under the age of fifteen are too immature to make this decision or that an abortion never may be in the minor's best interests without parental consent." Further, the Court found the Akron ordinance's provision that required disclosure to the pregnant woman of the viability, size, and weight of her second-trimester unborn child (or later) to be unconstitutional. "Informed consent" as defined by the Akron ordinance went too far "beyond permissible limits" (83, 85–87).

The Court also found unconstitutional the "litany of information that the physician must recite to each woman regardless of whether in his judgment the information is relevant to her personal decision." The Court ruled that less information may be better: "Akron has gone far beyond merely describing the general subject matter relevant to informed consent." The Court also found to be invalid the requirement of *Akron* to discuss more fully with the pregnant woman "…the particular risks associated with her own pregnancy and the abortion technique to be employed including providing her with at least a general description of the medical instructions to be followed subsequent to the abortion in order to insure her safe recovery" (87)—as well as whether in the physician's judgment she should proceed with the abortion or carry to term. Abortion may be the only medical procedure in which it is unconstitutional for the patient to have too much information.

With regard to the twenty-four-hour waiting period, the Court agreed with the Court of Appeals. Although the twenty-four-hour waiting period appeared to allow for a "cooling off" period in which to weigh such a momentous decision, the Court found that "a State may not demand that [the pregnant] woman delay the effectuation of [the abortion] decision."

O'Connor dissented formidably in this case, arguing that the *Akron* decision makes invalid the restrictions imposed by *Roe*. She found that, "The Court's analysis of the Akron regulations is inconsistent both with the methods of analysis employed in previous cases dealing with abortion, and with the Court's approach to fundamental rights in other areas." More than that, O'Connor called into question the usefulness of *Roe* altogether. "The decision of the Court today graphically illustrates why the trimester approach is a completely unworkable method of accommodating the conflicting personal rights and compelling state interests that are involved in the abortion context" (92). She further added that ". . . the lines drawn in [the *Roe*] decision have now been blurred because of what the Court accepts as technological advancement in the safety of abortion procedure. The State may no longer rely on a 'bright line' that separates permissible from impermissible regulation, and it is no longer free to consider second trimester as a unit and weigh the risks posed by all abortion procedures throughout that trimester." In other words, though *Roe* did not allow for an "unqualified constitutional right to abortion" the Court declared in *Akron* that it did. O'Connor went on to point out that *Roe* "was on a collision course with itself" (93ff).

PLANNED PARENTHOOD V ASHCROFT

The line of attack in *Ashcroft* proved to be nearly the same, but in a different state. In this case, two physicians and Planned Parenthood of Kansas City, Missouri, filed a complaint challenging as unconstitutional several sections of Missouri statutes regulating abortions. These required that abortions after twelve weeks be performed in a hospital; that a pathology report be performed after each abortion; that a second physician be present during abortions performed after viability; and that parental or judicial consent be obtained in advance. Citing *Akron,* the Court found hospitalization after the second trimester unconstitutional.

The requirement of a second physician safeguarded both mother and child in the event of a live birth. While the first physician would be responsible for the mother, the second would be responsible for child so that immediate medical care could be provided. The Court found this to be constitutional. Further, it found constitutional the requirement of a pathology report, since Missouri already required that all surgically removed tissues (tonsils, adenoids, hernial sacs, and prepuces) be examined by a pathologist either on the premises or by arrangement outside the hospital, and that a report be filed with the state Division of Health. The Court found this to be "an insignificant burden" and overturned the Court of Appeals, which had ruled this requirement to be unconstitutional (112). Justice O'Connor dissented with respect to the hospitalization, again citing the same issues she outlined in *Akron,* namely, that second-trimester hospitalization is not an undue burden and is in keeping with the state's compelling interest in citizens' health. With respect to parental consent, the Court found that constitutional.

Blackmun found the Missouri pathologist requirement "not justified by important health objective." While conceding that the existence of such a report may be necessary, he found the requirement meddlesome (116). The attending physician should be the only observer, he argued, and even then only to the extent of discovering abnormalities. On these issues O'Connor concurred in part and dissented in part, arguing that the hospitalization was hardly an imposition, especially since second-trimester abortions escalated the risk to a woman's health significantly. She also found the pathology report requirement to be constitutional "because it poses no undue burden on the limited right to undergo an abortion" (121).

THORNBURGH V AMERICAN COLLEGE OF OBSTETRICIANS AND GYNECOLOGISTS

Perhaps *Thornburgh* alacrified pro-life interests because it was decided by a slim 5–4 margin. Certainly by the mid-1980s, when the case was decided, and just months before Chief Justice Burger's retirement, the decision provided a different backdrop. No longer did abortion-related decisions end in a 7–2 unbeatable majority. Slowly the majority dwindled from 6–3 to 5–4, indicating to all observers that abortion, once favored by a clear majority on the Court, now held on by a single vote. The significance of this change was not lost on either side. Since presidents appoint Supreme Court Justices, the position of presidential candidates on the issue of abortion (or their position on how the Constitution should be read, either as a living document or as a unchangeable guide) became far more important than in the past.

In *Thornburgh,* the Court examined once more states' regulation of abortion—in this case Pennsylvania's statutes. The Abortion Control Act was of recent vintage and sought to limit abortion according to the *Roe* guidelines. Already Pennsylvania had lost restraints on spousal and parental consent, the choice of procedure for postviability abortion, and for the proscription of abortion advertisements. Only informed consent remained. In *Thornburgh,* the plaintiffs argued that the Abortion Control Act sought to provide protection for maternal health. The Court found informed consent to be "a guise" seeking to "intimidate women into continuing pregnancies" (143–144).

What the Court objected to was not "informed consent," which it found to be constitutional, but the *degree* of informed consent (in this case "seven explicit kinds of information" that had to be delivered to the woman at least twenty-four hours before her consent was given). Five of the seven (specified in the following list) had to be delivered by the woman's physician. The seven included (142)

1. The name of the physician who would be performing the abortion
2. The fact that there may be detrimental physical and psychological effects which are not accurately foreseeable"
3. "The particular medical risks associated with the particular abortion procedure employed"
4. The probable gestational age
5. The "medical risks associated with carrying her child to term"
6. The "fact that medical assistance benefits may be available for prenatal care, childbirth and neonatal care"
7. The "fact that the father is liable to assist" in child-care support, "even in instances where the father has offered to pay for the abortion"

Other sticking points included a printed statement to the effect that "[t]here are many public and private agencies willing and able to help you to carry your child to term, and to assist you and your child after your child is born, whether you choose to keep your child or place her or him for adoption" (142). The Court found that these statements "intended" not to get the woman's consent but to prevent her from getting it at all. Blackmun argued, "A woman's right to make that choice freely is fundamental. Any other result, in our view, would protect inadequately a central part of the sphere of liberty that our law guarantees equally to all" (148).

Chief Justice Warren Burger's dissent proved important to pro-life forces: "[E]very member of the *Roe* Court rejected the idea of abortion on demand. The Court's opinion today, however, plainly undermines that important principle..." (151).

WEBSTER V REPRODUCTIVE HEALTH SERVICES

Webster brings to a close the most important of abortion cases during the 1980s. Adjudicated on July 3, 1989, this Court brought a new face, and a new majority, to the bench. Burger had retired. The Court now consisted of Chief Justice Rehnquist, Justices White, O'Connor, Scalia, Kennedy, Brennan, Thurgood Marshall, Blackmun, and Stevens. *Webster* became the first decision since *Roe* that turned in favor of pro-life partisans. The 5–4 decision found in favor of *some* pro-life principles. What pro-life advocates failed, or refused, to see was the reaffirmation of the most important parts of *Roe*.

Missouri's Abortion Act of 1986 proved the pivotal matter. The Missouri Eighth Circuit Court had struck down Missouri's Abortion Act on the grounds that it violated the Court's decision in *Roe*. The Act included twenty provisions, five of which came before the Court. The five were:

1. That "the life of each human being begins at conception";
2. That "unborn children have protectable interests in life, health and well-being";
3. That the unborn have the same protections under the Constitution as everyone else;
4. That the physician performing the abortion must determine the gestational age if he or she suspects the pregnant woman is twenty weeks' pregnant or more; and,
5. That use of public employees and facilities to perform or assist in performing abortions not necessary to save the mother's life is prohibited, as is the use of public funds for the purpose of "encouraging or counseling" a woman to undergo an abortion not necessary to save her life. (179–180)

Under argument was the Reproductive Health Services agency, a public agency, and Planned Parenthood of Kansas City. Three employees—all public employees at public facilities in Missouri and supported by public funds—were named as defendants in the suit.

The Court did not address itself to the "human life begins at conception" issue. Rather, it claimed it had no power to decide "abstract propositions" or to declare principles not the result of laws. Due process, the Court argued, did not entitle one to an "affirmative right to governmental aid." Citing *Maher* and *Poelker v Doe,* the Court argued that it could provide publicly funded services for childbirth but not nontherapeutic abortions. The Court rejected the argument that to choose to favor childbirth over abortion was a political decision, especially since the Court determined that the right to an abortion was also not a political statement by the Court. The Court reaffirmed its *Maher, Poelker,* and *McRae* decisions by saying that choosing to encourage childbirth over abortion "places no governmental obstacle in the path of a woman who chooses to terminate her pregnancy" (184).

The Court also found that Missouri's claim that the stipulation for public funding was not directed to the abortion-seeker, but to those responsible for expending public funds, and well within constitutional rights. As for the viability clause in the Missouri Abortion Act, the Court argued, "We think the viability-testing provision makes sense only if the second sentence is read to require only those tests that are useful to making subsidiary findings as to viability" (188).

Scalia, while concurring, "strongly" dissented from the manner in which the decision came down. Scalia felt that the Court should have acted to either reaffirm *Roe,* overrule it explicitly, or overrule it *sub silentio,* that is, without comment. Instead, he felt the Court had simply avoided the question entirely.

Not to be outdone, Blackmun, now finding himself in the minority on the abortion question for the first time since *Roe,* stridently objected. "Never in my memory has a plurality announced a judgment of this Court that so foments disregard for the law and for our standing decisions" (202). He continued, "I fear for the future.... I fear for the liberty and equality of millions of women...[and] I fear for the integrity of, and the public esteem for, this Court" (203). Blackmun concluded, "For today, at least, the law of abortion stands undisturbed [b]ut a chill wind blows" (215). Almost never before had the Court found itself attacked by one of its own members so blatantly, or so the other Justices said.

The mainstream media reported on *Webster* weeks before it came down. *Time* devoted its cover story to the then-upcoming case: "The long emotional battle over abortion approaches a climax as the Supreme Court prepares for a historic challenge to *Roe v. Wade.*"[2] The story described the case as "a Supreme Court refashioned by Ronald Reagan [that] will hear arguments in *William L. Webster v. Reproductive Health Services,* a case that could lead to *Roe*'s being seriously weakened or even reversed."[3] Included were human-interest stories about women who had aborted their unborn for various reasons, most because they had gotten pregnant early (around eighteen years of age) or could not handle the financial demands of a new baby. *Newsweek* followed suit.[4] It argued, "The Supreme Court confronts *Roe v Wade* in a controversial case that could chip away at a right American women have come to take for granted." In sidebars, both magazines favored the pro-choice side of the argument.

RUST V SULLIVAN

Justice David Souter joined the bench for the first time in these deliberations, appointed by President George H. W. Bush in 1991. Gone from the bench were Justice Brennan and, of course, Chief Justice Burger. If pro-life advocates were uplifted it had to be because the party that aligned itself with the Right-to-Life movement now had on the bench *seven* of its nominees. President Reagan alone had appointed three: Justices O'Connor (the first woman), Scalia, and Kennedy. Joining them were Chief Justice Rehnquist.

The question in *Rust* involved whether the government could issue a "gag rule" on federally funded family planning agencies. Irving Rust represented Title X grantees (Public Health Service Act of 1970, hereinafter HSA) and physicians. Louis Sullivan, Secretary of the U.S. Department of Health and Human Services was the defendant. HSA authorized the Secretary to "make grants to and enter into contracts with public or nonprofit private entities to assist in the establishment and operation of voluntary family planning projects which shall offer a broad range of acceptable and effective family planning methods and services" (77). In 1988, Secretary Sullivan published new regulations that sought to define "clear and operational guidance to grantees about how to preserve the distinction between Title X programs and abortion as a method of family planning" (77). The "family planning" that Congress had in mind specifically excluded "pregnancy care."

The Court found that when ambiguous language appeared in regulations (as the Court deemed the language in these guidelines to be) the agency (in this case, the Department of Health and Human Services) had liberty to construe it as it deemed appropriate as long as the regulations did not violate or undermine the intent of Congress. The Court deferred to the "expertise of the agency" (82). The Court also found that the Secretary's revision of the regulations was justified since the guidelines clearly indicated that abortion was not a means of family planning. "It is well established," said the Court, "that legislative history which does not demonstrate a clear and certain congressional intent cannot form a basis for enjoining [stopping] the regulations." The Secretary based the need for the separation requirements "squarely on the congressional intent that abortion not be a part of a Title X funded program" (85). It therefore found the revisions to be constitutional, citing *Maher,* in which Medicaid recipients were entitled to receive funds for childbirth but not for nontherapeutic abortions. The Court added that, "To hold that the Government unconstitutionally discriminates on the basis of viewpoint...would render numerous government programs constitutionally suspect" (87).

Finally, the Court found that "[T]he regulations do not impermissibly burden a woman's Fifth Amendment rights..." (91). It found that by denying this in the case of Title X funds still left a woman "with the same choices as if the government had chosen not to fund family-planning services at all" (91).

Blackmun dissented on a number of grounds, joined in part by Justices Marshall, O'Connor, and Stevens. Blackmun thought the Court had overlooked or turned away from the constitutional question raised by *Rust.* Further, he argued that until *Rust,* the Court had never thought speech could be infringed upon or regulated by simply choosing one alternative over another. The Court, he said, had an "impermissible focus upon the viewpoint of regulated speech" (97). He charged the Court with "manipulating" the content of the doctor/patient dialogue. Blackmun continued, "Today's decision abandons that principle, and with disastrous results" (99).

THE SILENT SCREAM

Following *Thornburgh* but preceding *Webster* came a momentous and controversial event in the abortion debate since *Roe*. Nothing during this period came close to the hue and cry that arose from one small film that did not run even a full half-hour, the video *Silent Scream*. Pro-life proponents applauded its efforts to portray the harsh realities of abortion; pro-choice advocates questioned its facts and authority. Like most unbridled views, neither side may have had it *exactly* right. What we do know is that *The Silent Scream*, now nearly twenty years old, is not only still around, it is still stirring up virulent controversy.

The film depicts in high-resolution an ultrasound examination of a fetus in the womb. (There is some argument whether the woman shown during the ultrasound is the same woman undergoing the actual abortion later in the video.) After a discussion of fetal development, a description of the abortion ensues from "the victim's viewpoint." As the ultrasound runs, the narrator appears on screen using a plastic model of a fetus and actual instruments to show what is happening, mainly because the film is grainy and hard to follow. The narrator tells viewers when the fetus, or, in the words of the narrator, "baby," recoiled from the instrument inserted into the uterus. The mouth, we are told, forms a "silent scream" as the forceps are used to crush its head. The narrator then cues viewers about the "secret language" that goes on between the abortionist and the anesthesiologist: "Did you get number one?" (i.e., the head). As the camera pans to a grieving woman and a discarded unborn alternately, the narrator talks about victimized women who are sterilized and "castrated." There follows a discussion about the "destruction of human life" as a useless solution to a social problem, and the loss of regard for humanity.

What especially caught the attention of pro-choice advocates about the video was the familiar face of its narrator, the famed New York obstetrician and abortionist, Dr. Bernard Nathanson. Nathanson had headed up one of the most lucrative and largest abortion clinics in the country for more than a decade in the mid-1970s. At one point his clinic performed hundreds of abortions daily, and more than 60,000 annually.[5] Nathanson attributed his about-face on the abortion question to advancements in perinatology and the stark fact that he could not only see what he was doing, but see the expressions on the faces of fetuses, the thumb-sucking, and various other lifelike maneuvers. Nathanson later appeared in subsequent lecture tours. The film is graphic. Panning the plastic fetuses, the camera cuts to the stark and sterile abortion clinic where a woman lies, spread-eagle, on a table. Viewers know what comes next. The struggle, or what certainly looked like a struggle for life, was unmistakable.

"Now for the first time," Nathanson began, "we have the technology to see abortion from the victim's vantage point. We are going to watch a child being torn apart, dismembered, disarticulated, crushed, and destroyed by the unfeeling steel instruments of the abortionist."[6] When Nathanson concludes with, "All we see remaining are simply the shards, the broken fragments, the pieces of tissue which document there was once a living defenseless tiny human being there," it is clear he hopes to shake up his audience.

The effect of *The Silent Scream* proved nothing short of sensational. President Reagan urged a "complete rejection of violence as means of settling this issue." He also spoke to pro-life supporters and carried their message with him whenever the opportunity arose. Further, Congress took the film seriously. "Never have so many millions of Americans seen so graphic a representation of a baby being ripped apart," exclaimed Representative Robert Dornan (R–CA).[7]

Members of the press were less enthusiastic. "It's technical flimflam," *Time* reported.[8] It's full of "lurid logic" argued others.[9] Further, many argued that although the film depicted the twelve-week-old fetus as experiencing pain, it could not. Some rushed into print with those thoughts.[10] By the turn of the new decade, *The Silent Scream* ceased to be discussed in pro-choice circles. It was passé to them. Meanwhile, breakthrough medical evidence disputed the claim that fetuses could not feel pain; the evidence revealed that they do, and as early as twelve weeks.

Not all pro-choice advocates stayed in denial, however. "It's really quite moving," conceded Ron Fitzsimmons, lobbyist for the National Abortion Rights Action League. "I can see how it would affect people."[11] Fitzsimmons quickly added that left without rebuttal, "It could possibly do some damage." Nathanson continues today to be the film's best advocate and it's easy to see why an inveterate pro-choice advocate like Fitzsimmons could be swayed. Speaking about his own change of heart, Nathanson wrote, "[A]s a result of all this technology—looking at this baby, examining it, investigating it, watching its metabolic functions, watching it urinate [and] swallow.... I was a physician pledged to save my patients' lives, not to destroy them. So I changed my mind on the subject of abortion."[12]

The Silent Scream continues to make headlines today. When Republican Hal Turner ran against Democratic Representative Robert Menendez in the Hudson County district of New Jersey in the late 1990s, he made *The Silent Scream* central to his campaign.[13] Even in late 2000, *The Silent Scream* galvanized its proponents and embittered its enemies.

RU-486

Almost lost in the shuffle of abortion cases, sandwiched between *Webster,* the high-profile case on the one hand, and the much-anticipated *Roe*-amending

French Professor Etienne-Emile Baulieu, inventor of RU-486, the "morning after pill." (Photograph by Remy de la Mauviniere. AP/Wide World Photos.)

Casey, came the "morning after pill" known as RU-486. Roussel-Uclaf, the French distributors of the pill, hit the American scene in 1982, when Dr. Etienne-Emile Baulieu invented the pill. RU-486, an antiprogestin, breaks the fertilized egg's bond to the uterine wall and a miscarriage follows.[14] The pill immediately became known as "The French Pill." The progesterone antagonist (Mifepristone in the United States) had more going for it than mere pregnancy interruption. The pill's inventors touted its medicinal effects as both an anti-cancer agent and an anti-Cushing prohibitive.[15] Threats to the pill's sponsors, however, provided a sure obstacle to the drug's development as either.

RU-486 hit the French market in September 1988. After 2,115 women used 600 mg of RU-486 followed by the administration of one of two synthetic prostaglandins thirty-six to forty-eight hours later to terminate pregnancies, the French researchers found a 96 percent efficacy rate. The rate of expulsion of the unborn after administration ranged from four and half hours to nearly twenty-four. Problematic, however, proved the mean-bleeding rate of nearly ten days. The French government made the pill available after 17,000 women used it without major incident. But in 1991, an avid female smoker in her late thirties suffered a heart attack while using RU-486. After that, the pill was banned for any woman over thirty-five and for all smokers.[16]

RU-486 came under immediate attack from the Catholic Church. Other pro-life groups slowly responded, too, but by 1990 all that had changed and virtually every pro-life group had come out against RU-486. Drug distributors in the United States, such as Hoechst Marion Roussel (HMR), reluctantly fought these groups, which often sent postcards by the thousands, asking that the company keep its "death pill" out of the United States. Hoechst ultimately decided to leave the distribution to nonprofit organizations.[17] This only made sense since HMR's annual profit on RU-486 was only $3.5 million. Yet boycotts worldwide began to threaten its $7.5 billion portfolio. For companies that must make their livelihood on public goodwill, pharmaceutical companies faced with protest before the first pill was bottled and sold shunned the controversy straightway. The U.S. debate about RU-486 ended in September 1996, when the FDA approved its use but it kept the pill shrouded in secrecy, even refusing to release the name of the company that bought the rights to distribute it.[18] The pill became a restricted reality in 1997. Even with the secrecy and the potential risk, few companies lined up to market it, and no wonder. Early estimates pegged a $100 million market, not a high dollar figure for what could end with disastrous results.

President Clinton, faithful to his pro-choice constituents, ordered the FDA in 1993 to reassess its exclusion of RU-486 from importation via its Import Alert 66–47. In a memorandum to the Secretary of Health and Human Services, Clinton wrote, "I am informed that in excluding RU-486 from the personal use importation exemption, the FDA appears to have based its decision on factors other than an assessment of the possible health and safety risks of the drug. Accordingly, I hereby direct that you promptly instruct FDA to determine whether there is sufficient evidence to warrant exclusion of RU-486 from the list of drugs that qualify for personal use importation exemption."[19]

While the drug has been found to be effective against other illnesses, including estrogen-dependent uterine fibroids, endometriosis, and certain breast and uterine cancers, the drug has had difficulty gaining FDA approval for those uses. As late as June 2000, the Food and Drug Administration considered stringent standards that would track the drug from physician to user.[20] "The FDA is considering placing so many restrictions on doctors who want to use the drug that few will be interested in using it," said Vicki Saporta, director of the National Abortion Federation. While the FDA exercised its role on new drugs coming onto the market, most observers felt the RU-486 restrictions were too heavy-handed. Yet the drug continued to be plagued by anecdotal evidence of serious side effects, including prolonged bleeding that could lead to anemia or more serious conditions. Indeed, in some cases, it was said to be as difficult as surgical abortion.[21]

RU-486 has had trouble gaining acceptance both in the United States and overseas. Germany, France, and Spain have had full-scale boycotts over the drug. Indeed, HMR gave up on the drug for that very reason, as noted above.[22] "[The drug] reminds politicians and the chemical industry in Germany," said Cardinal Joachim Meisner of Cologne, "of their special historical and moral responsibility on such a topic. Among other things it certainly resurrected a shadow of the German past when the Hoechst company, a successor enterprise to IG Farben [the German company that patented the poison gas Zyklon B used in the gas chambers during World War II] obtained the patent to RU-486."[23]

The jury is still out on RU-486. If it can be proved that it works as advertised, it could provide a means of escape in the abortion debate by attacking the issue during the first days of the first trimester. Physicians have pointed to other alternatives, such as the drug Methotrexate, in lieu of Mifepristone.[24] Physicians argue that the alternative is as safe and as effective as RU-486. Moreover, not only is it as effective, but it's also less expensive. Doctors also argue that the pills broaden women's choices and make abortion safer by eliminating surgical abortion with anesthesia.[25] The American College of Obstetrics and Gynecology rushed an ad campaign together to remind the public and physicians of an older discovery: that the birth control pill, if taken within seventy-two hours of intercourse, would also prevent pregnancy.[26]

Either of the abortion pills, if widely distributed without physician supervision, could prove dangerous. The abortion pills' way of working is strikingly similar to that of the other, more famous "Pill." When the first birth control pill came on the market, proponents hailed it as the panacea for all things reproductive. If women merely went on the pill soon after they became sexually active (following their first menses), unexpected pregnancies, and the need for abortion would be diminished. But now, more than three decades after its debut, "the Pill" has done neither. First, a large majority of women cannot take the birth control pill without serious side effects, even death. Today, the pill cannot be prescribed for some women over thirty-five with circulatory problems, and it is not recommended for women who smoke or who have a history of heart disease.[27]

RU-486 has followed a similar track. Pro-choice advocates are convinced that RU-486 and its derivatives will make abortion nearly obsolete, making the question truly a private matter between pregnant women and their doctors.[28] Pro-choice advocates have backed this faith by pouring into the RU-486 effort a mountain of dollars. Peg Yorkin of the Feminist Majority Foundation (her personal worth has been estimated at $100 million) authorized $10 million to the fight to get RU-486 widespread acceptance.

Yorkin faces equally strong opposition, however, in the form of the Catholic Church and numerous Protestant groups. Violent pro-life activist Joseph Scheidler warned that his group, Chicago Pro-Life Leader, would discover which physicians planned to dispense it. "We'll go to their homes, to their offices, to their hospitals."[29] Not an empty threat from a man who has been associated with those who have murdered physicians for performing abortions.

CONCLUSION

On a philosophical level, it's easy to see why pro-life advocates expected so many great things from the Court in the 1980s and early 1990s. On an operational level, it is less easy to see why. *Akron* provided the first salvo for the pro-life forces. O'Connor uncharacteristically showed her hand when she wrote in her *Akron* dissent that *Roe* was "clearly on a collision course with itself" and that she found *Roe*'s mechanism for weighing competing rights of mother and state "completely unworkable."

Furthermore, pro-life advocates had to reconcile themselves to what had heretofore been an unbeatable history. When *Roe* was decided, the margin looked so comfortable as to be unbeatable: 7–2. The decision was made following a time of unrest in this country but even accounting for that, the 1960s really represented only about eight years of public protest, from about 1966 to 1973. By 1974, the country was headed in another direction at the state level.[30] The states, too, had made their mark in the abortion arena. Arizona, in contradiction to the Supreme Court's *Roe* decision, came within one vote of outlawing abortion entirely in the mid-1980s.[31] Perhaps federal politics was simply slower to catch up to state politics. In any event, *Akron* proved more than mere gunpowder to the pro-life debate.

Operationally, however, pro-life advocates missed the obvious. *Akron* was decided 6–3, only one vote less than the *Roe* decision more than a decade earlier. Clearly, not much had changed, including the Court's logic. Furthermore, Republican nominees to the bench had hardly proved predictably pro-life. Finally, nothing the pro-life side wanted had been granted. Uncannily, the Justices had decided against parental notification in *Akron*.

Ashcroft merely solidified the *Akron* arguments. As Sherry Matulis writes, "Without safe and legal abortion, many women will die and women will become reproductive slaves, it's as simple as that."[32] It seemed that the Supreme Court Justices, a majority of them anyway, went along with that reasoning, or something very similar to it. *Ashcroft* offered another point. Parental consent was not, per se, wrong, but in this case it was wrong. Pathology reports were eventually allowed, but even Blackmun found these to be cumbersome and "intended" to prevent abortion.

Thornburgh offered some further hope philosophically for the pro-life side, but again overturned pro-life hopes operationally. *Thornburgh* examined informed consent in detail. Informed consent could not be too informed. The Supreme Court Justices determined—granted by the slimmest of margins, 5–4—that informed consent was still intended to stop abortion and was therefore unconstitutional. What sort of informed consent *was* allowable could not be exactly ascertained. If a woman got the medical details of her second-trimester abortion, that might prove too much and she might choose not to abort. Dissents abounded, but in the end, *Roe* stood firm just as it had in *Akron* and in *Ashcroft*.

This is hardly surprising, given the parameters of the debate. Already, pro-choice advocates had come down hard on the detailed informed consent. *The Silent Scream* opponents argued that it offered too much "uneasy intimacy," and was designed to make women look like murderers and child-haters. Pro-life advocates countered that pictures of the unborn, especially pictures of the "fetus" sucking its thumb, would prove fatal to the pro-choice movement.[33] To pro-lifers, any attempt to provide anything but a funeral for the unborn must be categorically condemned.[34]

Thornburgh extended the discussions on the abortion theme by the various Justices. Justice Blackmun conceded the private nature of the abortion act, only to complain that this very private act—which occurred in a very public setting, often at public expense—could not be regulated in a manner in which anyone, other than the woman and her physician, would be aware. To pro-lifers, it seemed the height of tyranny to argue on the one hand that this highly controversial act was private, but on the other, that its funding should be at public expense. In other words, government had an obligation to provide access to the abortion but had no right to require anything in return. It was an unprecedented argument, especially for the highest court in the land.

With *Webster*, nearly everything changed, or seemed to change. Once *Webster* appeared, the media now kicked itself into high gear. When *Webster* came before the Court, the media began the debate in favor of *Roe*. The *Washington Post*, for example, ran five stories, five days before the decision, including a 6,550-word story in its magazine section, all pointing to a hoped-for favorable outcome to *Webster.* The same occurred when it came to reporting on the size of pro-life versus pro-choice marches: pro-life marches were often said to attract the lowest number of demonstrators reported, while pro-choice marches enjoyed the highest reported figures.[35]

This is an important point for anyone examining the issue, since some of the frustration of pro-life advocates can be traced to perceived media bias. *Webster* proved to be the biggest feather in the cap of pro-life advocates, but they felt that the media did everything it could to undermine the decision: first to prevent it, then to forestall it, and finally to ignore it. It is perhaps at this point that some pro-life advocates wrongly began to think that taking matters into their own hands was the only way to prove their point.

Clearly, both sides knew that much hung in the balance with *Webster.* Nearly eighty *amicus curiae* briefs (Friend of the Court briefs, submitted to the Court from either side, favoring a certain outcome) were submitted, more than in any other case ever considered in the history of the High Court.[36]

At first, some argued that *Webster* overturned *Roe.*[37] Others, contended that it mattered very little, settling a fraction of abortion law. *Webster* did send a message indicating the willingness of the Justices to re-examine *Roe.* It did not, however, change materially what the Justices would do concerning *Roe's* basic principle of abortion on demand. Law articles that proclaimed the end of *Roe,* or claimed an end to the fundamental right to abortion, as many did, signaled, wrongly, to the pro-life advocates that victory was within their grasp.

Webster indicated to pro-life groups that the Court might limit access to abortion (as, incidentally, *Roe* allowed) if those limitations proved not unduly burdensome or did not halt the procedure altogether. What pro-life advocates soon discovered, however, was that few if any limitations imposed by a state would be found as anything other than burdensome.[38]

One writer argued that "Future historians will describe the *Webster* ruling as the crucial moment in the right-to-life movement, the beginning of an era when the general public was forced to decide whether activists were pro-life or antiabortion."[39] Others argued that neither side won anything of significance in the *Webster* ruling. But both of these positions appear wrong in hindsight. *Webster* allowed for a few conceded positions (tests for viability, and lifesaving abortions in the second trimester performed at hospitals), but it did not change *Roe* at all. Pro-life advocates focused too narrowly on what was said rather than what was decided.[40] Too many focused on Chief Justice Rehnquist's written declaration indicating his readiness to jettison *Roe.* Too many fixated on Justice Scalia's desire to "more explicitly" overrule *Roe.* Further, Scalia's castigation of Justice O'Connor's on-again, off-again support of the overthrow of *Roe* clearly irked him and other Justices. They had won the day, or so they thought. Pro-choice advocates, on the other hand, felt a chill wind blowing and used *Webster* as a rallying point to turn up the heat on politicians.

This proved pivotal in the next ruling, *Casey.* With the press on its side, the pro-choice movement rescued a small victory from the pro-life camp and turned it into pro-life defeat. After *Webster,* pro-choice advocates saw that they could not longer count on the Supreme Court to provide 7–2 decisions in their favor. Rather than using this small defeat as a means of complaining, they used it as a means of gaining leverage everywhere. If they could use *Webster* as a rallying point, they just might be able to prevent further weakening of the cause. *Casey* would prove to be a challenge for them to do just that.

NOTES

1.   Maureen Harrison and Steve Gilbert, eds., *Abortion Decisions of the United States Supreme Court: The 1980s* (Beverly Hills, Calif.: Excellent Books, 1993), 75–76. All references in the text to the cases are from this source, cited by page number, unless otherwise indicated.

2.   Richard Lacayo, "Whose Life Is It?" *Time* 133, no. 18 (May 1, 1989): 20.

3.   Ibid.

4.   "The Battle Over Abortion," *Newsweek* (May 1, 1989): 28–32.

5.   Jefferson Morley, "Right-to-Life Porn: The Lurid Logic of 'The Silent Scream,'" *The New Republic* 192 (March 25, 1985), accessed via InfoTrac's Expanded Academic ASAP database, 1.

6.   Claudia Wallis, "Silent Scream: Outcry over Antiabortion Film," *Time* 125 (March 25, 1985), accessed via InfoTrac's Expanded Academic ASAP database, 1.

7.   Robert Zintl, "New Heat Over an Old Issue: Renewing the Abortion Fight," *Time* 125 (February 4, 1985), accessed via InfoTrac's Expanded Academic ASAP database, 1.

8.   Wallis, 2.

9.   Morley, 2.

10.   "The Abortion Debate," *The New Republic* 192 (April 8, 1985), accessed via InfoTrac's Expanded Academic ASAP database, 1.

11.   Julia Malone, "Graphic Film Raises Intensity Level of US Abortion Controversy," *The Christian Science Monitor* (February 14, 1985), accessed via InfoTrac's Expanded Academic ASAP database, 1.

12.   David Kupelin and Mark Mastos, "Pro-Choice 1991: Skeletons in the Closet," *New Dimensions: The Psychology Behind the News* (September/October 1991): 40.

13.   Chris Cillizza, "*The Silent Scream* in N.J.-13," *CongressDaily/A.M.* (February 28, 2000), accessed via InfoTrac's Expanded Academic ASAP database, 1.

14.   Jim Smolowe, "New, Improved and Ready for Battle," *Time* 141, no. 24 (June 14, 1993), accessed via InfoTrac's Expanded Academic Universe ASAP database, 2.

15.   R. M. Baum, "RU-486: Abortion Controversy in U.S. Clouds Future of Promising Drug," *Chemical & Engineering News* (March 11, 1991): 7–14.

16.   Smolowe, 2.

17.   "Abort, Retry, Sell?" *The Economist (US)* 343, no. 8012 (April 12, 1997), accessed via InfoTrac's Expanded Academic Universe ASAP database, 1.

18.   John Marks, "The Secret World of the Abortion Pill: Selling RU-486 Is a Delicate and Risky Venture," *U.S. News and World Report* 121, no. 13 (September 30, 1996), accessed via InfoTrac's Expanded Academic Universe ASAP database, 1.

19.   William Jefferson Clinton, "Memorandum on Importation of RU-486," *Weekly Compilation of Presidential Documents* 29, no. 3 (January 25, 1993), accessed via InfoTrac's Expanded Academic Universe ASAP database, 1.

20.   Rita Rubin, "RU-486 May Face FDA Limits," *USA Today* (June 7, 2000): 1D.

21.   Debra Rosenberg, "Blood and Tears," *Newsweek* 126, no. 12 (September 18, 1995), accessed via InfoTrac's Expanded Academic Universe ASAP database, 1.

22.   See, for example, John L. Allen Jr., "Abortion Debates Rock Germany," *National Catholic Reporter* 35, no. 15 (February 12, 1999), accessed via InfoTrac's Expanded Academic Universe ASAP database, 1.

23.   Ibid., 2.

24.   David A. Grimes, "A 26-Year-Old Woman Seeking an Abortion," *JAMA, The Journal of the American Medical Association* 282, no. 12 (September 22, 1999), accessed via InfoTrac's Expanded Academic Universe ASAP database, 1.

25.   "Pill Alters Abortion Debate," *The Christian Century* 17, no 3 (January 26, 2000), accessed via InfoTrac's Expanded Academic Universe ASAP database, 1.

26.   Andrew A. Skolnick, "Campaign Launched to Tell Physicians, Public about Emergency Contraception," *JAMA, The Journal of the American Medical Association* 278, no. 2 (July 9, 1997), accessed via InfoTrac's Expanded Academic Universe ASAP database, 1.

27.   "Smoking or the Pill," Planned Parenthood, www.plannedparenthood.org/BIRTH-CONTROL/Smoking.htm, Spring 2002.

28.   David Van Biema, "But Will It End the Abortion Debate?" *Time* 141, no. 24 (June 14, 1993), accessed via InfoTrac's Expanded Academic Universe ASAP database, 1.

29.   Ibid., 3.

30.   See, for example, Myron Magnet's excellent book *The Dream and the Nightmare: The Sixties' Legacy to the Underclass* (New York: William Morrow, 1993).

31.   Paul Reidinger, "Will *Roe v. Wade* Be Overruled?" *ABA Journal* (July 12, 1988): 66.

32.   Sherry Matulis, "Why Abortion *Must* Remain the Law of the Land," *The Humanist* 52(4) (July/August 1992): 35.

33.   See Valerie Hartouni, "Fetal Exposures: Abortion Politics and the Optics of Allusion," in *Cultural Conceptions: On Reproductive Technologies and the Remaking of Life* (Minneapolis, Minn.: University of Minnesota Press, 1997); and Carol Stabile, "Shooting the Mother: Fetal Photography and the Politics of Disappearance," in

Paula A. Treichler and Lisa Cartwright, eds., *The Visible Woman: Imaging Technologies, Gender, and Science.* (New York: New York University Press, 1998), 171–198. Hartouni's essay also appears in this book as well (198–216).

34.   See Janet Gallagher, "Collective Bad Faith: 'Protecting' the Fetus," in Joan C. Callahan, ed., *Reproduction, Ethics and the Law: Feminist Perspectives* (Bloomington: Indiana University Press, 1995), 380–398.

35.   Guido Cowden, "The Post-*Webster* Press," *National Review* 42, no. 22 (November 19, 1990): 37–38.

36.   Elizabeth Phillips, *Abortion and the Ethics of American Christianity,* Master's thesis, Abilene Christian University, Abilene, Tex., 1990, 50.

37.   A good discussion of this is found in James Bopp, and Richard E. Coleson, "What Does *Webster* Mean?" *University of Pennsylvania Law Review* 138, no. 1 (1989): 157–76.

38.   Karen J. Lewis, "Abortion Law: One Year After *Webster,*" *Supreme Court Review* (September/October 1990): 16–20.

39.   James Kelley, "Winning *Webster v. Reproductive Health Services:* The Crisis of the Pro-Life Movement," *America* (August 19, 1989): 83.

40.   Only Susan R. Estrich and Kathleen M. Sullivan, in their article "Abortion Politics: Writing for an Audience of One," *University of Pennsylvania Law Review* 138, no. 1 (1989): 119–155, seemed to understand this. Interestingly, both are devoutly pro-choice.

7

Another Casey Steps to the Plate: Planned Parenthood of Southeastern Pennsylvania v Casey

Casey, or by its formal name, *Planned Parenthood of Southeastern Pennsylvania v Casey,* is the one major case of the 1990s to be treated in this chapter. *Casey* is of major importance for at least two reasons. First, the case came from a most unconventional source: a pro-life Democrat. Second, the case made a larger media splash than *Webster* mainly because pro-choice personalities feared that *Webster* meant the end of *Roe* and so made certain the next Supreme Court case would not be ignored. In the end, however, *Casey* did little more than reaffirm *Roe,* and promised that all future pro-life challenges would be met with the same fate: a reaffirmation of *Roe* regardless of what else might be granted.[1]

PLANNED PARENTHOOD OF SOUTHEASTERN PENNSYLVANIA V CASEY

Casey would have been a pivotal court case even if its antagonists had been insignificant at the time. Backed by public funding, Planned Parenthood, known for fighting abortion battles it felt it was necessary to fight, would have made that certain. The Casey in *Casey* was the late Robert P. Casey, a pro-life Democrat and governor of a blue-collar state.[2] Casey's background is worth exploring briefly.[3] In his first winning campaign, he took on a sure winner and defeated him, but only after three previous failed bids.[4] After his victory, Casey got the worst news of his life: a diagnosis of familial amyloidosis. The disease, for which there is no known cure other than a transplant, degrades the organs, especially the heart, by turning their tissues into stonelike substances. Before his second term ended, Casey would undergo two transplant operations on the same day, receiving both a new heart and a new liver. Neither the disease nor the transplants slowed him down. The abortion issue was important to Casey because he wanted, as he put it, "to take back his party for life." He went on to say:

Leaving aside the Republicans, I would take the pro-life point even further. I believe that a qualified pro-life Democrat running for president cannot lose. Such a candidacy would have broad appeal. One of these days—I hope soon—the national Democratic Party will wake up and discover that abortion on demand is not only morally wrong, it is also a long-term loser in political terms.[5]

Even with language like this, Casey managed to win elections, even after his campaign manager, James Carville, later former President Clinton's campaign manager, begged him to withdraw his stance on abortion. 6. Ibid., p. 155. In the end, Casey's health proved too much of an issue and he dropped his presidential primary challenge against the incumbent Bill Clinton in 1996.

At issue in *Casey* were five provisions in the Pennsylvania Abortion Control Act of 1982. The case came before the Court in April of 1992. A decision came down in June of the same year. Those issues were: informed consent; a provision that certain information be provided to a pregnant woman at least twenty-four hours before her abortion is performed; parental consent for minors but with a judicial-bypass procedure if the consent could not be obtained or the minor did not wish to seek it; a requirement that the woman seeking the abortion must sign a statement that she had notified her husband of her intended abortion; and, a requirement that the facilities providing abortions file specified reports. Each of these was challenged as unconstitutional on *Roe* grounds. Most observers felt that *Casey* would be *Roe*'s undoing.

Justices O'Connor, Kennedy, and Souter disagreed that the Pennsylvania Act could be upheld without overturning *Roe*. Chief Justice Rehnquist argued to overrule the central holding of *Roe* and adopt in its place the "rational relationship" test as the sole criterion of constitutionality. In a most interesting opening cannonade, O'Connor, Kennedy, and Souter argued that "Liberty finds no refuge in a jurisprudence of doubt."[6] The Justices reaffirmed the "essential holding" of *Roe:* "a recognition of the right of the woman to choose to have an abortion before viability and to obtain it without undue interference from the State" (115). They also confirmed the state's power to restrict abortions after fetal viability, and the state's legitimate interests in protecting the life of the mother throughout. The Justices went on to say,

Men and women of good conscience can disagree, and we suppose some always shall disagree, about the profound moral and spiritual implications of terminating a pregnancy, even at its earliest stages. Some of us as individuals find abortion offensive to our most basic principles of morality, but that cannot control our decision. Our obligation is to define the liberty of all, not to mandate our own moral code. (117)

They added that while the Constitution serves human values, "[T]he effect of reliance on *Roe* cannot be exactly measured [and neither] can the certain cost of overruling *Roe* for people who have ordered their thinking and living around that case be dismissed" (122). Repeatedly, the Justices returned to the theme that *Roe* was *not* unworkable (only that its trimester rule was), or weakened at all by cases decided since. Most importantly, these Justices went on to say, "We conclude that the basic decision in *Roe* was based on a constitutional analysis which we cannot now repudiate" (130). When it was over, these three Justices had agreed with the Pennsylvania Abortion Act that informed consent was required; that certain information should be provided at least twenty-four hours before an abortion is performed, and that parental consent for minors was constitutional. They rejected spousal consent, however.

Chief Justice Rehnquist (joined by Justices White, Scalia, and Thomas) concurred in part and dissented in part. Rehnquist was perplexed that the Justices chose to leave the matter as divided as it had always been since *Roe,* and called the decision "an unjustified constitutional compromise, one which leaves the Court in a position to closely scrutinize all types of abortion regulations despite the fact that it lacks the power to do so under the Constitution" (173–174). Rehnquist went on to argue that even the "historical traditions of the American people support the view that the right to terminate one's pregnancy is 'fundamental'" (175). Rehnquist also pointed out that *stare decisis* (prior decisions) had always guided the Court. But in *Casey,* the Justices were treating the case as if previous decisions were an iron rule of law. However, prior courts had overturned decisions of previous ones. In one celebrated case that had remained in force for fifty-eight years (*Plessy*), *stare decisis,* thankfully, did not hold.

Plessy, Rehnquist pointed out, found the "separate but equal" doctrine constitutional, but *Brown* overturned it in 1954. In a most excoriating passage, Rehnquist concluded by saying, "Under this principle, when the Court has ruled on a divisive issue, it is apparently prevented from overruling that decision for the sole reason that it was incorrect, *unless opposition to the original decision has died away*" (180; emphasis in the original). He went on to point out that the propriety of overruling a divisive decision really depends "on whether 'most people' would now agree that it should be overruled." (180–182) In other words, *stare decisis* holds unless public political opinion dictates otherwise.

Justice Scalia (who was joined by the Chief Justice and Justices Thomas and White) agreed with his previous separate opinions espoused in *Webster* and *Akron*. In a biting rejoinder to the Justices' claim that "liberty can find no refuge in a jurisprudence of doubt," Scalia wrote, "Reason finds no refuge in this jurisprudence of confusion" (202). Scalia went on to argue that applying the doctrine of *stare decisis* to *Casey* was "contrived." Scalia pointed out that the "undue burden" rule being applied to *Casey* in the case of any restrictions on abortion forced "two of the three [in the joint decision], in order to remain steadfast, [had] to abandon previously stated positions. The only principle the Court 'adheres' to, it seems to me, is the principle that the Court must be seen as standing by *Roe*." Scalia continued:

I cannot agree with, indeed I am appalled by, the Court's suggestion that the decision whether to stand by an erroneous constitutional decision must be strongly influenced—*against* overruling no less—by the substantial and continuing public opposition the decision has generated. (207)

Scalia finished by addressing the position taken by Justices O'Connor, Kennedy, and Souter. He argued that the American people loved democracy and were "not fools." "The people know that their value judgments are quite as good as those taught in any law school—maybe better."[7] Scalia concluded that "We should get out of this area, where we have no right to be, and where we do neither ourselves nor the country any good by remaining" (211).

In some ways, Scalia and the dissenting Justices had their way. Scalia's argument is nearly the same as that put forward by Karen O'Connor.[8] While Supreme Court nominees were not necessarily put through a question-and-answer session, candidates were, and the 1992 elections proved especially helpful to pro-life Republicans, though George H. W. Bush did not benefit at all. Since *Casey*, pro-choice groups left nothing to chance. NARAL issued a state-by-state review of "anti-choice" congressional districts and what must be done about them.[9] Pro-choice advocates reading the *Casey* text realized that choice, as defined by *Roe*, now hung by a thread. NARAL did not want any compromise on any restrictions granted by *Webster*, *Casey*, or any other proposed set of measures that would in any way prohibit abortion on demand. Indeed, in 2001, pro-choice advocates were claiming that no pro-life Supreme Court Justice would make it through congressional examination.

It's not hard to see why pro-choice advocates feared *Casey*, especially when reviewed in conjunction with *Webster*. In *Akron*, O'Connor had written that *Roe* was on a collision course with itself. She had called the trimester framework of *Roe* unworkable. When *Casey* came before the Supreme Court, both sides prepared for a dismissal of *Roe*. What they got instead stunned both sides: an endorsement of *Roe*. Neither side expected this outcome. The Court affirmed *Roe* because, as it argued, the government could not go back and undo *Roe* conveniently. To do so, O'Connor argued, would make the Court

Supreme Court Justice Antonin Scalia. (Courtesy of the Library of Congress.)

look illegitimate. What had happened in three years since *Webster?* What took place that turned what looked to be the cancelation of *Roe* into its full endorsement by the Court?

Most observers say politics. Apparently the Court, and specifically Justices Kennedy and O'Connor, found the heat of politics involved in overturning *Roe* too much to bear. In the years leading up to *Casey, Roe* had, again and again, taken a beating in various cases, and in many of those, Justices Kennedy and O'Connor had signaled a willingness to overturn, or substantially change, *Roe.* Now with the chance at hand, they chose in *Casey* to let the matter stand. Further, O'Connor inserted an "undue burden" on the backs of all future abortion restrictions (replacing, in effect, the trimester standard), a burden that would in *Carhart,* the Nebraska case to outlaw partial-birth abortions, make clear that any proposed restriction would be found by this Court to be unduly burdensome.

The weight of *Webster* as a rallying cry for pro-choice advocates paved the way for *Casey*. Fears concerning a return to [supposed] back-alley abortions were brought to the forefront after *Webster*. By the time of the *Roe* decision, most abortions were being performed by licensed physicians, though not all were trained in abortion procedure. If they were being botched, they were being botched by physicians in medical facilities where women could get the care they needed if complications ensued.

Interestingly, one part of the Pennsylvania law reviewed in *Casey* did not get on the docket and was little publicized. Sex-selection abortions failed to fall under the Planned Parenthood challenge.[10] The Pennsylvania law contained a blanket prohibition against gender-selection abortions.[11] For pro-choice advocates, the matter must have been a difficult one, as difficult as it was for presidential contender Al Gore, the vice president, to answer a Tim Russert question on *Meet the Press* regarding abortions for women on death row.[12] ACLU leaders did not protest the Pennsylvania restriction, the only one in the country at the time, since they could not find a woman who claimed she had been injured by it.[13]

It proved difficult for pro-choice feminists because the vast majority of gender-selected abortions for first-time mothers were female. When questioned about this in connection with *Casey*, pro-choice leaders claimed it didn't occur. "It's an irrelevant issue," said then–vice president of the National Organization of Women, Rosemary Dempsey. Judith Lichtman, president of the Women's Legal Defense Fund, made the same claim. "It's a bogus issue. I'm not answering your question because I'm being cute but because it really trivializes a very momentous decision. There are a lot of real problems out there." Other leaders followed suit.[14] Pro-life advocates saw an inconsistency. Is this the one restriction, they said, that pro-choice advocates are willing to allow: no sex-selection abortions, at least when the sex selected for abortion is female? Yet if women are to be the sole decision-makers in this matter, why are they not challenged on this?

For most observers, however, *Casey* was an entirely political decision. The *New Republic* found this to be the case in its editorial following *Casey*.[15] It found the "undue burden" standard to be "less logical" and "more political" than *Roe*.

The most remarkable aspect of the *Casey* decision is that Justices O'Connor, Kennedy and Souter frankly acknowledge their political motives. They refuse to say whether or not *Roe* was rightly decided because overturning it "under fire" would make the Court look political and illegitimate. The circularity of their logic is exquisite. It was *Roe*'s lack of persuasive constitutional support that made the Court look illegitimate to begin with; and by affirming the result without defending the reasoning, the *Casey* majority not only appears, but stands exposed, as less legitimate than *Roe* itself.…

The *Casey* decision offers an embarrassingly intimate vision of the Rehnquist Court, in which the red velvet curtains are unexpectedly lifted and the Justices are exposed *in flagrante politico* [caught red-handed in politics]. We can imagine any number of plausible ways that *Roe* might have been clearly overturned, or perhaps even reaffirmed on different grounds.[16]

In the case of Justices Kennedy and O'Connor, the change of heart appears to have been exclusively politically motivated.[17] Prior to *Casey*, both Kennedy and O'Connor expressed their desire to see *Roe* changed in some way. As the arguments continued, Justice Kennedy worried aloud about his press coverage and how that might affect his political future. His change of view was so shocking to observers that law clerks in the Justices' office depicted Kennedy in their annual end-of-year parody of the Justices as "Flipper."[18]

When *Roe* came down, it forged a political framework in which the very moral and intensely personal debate would be ongoing. To attempt now to have a debate on these moral particulars would require an overturning of *Roe*, something the Justices determined in *Casey* to be impossible. In fact, it would appear with *Casey* that there was no turning back from abortion.[19] Two female observers, Estrich and Sullivan, called it "spin."

The danger was, quite simply, that a decision like *Webster* would lead the newly or about-to-be activated to conclude that the past months' political efforts had been so much ado about nothing. The July 3rd [referencing political work following the *Webster* decision] "spin" plainly avoided that danger. The losers, like the winners, described *Webster* as a major turning point. Both sides were saying the same thing, albeit for different reasons. And when that happens, the spin is the news, for better or for worse.[20]

In one sense, *Casey* overturned one aspect of *Roe*: the trimester conditions. Without saying as much, *Casey* replaced the trimester framework (which was never enforced, since abortions occurred in every trimester), with something O'Connor called "undue burden." When Justice O'Connor fell upon the idea, she struck gold for the pro-choice forces, wittingly or not. For "undue burden" can now be defined (and generally is) as *anything* that interferes with a woman's opportunity to get an abortion.

The vagueness of *Webster* allowed for the pro-choice clarity of *Casey*.[21] Although *vagueness* here usually refers to a statute the Supreme Court examines, the word refers rather to what the Justices wrought in *Webster* and defined in *Casey*. By granting the unstable nature of *Roe* in *Webster*, and essentially telegraphing the end of *Roe*, the Supreme Court provided an open door by placing the burden on the difficulty involved in *Roe*'s trimester framework. This allowed the Justices, and the countervailing parties, time to rethink a different framework. O'Connor came upon "undue burden" in *Casey*, which is more vague and ill-defined than the original trimester arrangement. As medicine continued to aid in the definition of trimesters, and thus allowed for restrictions by the states for various kinds of abortion based upon those trimesters, "undue burden" granted, as it were, an additional penumbra, or "constitutional emanation" in which *Roe* could find relief. Clearly what drove this issue, however, was not constitutional mandates or inherent rights, but what the Justices saw as the prevailing interests in the reproductive wishes of one segment of the electorate.

The Court's legitimacy, as Scalia pointed out, had been called into question with the change from *Webster* to *Casey*. If political pressure did not change the minds of some Justices, then whatever data did should be revealed, since it could change the minds of others.

In reviewing these different cases, it can be argued that it is the Court, as much as anything or anyone else, that has made this great debate over abortion last as long as it has. First, it established a principle in *Roe* that *Roe* had not been able to reveal, and established a right in the Constitution where many don't see one. Second, it confused the issue by making seemingly contradictory arguments in the two cases of *Webster* and *Casey*. The argument can be made that what *Casey* wrought is a signal to the country that future cases may be determined, not by the Constitution—really the only legal grounds on which such decisions can be made—but by forceful arguments made by the politically powerful.

It is important to understand that this *does not mean* that there is not an abortion right that can be legally and jurisprudentially made. Rather it means that, based on the evidence so far, that right cannot be located in *Roe*, or the decisions that followed. That being the case, the debate continues, and comes to another heated end in *Stenberg v Carhart*, the case to which our attention turns next.

NOTES

1. This is certain to remain the case unless the makeup of the Supreme Court changes to at least two more strict constitutionalists during the administration of George W. Bush.

2. Details of Casey's biography are taken from Robert P. Casey, *Fighting for Life: The Story of a Courageous Pro-Life Democrat Whose Own Brush with Death Made Medical History* (Dallas: Word Publishing, 1996).

3. The past tense is used because Casey passed away at the age of sixty-eight of prostate cancer in the spring of 2000.

4. Casey, 149.

5. Ibid., 150.

6. Maureen Harrison and Steve Gilbert, eds., *Abortion Decisions of the United States Supreme Court: The 1990s* (Beverly Hills, CA: Excellent Books, 1993), 114. All references in the text to the case are from this source, cited by page number, unless otherwise indicated.

7. Harrison and Gilbert, *Abortion Decisions*, 209.

8. Karen O' Connor, *No Neutral Ground? Abortion Politics in an Age of Absolutes* (New York: Westview Press, 1996).

9. NARAL and NARAL Foundation for Reproductive Freedom and Choice, *Who Decides? A State-by-State Review of Abortion and Reproductive Rights,* 9th ed. (Washington, D.C.: NARAL, 2000).

10. Helen Alvare, What's Wrong with Planned Parenthood?" http://members.aol.com/stacath/planned.htm. Accessed Spring 2002.

11. Charlotte Allen, "Boys Only," *New Republic* 206, no. 10 (March 9, 1992): 16–19, spoke directly to the matter but few other articles referenced it at all.

12. The interview aired on *Meet the Press,* June 30, 2000. Gore stumbled through his answer, apparently undecided about whether it mattered. The horns of his dilemma were palpable: if he answered yes, he appeared callous and uncaring; if he answered no, he appeared to believe that the unborn were, in fact, entitled to rights of some kind.

13. Allen, 16.

14. Allen, 17.

15. "The Case Against *Casey,*" *New Republic* 207, no. 5 (July 27, 1992): 17.

16. Ibid.

17. Lynn Wardle, "Thomas Jefferson v. *Casey,*" *Human Life Review* 20, no. 5 (Summer 1994): 55.

18. Ibid.

19. A similar point is implicitly made in "The America We Seek: A Statement of Pro-Life Principle and Concern," *First Things* (May 1996): 40–44.

20. Susan Estrich, and Kathleen Sullivan, "Abortion Polling: Writing for an Audience of One," *University of Pennsylvania Law Review* 138, no. 1 (1989): 121.

21. James Bopp, and Richard E. Coleson, "*Webster,* Vagueness and the First Amendment," *American Journal of Law & Medicine* 15, no. 2–3 (Summer–Fall 1989): 226. See also Charles H. Baron, "Abortion and Legal Process in the United States: An Overview of the Post-*Webster* Legal Landscape," *Law, Medicine & Health Care* (Winter 1989): 368–375. Baron called *Webster's* decision-making process full of "murkiness" (369). He also sees in *Webster's* claim of *Roe's* trimester unworkability a chance to ponder what would replace it.

8

Partial-Birth or Late-Term Abortions and the Bans

Although the decision itself is both a moral and a social one, the act of abortion has always been a medical procedure. Because of the health hazards inherent in abortion, even from the earliest of times, performing one has always required medical intervention, or rather should. When it did not—and for most of its history, qualified medical help was not available—the outcome remained in doubt. Midwives offering herbs might have had more success than quacksalvers selling useless nostrums, but both had high patient-mortality rates. Abortion remained both unsafe and ineffective until two events occurred: the discovery of a safe medical procedure for it, and the discovery of penicillin. Penicillin greatly reduced the number of deaths from illegal or self-induced abortions.[1]

Medicine is an art form that is constantly evolving. Fifty years ago, physicians began talking seriously about heart surgeries. Today, they are so commonplace as to be second nature, extending the lives of millions annually in a procedure that often requires only overnight hospitalization. Only thirty years ago, physicians began transplanting organs. Early transplant operations had an eerie Dr. Frankenstein cast to them. Today, however, the transplanting of organs, especially kidneys, is almost as routine as the removal of tonsils, though the former is, of course, a more serious medical procedure.

Obviously, it is the nature of science and medicine to perfect its art, its craft, and this is altogether a good thing in every sense of the word. Without this ongoing improvement of procedures and research, many would die in childhood and from commonplace diseases such as smallpox or the measles.

The question remains, however: are we prepared to accept whatever the outcome happens to be of this ongoing improvement? At first blush, the answer seems an obvious and resounding yes.[2]

Too often, however, science moves faster than a given culture's ethics or philosophy. The upshot of new medical procedures (fetal tissue transplants and cloning, for example) often shocks the ethical and philosophical sensibilities of some individuals before those new procedures become commonplace, if they ever do.

A current abortion-rights slogan is: "Keep abortions safe and legal!" The phrase fosters the assumption that, invariably, legal abortions are safe and illegal abortions are not. But even legal abortions have not always turned out safe. Pro-choice activist Mary Calderone points out that 90 percent of all abortions are performed by physicians, not butchers or the ham-handed.[3] The number of reported illegal abortions continues to be as low as 5,000 to 10,000 annually today.[4] Likewise, while abortion deaths have declined greatly, they have not vanished altogether, especially after the first trimester.[5] Because of the inevitability of complications following abortions after the first trimester, physicians looked for ways both to improve the procedure and to enhance the delivery of abortion services. In the process of all this refining and redoing, in the midst of this never-ending perfection-seeking, physicians have discovered both manifest and latent benefits. Latent benefits are those not necessarily pursued but accompanying a sought-after discovery.

Such is the case with late-term or partial-birth abortions. In the process of performing them, physicians fell upon a new procedure. For this discussion, the phrases, "late-term" and "partial-birth" will be used interchangeably. While the term "partial-birth" has gained currency through codification, it has also been a favorite of the pro-life crowd.[6,7] In order to maintain the pledge to impartiality, the preferred pro-choice phrase, will also be used.

According to Planned Parenthood, there are "roughly" 100,000 abortions performed annually after the fetus is twenty or more weeks. Our interchangeable phrases will not refer to all 100,000, but only to those in which a specific procedure is used.[8]

Because numerous abortions occur during the third trimester (though it is the term of pregnancy in which the fewest occur because the health risks are so high), it is necessary to explain the procedure to which our phrases "partial-birth" or "late-term" refer. Even among pro-choice advocates, the procedure does not enjoy full support, however. The late, former senator and devout pro-choice proponent, Daniel Patrick Moynihan (D–NY), described it like this: "as close to infanticide as anything I have ever come upon."[9] On the other hand, former President Bill Clinton allowed the procedure to stand, and, as we shall see, the Supreme Court has found its prohibition unconstitutional.

In strict medical language, the procedure is referred to as "intact dilation and extraction" and includes the following four elements as described by the American College of Obstetricians and Gynecologists:

1. Deliberate dilation of the cervix, usually over a sequence of days;
2. Instrumental conversion of the fetus to a footing breech;
3. Breech extraction of the body excepting the head; and
4. Partial evacuation of the intracranial contents of the living fetus to effect vaginal delivery of a dead but otherwise intact fetus.[10]

For the layperson, a picture may be worth a thousand medical words, so see Figure 8.1.

It is necessary to dilate the woman's uterus because at this stage of the pregnancy, the unborn is nearly fully formed. The head is too large for the uterus and so the uterus must be medically enlarged to allow for partial delivery. Because the dilation must take place over several days, the woman is at risk for infection. Once a woman has been dilated, the abortion can be commenced. The unborn is positioned for a feet-first delivery by the use of

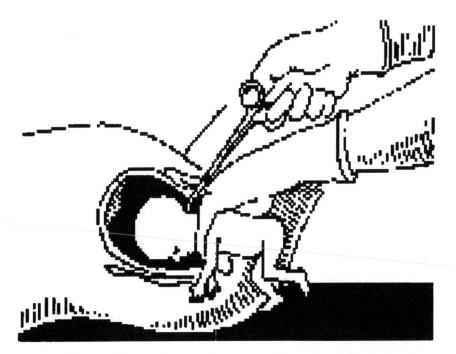

Figure 8.1 The partial-birth or late-term abortion procedure involves delivering the unborn and suctioning out the "inner-cranial contents" before delivery. This diagram not to scale. (Courtesy of National Right to Life, www.nrlc.org.)

instruments. The unborn is delivered until only the back of the skull is visible but it is still within the birth canal. A sharp instrument is inserted at the base of the skull and the "intracranial contents" of the unborn is suctioned out to allow for the soft skull to collapse and the fetus to be delivered intact. From a medical point of view, delivery of the full fetus is much to be preferred. Other methods used before the late-term or partial-birth procedure was discovered included dilation and evacuation, either the one- or two-day procedure. While these procedures are still used, they pose problems not posed by partial-birth abortion. Because they resemble partial-birth or late-term abortions, however, many pro-choice advocates fear that if one procedure were prohibited, others would be as well. In this sense, use of the partial-birth or late-term procedure reduced this possible infection risk dramatically.

Pro-choice advocates claim that the procedure is performed solely for the benefit of the mother's health. But former Surgeon General of the United States, C. Everett Koop, a strong pro-life defender, has pointed out that it is rarely, if ever, performed for this reason. The American College of Obstetricians and Gynecologists, however, noted that while it is sometimes used to save the life or health of the mother, the College's "select panel...could identify no circumstances under which this procedure...would be the only option to save the life or preserve the health of the woman."[11] The committee did, however, go on to point out that it *may* be the best or most appropriate procedure for mothers in fatal danger.

The number of partial-birth or late-term abortions performed annually is also highly disputed. Pro-life forces argue that there are 100,000. The National Abortion Federation, a pro-choice group, contends there are no more than 500 annually. The Centers for Disease Control, however, reported in 1996, for example, that just under 20,000 were performed at twenty-one weeks gestation, while just over 40,000 were performed at seventeen weeks gestation.[12] For our purposes here it is safe to say that there are more than 3,000 such abortions performed annually but fewer than 100,000.

Part of the reason for the confusion about numbers comes from both sides. For example, Pro-choice advocate, Ron Fitzsimmons, director of the National Coalition of Abortion Providers, said he intentionally misled Congress and the public about the procedure when he appeared on *Nightline* on ABC in November 1995.[13] In an article later published in the March 3, 1997, issue of *American Medical News,* Fitzsimmons said he "lied through my teeth" because he feared the truth would damage the cause of abortion rights. He came forward later because he felt the matter should rest on truth not fabrication. "The abortion-rights folks know it, the anti-abortion folks know it, and so, probably, does everyone else," Fitzsimmons claimed.

Hardly anyone on the pro-choice side agreed with Fitzsimmons's claims. He retained his position as executive director of the National Coalition of Abortion Providers, but not without controversy. Some pro-choice backers applauded Fitzsimmons's claims, of course. More often than not, however, pro-choicers agreed with the sentiment expressed by one: "When are you resigning?"[14] The normally pro-choice *Washington Post* called then–President Clinton's veto of the Daschle bill into question. Daschle had put forth an amendment to the Partial Birth Abortion Ban Act. This later became the Daschle-Durbin Amendment and gave President Clinton "plausible deniability" by providing for a ban but allowing for exceptions. Pro-life groups called it the "phony ban" because it allowed for so many exceptions, leading the *Post* to question Fitzsimmons as metaphor for all pro-choice opposition of partial birth abortions. "Mr. Fitzsimmons's revelation is a sharp blow to the credibility of his allies. These late-term abortions are extremely difficult to justify, if they can be justified at all."[15] The *Post* was not alone. Another normally pro-choice publication, the *New Republic,* published its editors' views: "The media's reticence [about the actual number of abortions by this method] is especially odd since the truths seem rather gettable. The difficult spade-work on the story was begun impressively last year by a few journalists who reported that the real number of partial-birth abortions did not jibe with the statements of abortions-rights advocates."[16] On the other hand, pro-life advocates often do not indicate the exact gestation of the pregnancy when referring to statistics, that is, whether at seventeen weeks, twenty, or more than twenty-one. Obviously, with each passing week, the number of such abortions being performed shrinks dramatically.

About four hundred to six hundred late-term abortions are performed annually at the third trimester because of severe fetal deformity or the mother's precarious health. If these six hundred are added to those being performed after the seventeenth week, the number of later-term or partial-birth abortions swells to six thousand or more annually; hence, our figure above. The vast majority of these are not done to preserve the health of the mother, or to abort a severely deformed fetus. They are done because the mother, for whatever reason, chooses late in the process to end her pregnancy.[17]

The numbers controversy has affected this part of the debate. Pro-choice Democratic Senators Patrick Leahy of Vermont, Daniel Patrick Moynihan of New York, and Thomas A. Daschle of South Dakota switched their votes from in favor of the late-term or partial-birth procedure, to votes against it.[18] Even devoutly pro-choice senators such as the late Paul Wellstone of Minnesota, Russ Feingold of Wisconsin, and Tom Harkin of Iowa, voted for the failed Daschle bill that outlawed partial-birth abortions except when the mother's death was imminent.

Late-term or partial-birth abortion bans began appearing in Congress in the mid-1990s. It's no secret that pro-life advocates are always seeking ways to reduce the number of abortions in this country (1.2–1.5 million every year since about 1975), and seek ways to restrict the procedure in one fell swoop. That is, if a given bill can be written in such a way as to restrict all or most abortions, so much the better from their point of view. The problem, of course, is that such sweeping restrictions are certain to be opposed at every turn, both legally and politically, as being unconstitutional according to *Roe*.

Partial-birth abortion bans gained wide acceptance in a number of state legislatures, and in the Republican-controlled Congress. Because many such abortions, indeed most of them, occur after twenty weeks, the issue of viability comes into play most significantly. Viability refers to the degree of "lung development necessary to permit sustained extra-uterine survival with neonatal intensive care."[19] This viability often comes at between twenty and twenty-three weeks. Certainly in today's sophisticated medical climate, it is not unduly excessive to claim that viability, with the proper neonatal care, can occur as early as eighteen to twenty weeks.

By 1998, more than twenty-two state bills, patterned after the Clinton-vetoed partial-birth-abortion ban act, had been enacted into law. The first court ruling on the merits was *Evans v Kelley*.[20] The *Kelley* case came to trial largely because of *Casey* and Justice O'Connor's "undue burden" claim as a replacement for *Roe*'s trimesters. But the partial-birth or late-term procedure itself did not become widely known until Dr. Martin Haskell explained it in the fall of 1992.

Haskell was a "family practitioner" and ran more than three abortion clinics. He added that he "routinely performed the procedure on all patients twenty through twenty-four weeks" (i.e., between four and five months). He testified before Congress on the medical procedure:

With a lower [fetal] extremity in the vagina, the surgeon uses his fingers to deliver the opposite lower extremity, then the torso, the shoulders and the upper extremities. The skull lodges at the internal cervical os [opening of the uterus]. . . . [T]he surgeon takes a pair of blunt curved Metzenbaum scissors in the right hand. He carefully advances the tip, curved down, along the spine and under his middle finger until he feels it contact the base of the skull under the tip of his middle finger. [T]he surgeon then forces the scissors into the base of the skull or into the foramen magnum. Having safely entered the skull, he spreads the scissors to enlarge the opening. The surgeon removes the scissors and introduces a suction catheter into this hole and evacuates the skull contents. With the catheter still in place, he applies traction to the fetus, removing it completely from the patient.[21]

Haskell told how the procedure came about. He found the D & Es to be "very tough," requiring three-quarters of an hour to perform.[22] In an interview with

American Medical News, he said, "[I]f I just put the ultrasound up there I could see it all and I would not have to feel my way around. Kind of serendipity" [meaning he stumbled upon it accidentally]. When asked if the unborn could be born alive, Haskell said yes but added, "The point here is to effect a safe legal abortion." Haskell pointed out that at least 80 percent were elective.[23]

In a 1993 interview with *American Medical News,* Dr. James McMahon, who had performed thousands of late-term or partial-birth abortions, said, "After 20 weeks where it frankly is a child to me, I agonize over it because the potential is so imminently there. On the other hand, I have another position, which I think is the superior hierarchy of questions, and that is: It's got to be the mother['s decision]."[24] McMahon's cited "maternal [health] indications" as the reason for aborting in 9 percent of over 2,000 partial-birth abortions he performed. The most common reason was depression, chicken pox, and vomiting. Of the remaining done for health reasons alone, most were done because the health or possible deformity of the infant was in question (cleft palate, for example). Haskell later revealed one reason for adopting the procedure: "Most surgeons find dismemberment at twenty weeks and beyond difficult due to the toughness of fetal tissues." He also revealed in later testimony that less than one-third are dead at the time of the procedure. Any abortion after the first trimester, Haskell explained to Congress, increases significantly the risk of permanent or serious injury to the mother.

Indeed, this was the very reason why the *Roe* trimesters were fashioned in the first place. A woman's right to decide for herself whether to terminate her pregnancy, at what time in the pregnancy, and for what reasons are *not,* according to *Roe,* absolute. Blackmun, when faced with this argument, wrote for the majority, "With this [that the woman has sole decision-making power when it comes to abortion] we do not agree."[25] Yet in every case examined by Congress it would appear that the woman decides at whatever point to have an abortion, and for what are called "elective" reasons.

Another argument posited is that the fetus feels nothing owing to anesthesia. Indeed, this part of the argument has made this form of abortion hard for pro-choice advocates to sell. Medical knowledge allows us to know that the fetus can feel pain.[26] How much pain, and to what extent, are unknown and widely debated. We do know, however, that the unborn reacts to certain intrusions into its space and gives visible or reactive responses to painful stimuli.[27] This point has generated much debate on both sides. During the congressional hearings cited above, anesthesiologists testified that the fetus does feel pain during late-term or partial-birth abortions.

Countering their claims is one brought to the fore that lack of fetal development constrains just how much pain a fetus can feel. Rebutting this, Robert J. White, a neurologist who testified before Congress, claimed that not only is there ample brain circuitry in place at twenty weeks to register pain, his studies and the studies of others indicate that some level of fetal pain detection can be ascertained as early as eight weeks.[28] Even if the eight weeks is discounted, there can be no question that his testimony, along with the testimony of others at the hearing, left only one impression: the fetus experiences pain to some degree and at an age long before the late-term or partial-birth abortions are performed.

Of course, it cannot be argued that the fetus feels pain the way a full-term infant does, or in the manner that you or I might feel it when we slam a door on our hand, or smash our thumb with a hammer. A fully developed, experienced human feels more pain than an infant, if only because the adult knows what is coming and the additional knowledge of previous experience serves to increase the pain. But in no case could it be argued that the pain of an infant is insignificant or small enough to be inconsequential.

PARTIAL-BIRTH ABORTION BANS

Bills to ban this procedure first began to be introduced in Congress in 1995. These came to Congress largely because the federal court could not make up its collective mind. Three federal courts held that bans in Illinois, Wisconsin, Virginia, and Georgia were *not* unconstitutional owing to vagueness. Different federal courts held that Arkansas, Iowa, Nebraska, Ohio, Louisiana, New Jersey, Florida, Kentucky, West Virginia, Arizona, Michigan, and Missouri stated that later-term or partial-birth abortion bans either were unconstitutional outright, or could be construed as unconstitutional owing to vagueness.[29] The idea behind the vagueness challenge was that if the definitions were too vague and yet allowed restrictions, it was conceivable that they could eventually allow for too many restrictions. In this case, the vagueness argument contended that "partial-birth abortions," as defined, were so broad as to allow for *any* abortion to be outlawed under its definition. This is often referred to as "overbreadth" of a vaguely worded statute.

The general standard of reasonableness in a statute is such that it is unconstitutionally vague if it "fails to give a person of ordinary intelligence a reasonable opportunity to know what is prohibited."[30] This has been the case in more than a number of laws, often because there is not a scienter (or defining, Latin for "to know") clause in the statute.[31] Even the presence of this clause, however, does not guarantee passage.[32] The phrases that often trip up these bans are worded along the lines of "a partially vaginally deliver[ed] living fetus before killing the fetus." The scienter clause often further explains the phrase, but apparently not to the satisfaction of the courts.

The first ban went to Congress in 1995 and was the result of a physician's (McMahon) ingenuity in figuring out how to deliver a partial birth, extract the skull contents, and deliver an intact but dead fetus. Dr. Haskell followed up with his how-to manual and then delivered an address about it to the National Abortion Federation (NAF) for study, both of which are discussed above. When the interviews with Haskell and McMahon became public via the *American Medical News*, confirming the procedure, NAF, apparently sensing the difficulties, charged *AMN* with having falsified the interviews, or at least the contents of those interviews. When a verbatim transcript was produced by reporter Diane Gianelli, NAF backed down. What troubled NAF most was the admission in the interview by both physicians that most of the partial-birth abortions (80 percent or more) were "elective."[33]

The matter might have remained closed had not Representative Charles Canady (R–FL) introduced the Partial-Birth Abortion Ban Act on July 1995. There followed a storm of controversy. Nearly every media outlet reported the figures for partial-birth abortion as both rare (four hundred annually) and extreme (when nothing else would work). This, too, might have closed the matter congressionally—sealed the vote against partial-birth abortion—had not two other events occurred.

First, reporter Ruth Padawer from *The Record* of Bergen County, New Jersey, called a local abortion clinic and asked how many partial-birth or late-term abortions were performed there. Padawer was astonished when she discovered that her own local clinic performed *more than three times* as many as the national figure of 1,500.[34] Further, she discovered that only a handful were done to save the mother's life. Forty-eight hours later, the *Washington Post* ran a long piece by its medical writer, Dr. David Brown, and reporter Barbara Vobejda. They concluded that it was not only possible but entirely probable that most partial-birth abortions were being performed on normal, healthy fetuses; that is, most were elective.[35]

The 1995 ban passed both houses but not by a margin wide enough to survive a presidential veto. A two-thirds majority is required to override a presidential veto of any bill. President Clinton vetoed the bill, as he said he would if presented with it, and the matter died for that session. To announce the ban, the president stood on stage with five women, who were told they had to have a late-term abortion for medical reasons. The issue still did not fade away after the veto. Within Clinton's own party, many were unhappy with his veto, including Al Gore's 2000 running mate, Senator Joe Lieberman (D–CT). Other Democrats also took umbrage. Wrote Sidney Callahan:

I am a prolife Democrat who's going to defect from my party. Come November, I plan to vote for Bob Dole. And how, pray tell, does an unreconstructed Humphrey-McGovern "pinko," "socialist," "big government," "bleeding heart," "peacenik" Democrat in favor of preferential option for the poor come to such a pass? Through

Former President Bill Clinton. (Courtesy of the Library of Congress.)

a bout of moral indignation, that's how. My multiple disillusionments with Bill Clinton have boiled over [on his veto of the partial-birth abortion ban].[36]

Although finding those who support partial-birth abortion as a form of abortion for certain cases is hard (in some polls, the percentage favoring the procedure is as low as 7 percent), there are those who do. In responding to the AMA's support of the partial-birth abortion ban by Congress, Janet Benshoof, president of the Center for Reproductive Law, said, "The AMA's endorsement of 'partial-birth abortion' legislation legitimizes anti-choice legislators' efforts to outlaw abortion, and jeopardizes the integrity of the physician-patient relationship. This ban on abortion turns responsible doctors into criminals and contributes to an environment in which hate crimes, like the

Table 8.1
President Clinton's Vetoes of All Partial-Birth Abortion Bans

Congress	House vote	Senate vote	Clinton Vote
104th, 1995–1996	Passed, 288–139	Passed, 54–44	Vetoed
	Overrode, 285–137	Sustained veto, 57–41	
105th, 1997–1998	Passed, 295–136	Passed, 64–36	Vetoed
	Overrode, 296–132	Sustained veto, 63–36	
106th, 1999–2000		Passed, 63–34	

Source: There are numerous sources for this data. See, for example, "Congress Has Tried to Ban Abortion Procedure," *Milwaukee Journal Sentinel* (April 24, 2000): final edition, 4A.

murder of Dr. Barnett Slepian, are committed."[37] Susan Yanow, of the Abortion Access Project, and Jeanne Clark, of Women Organizing for Change, agree that partial-birth abortion bans would be too broad and would hurt women who need them the most.[38]

Of course, Republicans complained to the media about the veto. Moreover, the vast majority of the people (more than 70 percent) were against partial-birth or late-term abortions.[39] Still, the ban was vetoed and had to wait until the next session of Congress convened. The Partial-Birth Abortion Act of 1997 met the same fate as the 1995 bill. In 1999, the Senate passed its version, and President Clinton promised his veto once again (see Table 8.1).

The bans themselves were very explicit. Depending on which ban was viewed, each contained language taken virtually intact from the description penned by the American College of Obstetricians and Gynecologists. It also contained a scienter clause providing further clarifying language. Nevertheless, President Clinton vetoed the bans.

What makes the vetoes so puzzling to many—both in the pro-life and the pro-choice camps—is the number of barriers that stood in the way of the vetoes. First, there was considerable public opinion against the procedures. In every poll taken to date, no matter how the question was worded, when the partial-birth or late-term abortion procedure was understood, the overwhelming majority expressed their opposition to it. Clinton's view of "triangulation" on policy matters, wherein public opinion is heavily weighted, militated steadfastly against his veto.[40] Second, from the first ban to the last, Clinton was well aware of the misrepresentation of PBA facts by pro-choice advocates. Even when Ron Fitzsimmons, the key pro-choice witness, recanted his testimony, Clinton still issued his veto. Third, the overwhelming medical evidence to date was strongly set against this particular abortion procedure.

Though there are still medical articles written in its favor for extenuating circumstances, no medical opinion weighed in its favor as an *elective* abortion procedure.[41]

Indeed, the American Medical Association has agreed with the need for some form of the ban. It is the first time ever in the AMA's history that it has declared a certain medical procedure off-limits. The AMA argued that in its examination of peer-reviewed medical literature, it could not find a single instance where it was listed as the preferred practice or the accepted medical procedure.[42] "Partial-birth abortion should be banned," wrote two prominent physicians, "because it is inhumane, unethical and could reasonably be labeled infanticide."[43] In the face of such evidence, why did the bans get vetoed, and why was Congress unable to override them?

President Clinton vetoed the bans owing to his lifelong allegiance to the pro-choice movement, and many in his party followed suit.[44] The ban survived an override, too, because many pro-choice Democrats, while voting *for* the ban, later voted *against* an override that would have overturned a veto by their own party's president. Although the vote in the House was veto-proof, and the one in the Senate only three votes shy of being veto-proof, the measure still failed. What made this veto and the subsequent failure to override unsurprising was former President Clinton's high popularity, not only among his own party, of course, but also among the general populace. Even after impeachment proceedings, Clinton enjoyed one of the highest approval ratings of any president in history. In political terms, it is very difficult to override the vetoes of a widely popular president of either party.

Roe provides yet another reason for the failure of the bans. Although *Roe* specifically allowed for certain bans, it clearly and unequivocally provided for two additional mandates:

1. No woman was the sole guarantor of her own body with respect to abortion.[45]
2. States restrict abortion because the government had a compelling interest and that interest became much more likely the longer a pregnant woman waited to have an abortion.

Many Members of Congress claimed their allegiance to *Roe* while voting against one of the two above-mentioned mandates. Furthermore, the failure of the ban pointed to a key problem between the two factions: if compromise could not be reached on this ban, there would appear to be no room for negotiation of any kind. Finally, because the partial-birth or late-term abortion procedure strongly resembles the D & E procedure (clearly allowed by *Roe*), many thought one could not be prohibited without banning the other. For this reason it is likely that the courts could not arrive at a consistent agreement either. Is no compromise possible?

Yes and no. Not all was grim. The "clash of absolutes" as Laurence Tribe has called the abortion debate, could not continue forever, or so it seemed. Although succeeding bans following the 1995 attempt met with the same presidential veto, a new and more remarkable trend began to emerge, as pointed out by Eliza Carney:

There was something odd about the press conference that a group of lawmakers held on the eve of the House's July 23 [1998] debate over the procedure known as "partial-birth" abortion.... The surprise lay in the cast of characters.... One of those who stood before the cameras that day was Rep. Steny H. Hoyer, D-Md., whose unfailing support for abortion rights has earned him a 100 percent approval rating from the National Abortion and Reproductive Rights Action League. By Hoyer's side were three more legislators who have, in the past, been dependably "pro-choice": Reps. Jim Moran, D-Va., Ellen O. Tauscher, D-Calif., and Robert E. Wise, D-W. Va. Even the two Republicans on hand—Reps. James C. Greenwood of Pennsylvania and Nancy L. Johnson of Connecticut—vote steadfastly for abortion rights.[46]

What made the story more newsworthy was not only the ban itself. Hoyer remained steadfastly against the ban, believing as he did that legislators should not be in the business of telling physicians what procedures to use or not. Rather, the group had gathered to call for more sweeping measures than the ban, one that would eliminate all late-term abortions, no matter what the procedure. This change in thinking, first touted by Senate Minority Leader Thomas A. Daschle (D–SD), would allow for exceptions to this late-term ban only if "serious, adverse health consequences" to the mother were present. Had common ground been found at last?

No. Pro-life groups, startlingly, opposed the Daschle bill, including both the Family Research Council and the Christian Coalition. Both hated the bill because the health exception, they argued, was much too broad, creating too large a loophole. This is understandable since the *Roe* version of the same health exception had already been defined broadly.

Nevertheless, a new trend began to grow, largely owing to the "incrementalism" being argued by social conservatives on both sides of the aisle.[47] While the bans were shot down in 1995 and 1997, the vote to override Clinton's veto (296–132 in the House in 1997–1998) passed with seventy-seven Democrats voting to override. Of that number, twenty-four had been solid pro-choice supporters. A Senate override failed in that chamber by only a few votes later that year, so the ban did not take effect. The end result was the defection of now pro-life Democrats who were outnumbered by pro-choice Republicans.

President George W. Bush has already agreed to sign a partial-birth abortion ban if presented with one. It will be interesting to watch, if a ban is introduced in Congress, who will and who will not support it. Also, it will be interesting to see if a successful ban survives an inevitable challenge in court.

If this all sounds confusing, it's because it is. Perhaps it serves to underscore the intense and confusing debate this issue has stirred up for the last quarter of a century. The incrementalism being used by Republicans in Congress has gained headway. Since 1995, Congress has voted more than ninety times on whether to restrict abortion or family planning. The pro-life contingent in Congress, Democrats or Republicans, has won all but thirteen of these.[48]

On April 29, 1999, Senator Rick Santorum (R–PA) introduced the third Partial-Birth Abortion Ban. The Senate approved Santorum's ban but it did not survive under former President Clinton.

While the federal legislation fell victim to President Clinton's vetoes, states such as Virginia and Wisconsin passed partial-birth abortion bans anyway. Pro-choice advocates, claiming the bans were but thinly disguised ploys to ban all abortions, vowed to fight them all the way to the Supreme Court.[49] This is exactly what they did. The Court chose to examine Nebraska's partial-birth abortion ban. In some cases, the distinctions between what constituted a partial-birth abortion and what did not defied any understanding. In an effort to draw these distinctions as narrowly as possible, pro-life advocates sought to define them so that they could not be misinterpreted to outlaw dilatation and extraction (D & E) abortions in this manner: the partial-birth abortion ban would outlaw only abortions in which the unborn was pulled into the vagina and dismembered intentionally, *not* those in which the fetus was dismembered *while* being pulled into the vagina. The Nebraska law went to great lengths to satisfy all concerned, including those who argued that *any* abortion at *any* time could be banned under a partial-birth abortion law. The most important partial-birth or later-term abortion case to date came before the High Court as *Stenberg v Carhart*.

STENBERG V CARHART

At issue in *Stenberg v Carhart* was whether Nebraska's partial-birth abortion law placed an "undue burden" (first mentioned by O'Connor in *Thornburgh* and later codified in *Casey* to replace the trimester arrangement of *Roe*) on a woman's decision to have an abortion. The Nebraska law prohibited any partial-birth abortion unless "that procedure is necessary to save the mother's [physical] life."[50] The Nebraska law defined partial-birth abortion as a procedure in which the doctor "partially delivers vaginally a living unborn child before killing the...child" and "intentionally delivering into the vagina a living unborn child, or a substantial portion thereof, for the purpose of performing a procedure that the [abortionist] knows will kill the...child and does kill the...child." Conviction under the law carried a felony charge and carried with it an immediate revocation of the convicted physician's state medical license. In *Stenberg*, Nebraska abortionist Leroy Carhart brought the suit seeking a declaration that the statute violated the Constitution as defined by *Roe*, *Casey*, and others. Both the District Court and the Eighth Circuit Court found the law to be unconstitutional.

The case centered on the method. As mentioned before, there are two such methods, D & E and D & X. The former procedure ("dilation and evacuation") involves dilation of the cervix and removal of some fetal tissue using nonvacuum surgical instruments. This method is used during the second trimester, twelve to fifteen weeks. Usually around the fifteenth week and beyond, it is necessary for some form of dismemberment to occur using surgical instruments. Once removed, the parts must be pieced back together, puzzlelike, into a fetus to be sure nothing has been left behind. When this dismemberment occurs, the physician pulls a portion of the fetus through the cervix into the birth canal.

Another similar form of D & E, known as "intact D & E," involves pulling the fetus through the cervix "intact," in one piece, as it were, rather than in pieces. This is normally used in the sixteenth week and later. This intact procedure occurs whether the unborn is positioned feet first or head first. It is here that the Nebraska law was called into question.

The feet-first method is often referred to as D & X or "dilation and extraction." It is this procedure that is most often associated with, or called, partial-birth or later-term abortion. Carhart claimed, and the lower courts agreed, that his D & X procedure was superior and safer than the typical D & E (mainly because D & E had a high potential for infection). D & E was not called into question by *Stenberg*. Nebraska argued that the "undue burden" claim would be applicable if it applied to both D & E and D & X. Since it did not (referring, as it did, only to D & X), Nebraska argued that another method still provided for both *Roe* and *Casey* without violating either.

The courts found that there was not enough in the Nebraska law to distinguish between the two procedures. The lower courts argued that the Nebraska law could mean both procedures. Nebraska's attorney general claimed that it was clear that it outlawed only one procedure, not both.

Supreme Court Justice Stephen Breyer delivered the High Court's opinion. Justice Breyer's opinion focused on three points:

1. "[B]efore viability...the woman has a right to choose to terminate her pregnancy."
2. "[A] law designed to further the State's interest in fetal life which imposes an undue burden on the woman's decision...is unconstitutional." And,

3. "[S]ubsequent to viability, the state in promoting its interest in the potentiality of human life may, if it chooses, regulate, and even proscribe, abortion except where it is necessary...for the preservation of the life and health of the mother."

Justice Breyer then argued that because the Nebraska law sought to ban one method of abortion in pregnancy,

...we must describe and then discuss several different abortion procedures. Considering the fact that those procedures seek to terminate a potential human life, our discussion may seem clinically cold or callous to some, perhaps horrifying to others. There is no alternative way, however, to acquaint the reader with the technical distinctions among different abortion methods and factual matters, upon which the outcome of this case depends.[51]

Justice Breyer then proceeded to enumerate the various forms of abortion. The first, encompassing over 90 percent of all abortions, occurred before twelve weeks and used "vacuum aspiration," in which the uterus was "vacuumed" of its "contents." About 10 percent occurred between twelve and twenty-four weeks. In the 1970s, for these second-trimester procedures, saline was injected into the uterus, the fetus burned to death, and was delivered dead. Today, the favored procedures are D & X and D & E. Since there are about 1.5 million abortions annually, 10 percent would mean about 150,000 annually are performed using this method. About 5 percent of this group (or 7,500) fall under the D & X method because D & E involves too many inherent risks (infection, for example).

Although the American College of Obstetricians and Gynecologists described the D & X procedure as different from the D & E method, Justice Breyer in his opinion, acknowledging this, argued that, "Despite the technical differences...intact D & E and D & X are sufficiently similar for us to use the terms interchangeably."[52] This point is important: on the one hand, the Court defers to the medical profession on certain points, while, on the other hand, the Court distances itself from the medical profession.

Justice Breyer and the Court concluded that, at least on two points, the Nebraska law violated the federal Constitution as interpreted in *Casey* and *Roe*. First, it found that the law lacked an exception for the preservation of the health of the mother. Although the Nebraska law allowed for the life exception, the Court found that the omission of the word *health* made it fail both the *Casey* and the *Roe* standards. Clearly, if ever there were any doubt that the Court would define *health* as any reason a woman wished, *Stenberg* dispelled it.

Second, the Court, while agreeing that the Nebraska law sought to single out one form of abortion, nevertheless placed an "undue burden" on any woman seeking an abortion. The Court's logic here implied that if one form or method of abortion were removed from the list of a woman's options, then it was an undue burden. The Court remained unpersuaded of Nebraska's argument that by seeking to ban partial-birth abortion it "prevents cruelty to partially born children" and "preserves the integrity of the medical profession."

Although Nebraska did bring forward considerable evidence that the piercing of the fetal skull amounted to a "blind" use of instrumentation, the Association of American Physicians agreed with Nebraska, citing further evidence of special risks imposed on the mother by this method. Further medical testimony on behalf of Nebraska that could not establish the safety of the D & X procedure proved unpersuasive to the Court. The Court, while admitting that most of these abortions were elective, found that "a rarely used treatment might be necessary to treat a rarely occurring disease that could strike anyone."[53] It appeared that the Court argued that if even one woman could be found who was prohibited from securing a wanted abortion, the proposed law was unconstitutional.

If this appears to allow abortion owing to exception, that is because no other reason satisfies. The Court cited the American College of Obstetricians and Gynecologists' own *amici* brief that "in the hands of a skilled and experienced" physician, D & X "can be the most appropriate." But given this, pro-life advocates argued, it appears that the opposite would be equally true: in the hands of an unskilled and inexperienced physician, it could be, at worst, deadly; at best, highly unsafe. The Court has never been bashful in limiting certain practices that may be safe in one situation but dangerous in others. Since so few of these procedures are performed (7,500 or less), the number of skilled and experienced physicians who could perform them safely would be small. No reputable general practitioner would, for example, undertake even a "routine" heart catheterization because of the safety issue. Because many who perform abortions are not by training abortion specialists, this allowance of the Court is at best highly confusing. Furthermore, for the very small fraction of women whose health considerations are such that they have no alternative to resort to but partial-birth abortion, it would seem that the Court, given earlier rulings, could have made those conditions the only exceptions. It chose not to.

The Court also found the Nebraska law to be unconstitutional because it had, per *Casey*, the "effect of placing a substantial obstacle in the path of a woman seeking an abortion of a nonviable fetus."[54] This is, of course the "undue burden" that O'Connor intimated into the law in *Thornburgh*, agonized over its absence in *Webster*, and codified in *Casey*. But the Court did not find that restricting women from federally funded abortions constituted an "undue burden" (*Maher*) In fact, the Court argued there that the restriction did not, in fact, limit a woman's alternatives to abortion. Yet to restrict even one method of elective abortions, even though this particular method was chosen in fewer than 5 percent of all abortions, nevertheless placed an undue burden, not on all women, but on a very select few.

Finally, the Court attacked the Nebraska ban because it attempted to outlaw more than one method, though the D & X method was the only one cited. Apparently, the Court read into the attorney general's comments that another form of abortion, or all forms of abortion, were being cloyed (hidden) in the law. It would not, of course, be surprising to discover that pro-life proponents secretly hoped for some peg upon which to hang all abortion procedures to impose a possible ban. But a simple nonpartisan reading of the ban's language would require a highly contentious mind to glean from it an attempt to restrict some, all, or more than the one method under discussion.

O'Connor concurred but wrote further to clarify her reasons for affirming the lower courts' ruling. She cited the fact that the Nebraska law had no instance of exception for the health of the mother. O'Connor indicated her eagerness to embrace the term *health* by arguing that the Nebraska law did not contain an exception beyond one in cases where the physical life of the mother was at risk. Stevens's written concurrence criticized further the intent of the Nebraska law: "[T]he law prohibits the procedure because the State legislators seek to chip away at the private choice shielded by *Roe v. Wade,* even as modified by *Casey.*"[55] He continued:

Although much ink is spilled today describing the gruesome nature of later term abortion procedures, that rhetoric does not provide me with a *reason* to believe that the procedure Nebraska here claims it seeks to ban is more brutal, more gruesome, or less respectful of "potential life" than the equally gruesome procedure Nebraska claims it still allows.[56]

In other words, all abortions are fearsome and brutal from the fetus' point of view. If we ban partial-birth abortion on this logic, then we must ban all forms of abortion. Judge Richard Posner of the Seventh Circuit Court made the same point when he wrote:

From the standpoint of the fetus and, I should think, of any rational person, it makes no difference whether, when the skull is crushed, the fetus is entirely within the uterus or its feet are outside the uterus. Yet the position of the feet is the only difference between committing a felony and performing an act states consider is constitutionally privileged... There is no meaningful difference between the forbidden and the privileged practice. No reason of policy or morality that would allow the one would forbid the other.[57]

Pro-life advocates pointed out that while both judges saw the procedures as "gruesome" neither argued that they should be outlawed.

Justices Rehnquist, Scalia, Kennedy, and Thomas all dissented. Scalia began, "I am optimistic enough to believe that, one day, *Stenberg v. Carhart* will be assigned its rightful place in the history of this Court's jurisprudence beside *Korematsu* and *Dred Scott*. The method of killing a human child—one cannot even accurately say an entirely unborn human child—proscribed by this statute is so horrible that the most clinical description of it evokes a shudder of revulsion."[58] Scalia went on to point out that the Justices knew full well in *Roe* that to demand a health exception meant abortion on demand. Scalia's fury did not end there. He went on to complain that *Stenberg* means five Justices respect a woman's right to kill her own child more than they respect the obligation she has to give it life. Scalia finished by arguing that *Stenberg* was nothing more than "policy-judgment-couched-as-law" and, further, "that *Casey* must be overruled."[59]

Justice Kennedy reminded the Court that *Roe* did provide for an occasion in which states could limit or restrict abortions. Kennedy went on to point out that *Stenberg* removed from the states any such right, even though there was no undue burden in place, and denied no woman the right to an abortion. Justice Kennedy also wanted it known across the nation, as he put it, what took place in these abortions, and took pains to make the matter clear.[60]

Justice Kennedy's dissenting opinion showed the larger Court's misreading of *Casey*. He felt that the states did have a compelling interest in certain forms of abortion, and that by having such an interest were within their right to seek to restrict it. He also found that "Those who oppose abortion would agree, would insist, that both procedures are subject to the most severe moral condemnation, condemnation reserved for the most repulsive human conduct." He further found that it was *not* inconsistent, however, to seek to restrict only one procedure. Kennedy pointed out what appeared to be an important piece of information: that Dr. Carhart's experts, testifying to the procedure, had not, in all their years of practice, ever performed one or found the need to.

Justice Kennedy found this reason to support upholding the ban. He pointed out that the Nebraska law spells out its ban in clear language. He also pointed out that O'Connor's health exception was a flight of fancy that would merely allow for partial-birth or later-term abortions to proceed unimpeded. Justice Kennedy concluded by pointing out that *Casey* upheld informed consent and that the opinion of the physician was neither exclusive nor unitary. It must be taken in conjunction with the mother's informed consent. He charged the Court with ignoring *Casey* and following *Akron*, which *Casey* supposedly corrected.

Justice Thomas pointed out in his dissent that the Court's opinion about abortion should have nothing to do with the case, since that is not grounded

Supreme Court Justice Anthony Kennedy. (Photograph by Marcy Nighswander. AP/Wide World Photos.)

in the Constitution. He charged that the standard applied in *Casey* and *Stenberg* were equivalent to the Justices' own philosophical opinions and were as illegitimate as the standard they sought to replace. He went on to add, "Today, the Court inexplicably holds that States cannot constitutionally prohibit a method of abortion that millions find hard to distinguish from infanticide and that the Court hesitates even to describe."[61] Indeed, Justice Thomas cited circumstances in which overdilation occurs and the unborn must be "trapped" inside the womb until the abortion is completed. Nebraska law, he argued, had been written in such a way as to prevent any confusion between D & X and D & E. Thomas accused the Court and Justice O'Connor of misunderstanding the plain language of the ban.

Thomas reminded the Court that "*Casey* professed to be, in part, a repudiation of *Roe* and its progeny. The *Casey* joint opinion expressly noted that prior case law had undervalued the State's interest in potential life."[62] Yet *Stenberg*, Thomas now asserted, seemed to be saying just the opposite. Further, Thomas argued that Nebraska made clear its intent that partial-birth abortion was akin to infanticide and that the law does not require further arguments: "In a civilized society, the answer is too obvious, and the contrary arguments too offensive to merit further discussion."

CONCLUSION

The Court certainly came under attack in *Stenberg*. It is clear from testimony given on both sides, from the testimony of both Democrats and Republicans, that partial-birth abortion is considered infanticide by many. Indeed, *Stenberg* allows for abortion up to the very moment of birth, but not one hour after. This is clear from a number of vantage points but perhaps none so compelling as the ones issued by the *New York Times* and other national newspapers.[63]

The national media, including Dan Rather, PBS, CBS, National Public Radio, the *New York Times,* Planned Parenthood, and the National Abortion Federation all misled the public and decision-makers regarding the number of late-term or partial-birth abortion procedures performed each year. When this later came out, it cast a shadow over the entire discussion, as noted above.

The failure of late-term or partial-birth abortion bans in *Stenberg* serves to underscore how contentious abortion will remain. If *this* method of abortion cannot be restricted, then, really, is there any method of abortion that states have a right to proscribe? If states cannot prohibit abortions that execute the unborn shortly before delivery, then what form of abortion can ever be devised that would be "too much"?

In *Stenberg*, the Court overrode itself in order to arrive at an opinion in which it could continue abortion on demand. When Justice O'Connor substituted "undue burden" for the trimester approach in *Casey,* it may well be that she had in mind the prevention of any restriction on abortion at all. Not only was the Nebraska law written to order, but it abided by the contingencies of the Court's earlier rulings. Yet the Court in *Stenberg* proves that it cannot be counted on to abide by those views it says it will allow.

The fallout from the *Stenberg* case is only now being felt as this book is being written. There has been plenty of negative reaction. Columnist John Leo argued that *Stenberg* proved *Casey* "was a bait-and-switch effort to placate people who expected *Roe v Wade* to be overturned, the court said it would allow abortion, but after [*Stenberg*] we know it has no intention of allowing any important dent in the country's abortion machine."[64] Another columnist,

Linda Bowles, complained that "These five unelected lawyers instructed the American people that as far as the law is concerned, life in the womb is sub-human, if human at all, and as such, is unworthy of protection by human conscience, and unentitled to protection by the Constitution."[65] Echoing that claim was Dallas pundit William Murchinson, who argued that the High Court arrogated to itself the power of the legislature, leaving the people no re-course at the voting booth.[66] Following *Stenberg,* those who approved it did not rush into print. However, there are those who do support the Court's rul-ing, such as the Center for Reproductive Law and Policy and, of course, NARAL, the National Abortion and Reproductive Rights Action League.[67]

Of all the cases covered in this book, clearly *Stenberg* is the most discon-certing. It provides a case study in which a highly politicized body, not itself subject to the will of the people through election, assumes a role not granted to it under the Constitution. Moreover, *Stenberg* sounds an ominous note that may prove just how unresolvable the abortion controversy will forever re-main.

NOTES

1.   Olasky, *The Press and Abortion,* 82.

2.   For an excellent discussion of this, see Leon Kass, "*L'Chaim* and Its Limits: Why Not Immortality?" *First Things,* no. 113 (May 2001): 17–24.

3.   Paige Comstock Cunningham and Clarke D. Forsythe, "Is Abortion the 'First Right' for Women?: Some Consequences of Legal Abortion." In J. Douglas Butler and David F. Walbert, eds., *Abortion, Medicine, and the Law,* Fourth Edition (New York: Facts on File, 1992), 12.

4.   This number is in wide dispute. For example, the National Center for Health Statistics reports that the number of deaths from illegal abortions is less than one hundred annually and has been since 1973. Finding a source that either side is willing to accept without qualification is, however, hopeless, so both are cited. See, for example, http://www.cdc.gov.mmwr/PDF/ss/ss4804/pdf, page 1. Accessed Spring 2002.

5.   Cunningham, 128. Christopher Tietze, Planned Parenthood's statistician, wrote, "Abortion-related deaths are of course only the proverbial tip of the iceberg. Nationwide information on the incidence of nonfatal complications of legal abor-tion, including major complications requiring patient care, is far less complete than information on abortion-related mortality. This is so because there is no agreement among investigators as [sic] to what constitutes a major complication, and there is no system of surveillance in place." In other words, abortion *may* be *said* to be less dan-gerous than childbirth, not because it necessarily is, but because no one is counting the complications because the complications are undefined.

6.   It is altogether unclear if this is, in fact, not a tactical decision by pro-choice advocates in the selection of terminology. If *late-term abortion* becomes the preferred

term, it is unlikely that the procedure will ever be banned for the simple reason that the term encompasses so many other abortions not covered by partial-birth abortion bans. The *partial-birth abortion* term is a specific term referring to a specific kind of procedure.

7. Teresa R. Wagner, "The Partial-Birth Abortion War," *The World and I* 14, no. 1 (September 1999), accessed via InfoTrac Expanded Academic ASAP database, 1.

8. To make matters even more confusing, however, the American College of Obstetricians and Gynecologists described the partial-birth procedure in 1997 as one that could be performed as early as sixteen weeks. See George J. Annas, "Partial-Birth Abortion, Congress, and the Constitution," *New England Journal of Medicine* 339, no. 4 (July 23, 1998): 280.

9. Quoted in numerous sources, one being Annas, "Partial-Birth Abortion," 280.

10. American College of Obstetrics and Gynecology, "Statement on Intact Dilation and Extraction, January 12, 1997," quoted in Annas, "Partial-Birth Abortion," 280–281.

11. Annas, 280.

12. http://www.cdc.gov/mmwr/PDF/ss/ss4804/pdf. Accessed Spring 2002.

13. David Stout, "An Abortion Rights Advocate Says He Lied About Procedure," *New York Times,* February 25, 1997.

14. Ibid., 2.

15. Ibid., 5.

16. William Powers, "Partial Truths," *The New Republic* 216, no. 12 (March 24, 1997), accessed via InfoTrac Expanded Academic ASAP database, 2.

17. Ibid., 1.

18. Melanie Conklin, "So I Lied: Whatever Happened to the Abortion Lobbyist Who Repented?" *Progressive* 61, no. 9 (September 1997), accessed via InfoTrac Expanded Academic ASAP database, 1.

19. James Bopp, and Curtis R. Cook, "Partial-Birth Abortion: The Final Frontier of Abortion Jurisprudence," *Issues in Law & Medicine* 14, no. 1 (Summer 1998), accessed via InfoTrac Expanded Academic ASAP database, 1.

20. Ibid., 2. The states with bans were Alaska, Arizona, Arkansas, Florida, Georgia, Idaho, Illinois, Indiana, Iowa, Louisiana, Michigan, Mississippi, Montana, Nebraska (which would figure largely in this history later), New Jersey, Rhode Island, South Carolina, South Dakota, Tennessee, Virginia, West Virginia, and Wisconsin. Another twenty-one had bans pending in their legislatures prior to *Stenberg v Carhart.*

21. Ibid., 2–3.

22. The pertinent question to ask at this point is "Why the hurry?"

23. "Second Trimester Abortion: An Interview with W. Martin Haskell, M.D.," *Cincinnati Medicine* 16 (1993): 18, 19. Also quoted in Bopp.

24. Bopp, 5–6.

25. See also the fiercely pro-choice Harvard lawyer, Laurence H. Tribe, *Abortion: The Clash of Absolutes* (New York: W.W. Norton & Company, 1990), chapter 5, where he makes the same point about *Roe.*

26.   R. Frank White, "Are We Overlooking Fetal Pain and Suffering During Abortion?" *American Society of Anesthesiologists Newsletter* 6, no. 10 (October 2001). www.asahq.org/Newsletters/2001/10_01/white.htm.

27.   U.S. House of Representatives, *Committee on the Judiciary, Testimony of Jean A. Wright, M.D. M.B.A., Associate Professor of Pediatrics and Anesthesia Division Doctor, Pediatric Clinic & Care Emergency Medicine, Emory University School of Medicine,* Subcommittee on the Constitution, March 21, 1996. Wright added, "Anatomic studies have shown that the density of cutaneous nociceptive nerve endings in the late fetus and newborn infant may equal or exceed that of adult skin."

28.   *Partial-Birth Abortion: Hearing Before the Subcommittee of the Constitution of the House Committee on the Judiciary, 104th Congress, 1st Session, 110–115* (June 15, 1995), 67. Also quoted in Bopp and Cook, 8.

29.   Maureen L. Rurka, "The Vagueness of Partial-Birth Abortion Bans: Deconstruction or Destruction?" *Journal of Criminal Law and Criminality* 89, no. 4 (Summer 1999), accessed via InfoTrac Expanded Academic ASAP database, 2, Spring 2001.

30.   Ibid., 6. Appears in *Grayned v. City of Rockford,* 408 U.S. 104, 108 (1972).

31.   See, for example, Joyce Frieden, "Partial-Birth Ban Overruled in Three States," *Family Practice News* 29, no. 21 (November 1, 1999): 51, accessed via InfoTrac Expanded Academic ASAP database, 1, Spring 2001.

32.   Rurka, 3.

33.   This and the succeeding chronology come from Matthew Scully, "Partial Truth," *National Review* 50, no. 11 (June 22, 1998), accessed via InfoTrac Expanded Academic ASAP database, 1, Spring 2001.

34.   Mike Hoyt, "Abortion: Partial Truths," *Columbia Journalism Review* 36 (1) (May–June 1997): 12–14.

35.   Ruth Padawer, "The Facts on Partial-Birth Abortion: Both Sides Have Misled the Public," *The Record Online,* Sunday, September 15, 1996, at www.bergen.com/ abortion/abort/199609191.htm. Accessed Spring 2001.

36.   Sidney Callahan, "Dear Mr. Clinton: I'm Returning Your Veto," *Commonweal* 123, no. 14 (August 16, 1996), accessed via InfoTrac Expanded Academic ASAP database, 1, Spring 2001.

37.   "American Medical Association Should Rescind Support for Abortion Ban," *CRLP Press* (December 4, 1998), available at http://www.crlp.org/pr_98_1204ama.html. Accessed Spring 2001.

38.   Susan Yanow, and Jeanne Clark, "The Latest Attack on Women's Lives: The Partial Birth Abortion Ban," The Abortion Access Project, www.repro-activist.org/ AAP/publica_resources/commentaries/latest.htm.

39.   Greg Langer, "Support for Legal Abortion Depends on the Circumstance," ABCNEWS.com, January 22, 2001, Abcnews.go.com/sections/politics/Daily News/poll_abortionrights010122.html. See also www.gallup.com/poll/topics/abortion2.asp. Accessed Spring 2002.

40.   Triangulation is a political concept used during Clinton's presidency. It involved taking two opposing sides and working them against the middle. For example, if 30 percent opposed a measure and 30 percent favored it (with 40 percent remain-

ing who could go either way), Clinton attempted to push members of the two 30 percent camps in one direction or another to achieve a clear majority position (51 percent). See "The Clinton Years: Interview with John Podesta," *NightLine, Frontline*, available at www.pbs.org/wgbh/pages/frontline/shows/clinton/interviews/podesta. html (accessed Spring 2002). A more jaundiced view of this policy is found in a book by a former Clinton supporter: Christopher Hitchens, *No One Left to Lie To: The Triangulations of William Jefferson Clinton* (London: Verso, 1999).

41.   David A. Grimes, "The Continuing Need for Late Abortions," *JAMA, The Journal of the American Medical Association* 280, no. 8 (August 26, 1998), accessed via InfoTrac Expanded Academic ASAP database. Even in this case, it is clear that Grimes is calling for the procedure to be allowed only for late-term abortions in which there is no alternative way to preserve the mother's health.

42.   J. E. Epner, Janet E. Gans, Harry S. Jonas, and Daniel L. Seckinger, "Late-Term Abortion," *JAMA, The Journal of the American Medical Association* 280, no. 8 (August 26, 1998), accessed via InfoTrac Expanded Academic ASAP database. In this case, the AMA recommends the procedure "not be performed unless alternative procedures pose a greater risk to the mother."

43.   M. LeRoy Sprang and Mark G. Neerhof, "Rationale for Banning Abortions Late in Pregnancy," *JAMA, The Journal of the American Medical Association* 280, no. 8, (August 26, 1998), accessed via InfoTrac Expanded Academic ASAP database.

44.   "Partial-Birth Abortion: A Chink in the Pro-Abortion Armor," April 3, 2000, available at www.cwfa.org/library/life/1999-10_pp_pba.shtml. Accessed Spring 2002.

45.   See, for example, Eva Rubin, *Abortion, Politics, and the Courts: Roe v. Wade and Its Aftermath* (Westport, Conn.: Greenwood Press, 1982).

46.   Eliza Newlin Carney, "Choosing Sides," *National Journal* 30, no. 31 (August 1, 1998), accessed via InfoTrac Expanded Academic ASAP database.

47.   Again, such a technical political term cannot get as much attention as it deserves since this book is about abortion and not about politics, per se. The idea behind "incrementalism" is to get whatever you can politically, then return later to get more. Eventually, step by step (or increment by increment) you get everything you seek politically. Young people have often used this approach. Perhaps they cannot get their parents to buy a car but can get permission to use the car every Friday. Later this becomes every Friday and every Saturday; later still, every Friday, Saturday, and Sunday. Before long, a new car seems more agreeable than loaning it out three and four nights a week.

48.   Carney, 6.

49.   Stuart Taylor, "When Abortion Laws Defy Common Sense," *National Journal* 31, no. 41 (October 9, 1999), accessed via InfoTrac Expanded Academic ASAP database. Lest those think this too one-sided, Taylor concludes that he would, nevertheless, get his daughter a partial-birth abortion.

50.   *Don Stenberg, Attorney General of Nebraska, et al. v. Leroy Carhart.* No. 99–830. U.S. Supreme Court, 2000 U.S. Lexis 4484 [accessed via Academic Universe Lexis-Nexis database].

51.   *Stenberg v Carhart,* 6.

52.   Ibid., 9.

53.   Ibid., 12.

54.   Ibid., 13.

55.   Ibid., 20.

56.   Ibid., 17.

57.   Richard John Neuhaus, "So What's the Big Deal about Partial Birth Abortion?" *First Things* 104 (June/July 2000): 84.

58.   Ibid.

59.   *Stenberg v Carhart*, 22.

60.   Ibid., 23.

61.   Ibid., 34.

62.   Ibid., 47.

63.   George Will, "The Press Overprotects the Public," *Charlotte Observer* (August 20, 2000): 20.

64.   John Leo, "Playing Bait-and-Switch in Abortion Cases," *Conservative Chronicle* 15 no. 8 (July 4, 2000): 11.

65.   Linda Bowles, "Supreme Court Ignores the Will of the People," *Conservative Chronicle* 15 no. 8 (July 4, 2000): 15.

66.   William Murchinson, "Supreme Court: Legislators in Black," *Conservative Chronicle* 15 no. 8 (July 4, 2000): 20.

67.   NARAL submitted "Brief Amicus Curiae" of Virginia, Alabama, Idaho, Iowa, Michigan, North Dakota, Ohio, Pennsylvania, South Carolina, South Dakota, Utah, The Governor of Rhode Island, The Governor of West Virginia and The State of New Jersey in Support of Petitioners, *Stenberg v. Carhart*, 530 U.S. 968 (2000) (no. 99–830).

9

Pro-Life/Pro-Choice Questions: Quo Vadis?

A number of unanswered questions remain regarding the future of this debate. Perhaps this concluding discussion will anticipate the direction this debate is headed. As this chapter is being written, the country is still recovering from the fallout of the September 11 terrorist attacks on the World Trade Center, the Pentagon, and the aborted attack on another Washington target. The country has taken a decidedly more patriotic turn since that fateful day and this shift may yet influence the debate on abortion.[1] Certainly, the midterm elections of 2002 fell decidedly in favor of Republicans, the party that leans more toward limiting abortion on demand. Abortion remains a seminal issue for most Americans. Since the September 11 attacks, however, most debates on political and social issues have been shelved for a future date, in favor of a focus on homeland security and a Middle East war. Even during the most recent elections, Democrats could not mobilize their own constituency on bedrock issues like the economy. It is unlikely that the kind of heated debate the country experienced regarding abortion will return quickly without a galvanizing event. Of course, we will no doubt return to it eventually. For example, it is clear that there will be a partial-birth ban passed by Congress and signed by President Bush by summer 2003.

For now, a Republican president, George W. Bush, sits in the White House and is experiencing near record levels of support. President Bush is on record as opposing abortion. During his campaign, he stumped on a pro-life platform and promised to sign into law a late-term or partial-birth abortion ban if presented with one. Not thirty days in the White House the President cut funding for overseas abortions. Known informally as the "global gag rule" or the "Mexico City Policy," it restricts foreign nongovernmental organizations (known as NGOs) that receive family planning funds "from using their own non-U.S. funds to provide legal abortions services, lobby their own governments for abortion law reform, or provide medical counseling or referrals regarding abortion."

On the one hand, Democrats, who generally favor the pro-choice side, controlled the Senate for George W. Bush's first two years in office. Any attempt to change the current stance on abortion will doubtless face an uphill battle in Congress, as evidenced by the unprecedented refusal of Senate Judiciary Committee Chairman Patrick Leahy's to let Bush's judicial nominees move forward.[2] With the sweep by Republicans into control of both Houses of Congress in November 2002, chances are better than even that some pro-life abortion bill will be introduced.

At the state and local levels, it appears that pro-life candidates have had more success than those who favored the pro-choice line. But such things are very hard to generalize about. Sometimes voters pick a candidate for an entirely different reason than his or her stance on the abortion question. The rising number of Hispanics in the United States, though traditionally very family oriented, has been shown to favor a pro-choice stance as evidenced by their very high abortion rates.[3] Whether this will continue, or is merely the preference among current voting Hispanics, is anyone's guess.[4]

It is true that divorce rates have leveled off. Meanwhile, premarital sexual activity remains constant or is leveling off. A 1997 Louis Harris Poll found an overwhelming percentage (94 percent) of college freshmen seeing a "happy marriage" as one of life's most important goals.[5] Furthermore, in some states, such as Oklahoma, legislatures have taken steps to make divorce much harder to obtain.[6] The number of abortions in recent years has declined.[7] All of this seems to point to a climate more favorable to the pro-life stance than the pro-choice line. As we have seen, however, public opinion is fickle and can change, literally overnight. Under President Clinton's tenure, the climate seemed more agreeable to the pro-choice side of the debate. Moreover, the latest figures indicate that from 1994 to 2000, the overall abortion rate fell from 24 abortions per 1,000 women to 21.

The administration of the drug RU-486 is now available in the United States. While American opinion remains divided over RU-486, its presence allows the number of abortions to drop while not really favoring the pro-life side of the argument.[8] Currently the division between those who favor RU-486 and those who oppose it is wide, 39 percent to 47 percent, respectively.[9] Finally, a new morning after pill (MAP) will also be offered, possibly without a prescription requirement. MAP also goes by the name "Yuzpe 212 regime." MAP works by interrupting the process of fertilization within seventy-two hours. Although opposition to this is also strong and will doubtless remain so, most of the controversy surrounds the lack of testing done by the Food and Drug Administration on the pill. Some argue that MAP is harmless; others cite side effects such as vomiting and bleeding.[10] Some school systems in the United Kingdom are now handing out MAP to teenagers.[11] With Republican pro-choice senators in Congress teaming up with pro-choice Democrats, not even formidable opposition will prevent the U.S. distribution of the pill, though it's unlikely that either MAP or RU-486 will ever be given out in U.S. high schools. In February 2001, however, the Virginia legislature, a Republican stronghold and therefore largely favoring pro-life causes, voted to sell the so-called "morning-after" abortifacients *without* a prescription. It has been labeled an "emergency contraception." Critics, however, argue that the drug does not prevent conception but, rather, prevents the implantation of the fertilized egg in the uterine wall. The Virginia state Senate vote to legalize free access was convincing (25–12); it followed a state House vote 58–40 in favor of the legalization. Although the House version requires minors to obtain parental consent, the Senate version dropped that requirement.

The *National Abortion Federation v Operation Rescue* (1993), and the use of the RICO Act (in *National Organization of Women (NOW) v Scheidler, 1994*) against pro-life protesters both made decisive cases against the violent activities of pro-life advocates. The rulings made protesting at abortion clinics more difficult. We have not heard the last of these laws, doubtless propelled by the murderous acts against physicians by pro-life advocates. Indeed, recently (March 2003) RICO was held by the SC to be inappropriate for use against abortion foes.

The debate over whether abortion is psychologically damaging, referred to as post-abortion syndrome, remains highly controversial. The most celebrated evidence of this syndrome was that submitted by President Reagan's Surgeon General, C. Everett Koop, a long-time defender of the pro-life position. Koop's report claimed that while there was evidence suggesting that post-abortion syndrome does occur, there wasn't enough to determine just how many cases of it there are or how significant they are.[12] Anecdotal evidence in support of its presence is, however, easily found.[13]

Roe continues to be defended and defamed since *Roe*. Between 16 percent and 27 percent of all Americans support abortion as *Roe* defined it under any circumstances.[14] On the other hand, between 13 percent and 22 percent (since 1996, 16 percent and 17 percent) wish to see *Roe* overturned.[15]

State law also appears divided even to this day. While every state in the union allows for abortion, most states do not allow female convicts to obtain abortions.[16] Amy Grossberg and Brian Peterson, two teenagers who delivered their unborn and threw it in a dumpster, faced the death penalty in the state of Delaware in 1998 and consequently brought the abortion debate to another level. As observers pointed out, had they gone to an abortion clinic, even a few weeks before, they would have faced no charges at all. In a case more clearly connected with abortion, famed football star Rae Carruth was charged with the murder of his pregnant wife and faced a second count of murder if the unborn child died (the child lived).[17] When the House passed the Unborn Victims Act in May of 2001, making it a crime to harm an unborn child in the course of an assault on the mother, pro-choice groups rose up in arms, calling the law a thinly veiled attempt to overturn all abortion laws.[18] The recent Lacie Peterson murder has set the pro-choice forces on edge as her death also took the life of her unborn child. Police may charge her husband with a double murder.

Pro-life advocates have favored a similar approach used in *Alexander v Whitman* (118 S. Ct. 367, 1997). Karen Alexander, who was eight-and-one-half-months' pregnant, was admitted to the Jersey Shore Medical Center in Neptune, New Jersey, to give birth. While everything seemed to go according to plan, the child was stillborn. The case attempted to establish the personhood of the fetus, and this approach appears to be gaining favor. But even conservative Justices are opposed to this approach.[19] Even so, with both houses of Congress controlled by Republicans, and a Republican president sympathetic to pro-life concerns, it's a safe bet that some form of a bill defining personhood will emerge. Will it be declared unconstitutional? President Bush will most likely appoint as many as two Supreme Court Justices in addition to hundreds of federal judges throughout the country, so it's not an easy call.

Fetal-tissue transplants continue to stir up the abortion debate, as did President Bush's ban on stem cell research in late 2001.[20] Tissue harvesting commands as much as $4,198 for good specimens.[21] How such cases should be adjudicated (legally decided) in light of *Roe* confuses just about everyone, including judges. The arguments for tissue transplants for horribly debilitating diseases such as Parkinson's, are compelling; a woman becoming pregnant just to harvest the tissues not nearly so.

One issue raised by former President Clinton's Surgeon General, Jocelyn Elders, continues to be hotly debated: namely, that if all the children who were aborted had been born, the economy would have suffered a considerable setback.[22] Pro-life proponent John Noonan argued that it was this population argument that gave the abortion issue its feet.[23] This is more than passing fancy, for just five years after Paul Ehrlich's blockbuster best-seller *Population Bomb* hit the best-seller list, abortion was made legal. Ehrlich made the same argument—that we were having so many children that we had overpopulated the earth. Since his book's publication, and the contemporary abortion debate, fertility rates have dropped and continue to drop, except in the poorest of countries.[24]

On the other hand, noted economist Marvin DeVries argued in 1983, using economic models, that the monetary addition of 1.5 million people annually would render an economic impact of nearly $9 trillion.[25] According to DeVries, economic gains would have been monumental if abortion had not been legal.

Controversial arguments abound in connection with this argument. Princeton philosopher Peter Singer calls for the abortion of the severely handicapped in his *Writings on an Ethical Life*.[26] Singer contends that killing infants immediately *after* birth, or *three years later* when severe handicaps are present, is not morally prohibitive. His remarks are defended by some and criticized by many. Statistician David Murray of the Statistical Assessment Service contends that the John J. Donohue III and Steve D. Levitt study on crime and abortion (in Harvard's *Quarterly Journal of Economics*) is fatally flawed.

Science has offered as much help as it has added confusion to the abortion debate. We now know, for example, that fetal formation is all but complete at the end of fifty-six days.[27] Fetaloscopy has helped physicians determine viability for prenatal infants facing life-threatening complications.[28] More

Table 9.1
Potential Economic Gains if *Roe* Had Failed

Item	Dollars, in *Billions*
Food	$7.7
Housing	$7
Transportation	$2.8
Clothing	$2.4

Item	Dollars, in *Billions*
Medical	$1.8
Miscellaneous	$1.5
Savings	$1.3
Social Security	$2
Taxes	$5.3

and more physicians are making the case that "personhood" begins on the fifty-seventh day of fetal formation and continues through adulthood.[29] How much personhood remains central to the debate. For example, we know scientifically that, through the first twenty weeks, the chances that a fetus could survive outside the womb is all but nil. Some biologists contend that a human embryo is a living organism by the time it is implanted in the womb, fourteen days after conception.[30] Others argue that we simply do not know.[31] Pro-choice groups have complained about the use of fetal imagery, charging that it is too graphic and too gruesome and therefore should not be allowed.[32] On the other hand, pro-life forces have overused science, often drawing fetuses the size of newborns in their materials, regardless of the gestation time.[33]

Neither side has answered well the charge made recently that the abortion debate is good for business, both pro-life and pro-choice business. Pro-life forces garner *half a billion dollars* annually ($500 million) while the pro-choice side does somewhat better at $660 million. Taken together, both sides make more than $1 billion annually, placing the two in the ranks of the top one thousand companies in the world.[34]

This accounts for only what both sides raise through solicitation, not the amount of money made by ancillary causes. For example, both sides know that any article about abortion sells magazines. The same holds true for politics on both sides. The pro-life argument does extremely well in the South and Midwest, while the pro-choice argument does well on the Eastern Seaboard and the West Coast.[35]

Throughout this debate, little has been made of the question of adoption. Are we forced, as some believe, either to save babies or punish women?[36] Both sides talk about it but it is not always a clear agenda item on either side. Pro-life forces are, however, making more of the adoption argument than they did earlier. Texas and South Carolina now have laws that allow parents of newborns to turn them over to hospital officials, free of intense interrogation, free of prosecution, free of any inquiry. This idea, now being examined by more than half the states, has as its goal reducing the number of abandoned infants. This is legislation both sides should rush to embrace. Most proposed bills usually allow hospitals custody of newborns for up to thirty days.[37]

Can a compromise be found? This question appears almost arrogant in the extreme, since, in more than thirty years of this controversy, we are no closer to resolving the debate than we were when the Supreme Court gave birth to *Roe*. Given the tenacity with which both sides hold their positions, compromise does not seem likely. Clearly, however, it appears that both sides could give up something in exchange for a more reasonable abortion policy in the United States. For example, pro-choice advocates could give in on the partial-birth abortion matter. They could also agree to a stricter interpretation of *Roe*, which, it will be recalled, did find that states *could* prohibit abortion. Public sentiment also favors this kind of compromise.[38]

Pro-life advocates could strive to find judicial consensus wherein abortion would be safe, available, and rare by agreeing to a timetable during which some abortions could occur. For example, abortion could be limited to the first trimester. Not only would this eliminate numerous abortions but it would bring American abortion policy more in line with that of all other democratic, industrialized nations.[39] Pro-life advocates could also give in on allowing abortion for the unborn who are certain to be severely and untreatably disabled at birth. This would also reduce the number of sex-selected abortions.

Such a compromise would not only make abortion available, it would also make it more rare. In Tennessee, for example, where this was proposed by pro-life advocates but later opposed by different pro-life groups, it would have reduced the number of abortions by more than 80 percent, reducing the then—twenty thousand abortions a year to fewer than four thousand. Although it would still allow for abortion, it surely would be better than twenty thousand. Surely, even from a pro-life perspective, reducing abortion by 80 percent would be a step in the right direction. Pro-life advocates could also allow abortions when the mother's health was in fatal jeopardy, and when the pregnancy was the result of rape or incest. Since these have historically amounted to less than 10 percent of all abortions since *Roe*, it would not be allowing for many.

Pro-life and pro-choice advocates should also team up to increase adoption options for all women by creating special funds to take care of mothers from the moment they learn of their pregnancies until twelve weeks or so following delivery. Job training programs for pregnant women sponsored by pro-life groups would underscore their concern for life, whether born or unborn. Both groups could also work much harder to establish programs that focus on abstinence among teens and young women. Contrary to popular modern belief, sexual activity is not a "do or die" proposition. We know, for example, that when abstinence is not combined with free distribution of condoms, premarital sexual activity declines precipitously and dramatically.[40]

How likely is it that some form of compromise will be reached? Sadly, not very. Both sides appear implacable on almost every aspect of the issue. Some pro-choice advocates are not willing to limit even one abortion, while some pro-life advocates think one abortion is too many. Perhaps the only hope is that continued discussion of the facts, such as those addressed in this book, will give rise to a new generation of advocates willing to hear the other side out.

NOTES

1.   Although it has been widely remarked that there have been "near record levels" of church or synagogue attendance since September 11, that is not the case according to the Gallup Poll. A survey on this very question (a regular for the Gallup Poll) showed very little change. In May, September, and December of 2001 the figures were 57 percent, 64 percent, and 60 percent, or little if any change. See www.gallup.com.poll/releases/pr011221.asp. Accessed Spring 2002.

2.   See Bob Egelko, "GOP Win Puts Focus on Supreme Court," *San Francisco Chronicle* (November 7, 2002), www.sfgate.com (accessed Spring 2002). Also see, Diane West, "Medal of Diss-honor," *Jewish World Review* (April 24, 2002), www.jewishworldreview.com/0402/west042402.asp. Accessed Spring 2002.

3.   "Abortion Rate Figures Mixed," *CBSNews.com* (October 8, 2002). This article calls it "disproportionately high," especially since the overall rate fell.

4.   See sample questions on abortion at www.gallup.com. Accessed Spring 2002.

5.   Dana Mack makes the same argument in "Educating for Marriage, Sort of," *First Things* 111 (March 2001): 18. A 2000 Gallup poll (gallup.com) found most teens more conservative than before but did not ask these questions.

6.   Oklahoma, which has the second-highest divorce rate in the country, is a state dominated by conservative Baptists. Divorces are obtained there by everyone, including Baptist fire-and-brimstone preachers.

7.   See "Number, Ratio and Rate of Legal Abortions Performed by Year, United States, 1976–1996," Centers for Disease Control, www.cdc.gov/nccdphp/drh/prf/48ss4_fig1.pdf (accessed Spring 2002). In 1990 the number was just over 1.4 million, declining to 1.2 million in 1996, and down to just over 1.1 million in 2000.

8.   Gallup News Service, "Approval of Controversial Abortion Drug RU-486 Proposed," www.gallup.com/poll/releases/pr00607b.asp. Poll conducted June 7, 2000.

9.   But see Michael Golay, *Where American Stands 1997* (New York: John Wiley & Sons, 1998), 86. Golay asks the question differently and the gap is only 1 percentage point.

10.   Preven and Plan B are two FDA-approved drugs and have between a 75 percent and an 85 percent effectiveness rate. Some women simply take twice the dose of birth control pills and forgo Preven or Plan B. It is known by less than 15 percent of women surveyed. See Janelle Brown, "High Noon for the Morning-After Pill," *Salon.com* (June 20, 2001), www.salon.com.mwt/feature/2001/06/20/pill (accessed Spring 2002). For the other side of the debate, see www.morningafterpill.org (accessed Spring 2002). This site features physician testimony that is less favorable than the *Salon.com* article.

11.   "Schools Give out Morning After Pill," (January 8, 2001), http://news.bbc.co.uk/hi/english/health/newsid_1106000/110612.stm. Accessed Spring 2002.

12. "Surgeon General C. Everett Koop's Statement on Post-Abortion Syndrome," *Life Cycle* (September 1989): 2.

13. "Revisiting the Koop Report," *The Post Abortion Review* (Summer 1995): 1–3; and C. McCarthy, "The Real Anguish of Abortions," *Washington Post* (February 5, 1989): F2. In the latter, Dr. Julius Fogel, who has performed more than twenty thousand abortions, claims that it is not "as harmless or casual an event" as pro-life advocates insist.

14. See www.gallup.com/poll/topics/abortion.asp. Accessed Spring 2002.

15. Ibid.

16. "Attention to Concerns of Female Prisoners," ACLU, www.aclu.org/issues/prisons/npp_policy. html. Accessed Spring 2002.

17. See http://crime.about.com/library/blfiles/blrae2.htm. Accessed Spring 2002.

18. In one sense, this takes us back to chapter 1 and Exodus 21:22, in which Jewish law penalized those who killed a woman when she was with child. Everything changes while remaining the same.

19. Paul Benjamin Linton, "How Not to Overturn *Roe v Wade*," *First Things*, no. 127 (November 2002): 15–16.

20. Maureen L. Condic, "The Basics About Stem Cells," *First Things*, no. 119 (January 2002): 30–34.

21. Celeste McGovern, "Secrets of the Dead Baby Identity," *Alberta Report* (August 23, 1999), SIRS Online Researcher.

22. Karen Brandon, " Study Links Abortion, Reduced Crime," *Chicago Tribune* (August 9, 1999): 1.

23. John Noonan, ed., *Morality of Abortion: Legal and Historical Perspectives* (Cambridge, Mass.: Harvard University Press, 1970).

24. Julian Simon has disproved Ehrlich's projections, especially as they relate to the earth's resources. The most recent work to address itself to Ehrlich's misinformation about the population explosion is Nicholas Eberstadt, "The Population Implosion," *Foreign Policy* (March 2001).

25. Marvin G. DeVries, "The Economic Impact of 1.5 Million Additional People per Year," in United States Senate, *Legal Ramifications of the Human Life Amendment. Hearings Before the Subcommittee on the Constitution of the Committee on the Judiciary*, 245–255. United States Senate, 98th Congress, First Session, S. J. Res. 3, "Joint Resolution to Amend the Constitution to Establish Legislative Authority in Congress and the States with Respect to Abortion, February 28 and March 7, 1983, Serial no. J-98-12 (Washington: GPO, 1983). Table 9.1 has been adapted from DeVries.

26. Peter Singer, *Writings on an Ethical Life* (London: Fourth Estate, 2001).

27. For this, what follows, and more, see Robert H. Blank, "Judicial Decision Making and Biological Fact: *Roe v Wade* and the Unresolved Question of Fetal Viability," *Western Political Quarterly* 37 (1984), especially 584, 586, and 598.

28. Agota Peterfy, "Fetal Viability as a Threshold to Personhood," *Journal of Legal Medicine* 16 (Dec. 1995): 607–637 n. 307.

29.   Ibid.

30.   Golay, 89.

31.   The best way to see the outlines of this debate is to surf pro-life and pro-choice Web sites and look through them. Sites advocating for each side offer evidence for their views on this debate.

32.   Rosalind Pollack Petchesky, *Abortion and Woman's Choice: The State, Sexuality, and Reproductive Freedom* (Boston, Mass.: Northeastern University Press, 1984), xii.

33.   See, for example, National Right to Life diagrams at http://www.nrlc.org/abortion/pba/diagram.html (accessed Spring 2002). The fetus in the diagrams is disproportionately large for the time of the pregnancy.

34.   Dana Kennedy, "Abortion, Inc." *George* 5, no. 10 (2000): 90–92, 100–101.

35.   These are typically strongholds for Republicans and Democrats, respectively.

36.   Cindi Ross Scoppe, "Our Choice Comes Down to This: Save Babies' Lives or Punish Women," *The (Columbia) State* (April 11, 2000): A78.

37.   Ibid.

38.   See www.gallup.com under topics and then abortion (accessed Spring 2002). On the extreme ends of the pro-life/pro-choice spectrum, there is little support for any abortion at any time (less than 20 percent) or for the criminalization of abortion, regardless of the trimester or the circumstances (17 percent). On the other hand, around 55 percent favor *some* restrictions.

39.   See   www.plannedparenthood.org/library/facts/abotaft1st_010600.html (accessed Spring 2002). For other countries and abortion rates, see Mary Ann Glendon, *Abortion and Divorce in Western Law* (Cambridge, Mass.: Harvard University Press, 1987), 23–24. Glendon points out that the United States has the most liberal abortion policy of any industrialized nation in the world, save China.

40.   "Abstinence Education Helps Reduce Early Sexual Activity, Analyst Says," *The Heritage Foundation Press Room News Releases* (April 8, 2002), http://www. heritage.org/Press/ NewsReleases/NR040802.cfm (accessed Spring 2002). Even the federal government is encouraging this with 93.235 Abstinence Education in *The Catalog of Federal and Domestic Assistance.* (See the Web site description at http://www.cfda.gov/public/viewprog.asp?progid=1214, accessed Spring 2002.)

Index

About the Author

MARK Y. HERRING is Dean of Library Services, Dacus Library at Winthrop University in South Carolina.